# Research Series on the Chinese Dream and China's Development Path

Drawing on a large body of empirical studies done over the last two decades, this Series provides its readers with in-depth analyses of the past and present and forecasts for the future course of China's development. It contains the latest research results made by members of the Chinese Academy of Social Sciences. This series is an invaluable companion to every researcher who is trying to gain a deeper understanding of the development model, path and experience unique to China. Thanks to the adoption of Socialism with Chinese characteristics, and the implementation of comprehensive reform and opening-up, China has made tremendous achievements in areas such as political reform, economic development, and social construction, and is making great strides towards the realization of the Chinese dream of national rejuvenation. In addition to presenting a detailed account of many of these achievements, the authors also discuss what lessons other countries can learn from China's experience.

More information about this series at http://www.springer.com/series/13571

Qizi Zhang
Editor

# Transforming Economic Growth and China's Industrial Upgrading

SSAP

Springer

*Editor*
Qizi Zhang
Chinese Academy of Social Sciences
Beijing, China

ISSN 2363-6866 ISSN 2363-6874 (electronic)
Research Series on the Chinese Dream and China's Development Path
ISBN 978-981-13-0961-8 ISBN 978-981-13-0962-5 (eBook)
https://doi.org/10.1007/978-981-13-0962-5

Jointly published with Social Sciences Academic Press, Beijing, China

The print edition is not for sale in China Mainland. Customers from China Mainland please order the print book from: Social Sciences Academic Press.

Library of Congress Control Number: 2018944329



This Springer imprint is published by the registered company Springer Nature Singapore Pte Ltd.
The registered company address is: 152 Beach Road, #21-01/04 Gateway East, Singapore 189721, Singapore

# Preface

Since the reform and opening-up, the Chinese government has always attached great importance to transforming the traditional pattern of economic growth. In 1981, the Fourth Session of the Fifth National People's Congress adopted the ten principles for developing the national economy in the Report on the Work of the Government, which focused on improving economic efficiency. This can be seen as the beginning of high attention to an attempt in this regard. Following this, the central government initiated numerous attempts to transform the pattern of economic growth and increase economic returns throughout the 1980s. In the 1990s, China put forward two "fundamental transformations." For example, the Ninth Five-year Plan and the Long-Range Objectives to the Year 2010, adopted on March 5, 1996, pointed out that "to transform from a planned economy to a socialist market economy and change the pattern of economic growth from an extensive one to an intensive one is the key to achieving our objectives over the coming fifteen years." Entering the twenty-first century, the central government proposed the "new industrialisation" path; this is another significant leap in China's transformation of its pattern of economic growth. In September 2002 at the 16th National Congress of the Communist Party of China (CPC), the path of "new industrialisation" was officially defined as follows: "we shall persist with IT development to drive industrialisation, which in turn promotes IT development, leading towards a path of new industrialisation featuring high technology, high economic efficiency, low resource consumption, less environmental pollution, and giving full play to the advantages of human resources." After 2003, China began to shift its focus from transforming the model of economic growth towards changing the pattern of development. Despite efforts and progress made, China still faced great pressure because the transformation of the development pattern affected economic and industrial development for some time.

The transformation of the development pattern is manifested in industrial restructuring and upgrade at the industry level. The aim of this book, given the requirements to transform the model of economic growth, is to come up with a rationale for China's industrial upgrade and the appropriate policies to adopt. The book consists of two parts. Part I analyses and evaluates the impact of the model of economic growth on industrial development. In evaluating the impact of the transformation, the focus is on the revision of the export policy, wage increase, and low-carbon economy, which will help our understanding of the difficulties that may arise during the process of transforming the growth pattern. Part II studies the method for China's industrial upgrade and the policy options.

This research is supported by the funding program of the Ministry of Human Resources and Social Security for selected projects of overseas students, the Innovation Project of Chinese Academy of Social Sciences, the 973 Program, and the National Science and Technology Support Program. The research group expresses its sincere gratitude to parties that have offered kind support.

Beijing, China Qizi Zhang

# Acknowledgements

After a relatively short gestation period, the *Research Series on the Chinese Dream and China's Development Path* has started to bear fruits. We have, first and foremost, the books' authors and editors to thank for making this possible. And it was the hard work by many people at Social Sciences Academic Press and Springer, the two collaborating publishers, that made it a reality. We are deeply grateful to all of them.

Mr. Xie Shouguang, President of Social Sciences Academic Press (SSAP), is the mastermind behind the project. In addition to defining the key missions to be accomplished by it and setting down the basic parameters for the project's execution, as the work has unfolded, Mr. Xie has provided critical input pertaining to its every aspect and at every step of the way. Thanks to the deft coordination by Ms. Li Yanling, all the constantly moving parts of the project, especially those on the SSAP side, are securely held together, and as well synchronised as is feasible for a project of this scale. Ms. Gao Jing, unfailingly diligent and meticulous, makes sure every aspect of each Chinese manuscript meets the highest standards for both publishers, something of critical importance to all subsequent steps in the publishing process. That high-quality, if also at times stylistically as well as technically challenging scholarly writing in Chinese has turned into decent, readable English that readers see on these pages is largely thanks to Ms. Liang Fan, who oversees translator recruitment and translation quality control.

Ten other members of the SSAP staff have been intimately involved, primarily in the capacity of in-house editor, in the preparation of the Chinese manuscripts. It is time-consuming work that requires attention to details, and each of them has done this and is continuing to do this with superb skills. They are in alphabetical order: Mr. Cai Jihui, Ms. Liu Xiaojun, Mr. Ren Wenwu, Ms. Shi Xiaolin, Ms. Song Yuehua, Mr. Tong Genxing, Ms. Wu Dan, Ms. Yao Dongmei, Ms. Yun Wei, and Ms. Zhou Qiong. In addition, Xie Shouguang and Li Yanling have also taken part in this work.

Mr. Ren Wenwu is the SSAP in-house editor for the current volume.

Our appreciation is also owed to Ms. Li Yan, Mr. Chai Ning, Ms. Wang Lei, and Ms. Xu Yi from Springer's Beijing Representative Office. Their strong support for the SSAP team in various aspects of the project helped to make the latter's work that much easier than it would have otherwise been.

We thank Ms. Somui Cheung for translating this book and Ms. Wang Yuxin for her work as the polisher. The translation and draft polish process benefited greatly from the consistent and professional coordination service by Global Tone Communication Technology Co., Ltd. We thank everyone involved for their hard work.

Last, but certainly not least, it must be mentioned that funding for this project comes from the Ministry of Finance of the People's Republic of China. Our profound gratitude, if we can be forgiven for a bit of apophasis, goes without saying.

Social Sciences Academic Press
Springer

# Contents

# Contributors

**Mei Bai** Chinese Academy of Social Sciences, Beijing, China

**Chaoxian Guo** Chinese Academy of Social Sciences, Beijing, China

**Gang Li** Chinese Academy of Social Sciences, Beijing, China

**Hao Li** Chinese Academy of Social Sciences, Beijing, China

**Keting Shen** Zhejiang Gongshang University, Hangzhou, China

**Lei Wang** Chinese Academy of Social Sciences, Beijing, China

**Yejun Wu** Chinese Academy of Social Sciences, Beijing, China

**Liu Yu** Chinese Academy of Sciences, Beijing, China

**Qizi Zhang** Chinese Academy of Social Sciences, Beijing, China

# Part I
# Transforming the Growth Pattern: Industrial Impact Analysis

# Chapter 1
# Evolution of Competitive Advantages of Chinese Industries

**Qizi Zhang, Yejun Wu and Hao Li**

According to the theory of economic growth projections, development in countries around the world tends to converge. However, the reality in economic development is that for the majority of countries, once they move into the middle-income range as a country, the pace of growth does not continue: they fall into the 'middle-income trap' in the middle-income club instead of moving on to the high-income club. In 2010, China's per capita GDP went above USD 4000, which placed it into the upper middle income category. Will China also fall into the "middle income trap"? This question received widespread attention. However, there is still much debate about why there is a middle income trap and how to avoid it and thus, little guidance can be expected. This chapter attempts to explain the mechanisms of how a 'middle income trap' is formed from the perspective of industrial upgrade based on an evolution of comparative advantage, so as to provide meaningful insights to help China avoid the middle income trap.

## 1.1 Structure of Chinese Industrial Competitiveness

A country's capabilities can be evaluated by measuring the input or the output. The capability of a country for industrial upgrade is seen in the country's industrial competitiveness and its structure.

---

Q. Zhang (✉) · Y. Wu · H. Li
Chinese Academy of Social Sciences, Beijing, China
e-mail: zhangqizi65@126.com



Q. Zhang (ed.), *Transforming Economic Growth and China's Industrial Upgrading*, Research Series on the Chinese Dream and China's Development Path,
https://doi.org/10.1007/978-981-13-0962-5_1

1. **China's overall industrial competitiveness is on the rise**

China's export as a proportion of the total global export, i.e. a share in the international market, has been growing fast since 1990, and the international market share exceeded 10% in 2010. The figure of 2011 was roughly the same as that in 2010, at 10.43%, up by 5 percentage points over 2002, and 10 times the figure in 1950 when China's export accounted for less than 1% of the global total. In 2012, the rise continued and China's international market share reached above 11% as of September. At 11.6%, the figure was already higher than the level of the USA, Germany and Japan, but only 45% of the USA's 1948 figure. China's trade competitiveness index dropped for three consecutive years from 2008, and rebounded slightly in 2012 (see Fig. 1.1).

2. **Market share of China's service industry exports have rising slightly but the competitiveness has been going down**

An important mission in transforming China's development pattern is to raise the proportion of service industry in the overall industrial structure and its contribution to economic growth. However, completing this task is not easy because whether an industry can develop quickly is mainly determined by its competitive edge against other industries, but China's service industry is quite uncompetitive compared with its secondary industry.

Since the 1980s, China's service industry has seen a growing trend as a proportion of the global service industry, but by 2010, the share remained under 5%, much lower than the share of product export. Although this figure is roughly the same as that of Japan, Germany and France and much higher than that of other developing countries, it is far below the figure of the USA—only about one third of it (see Figs. 1.2 and 1.3 and Table 1.1).

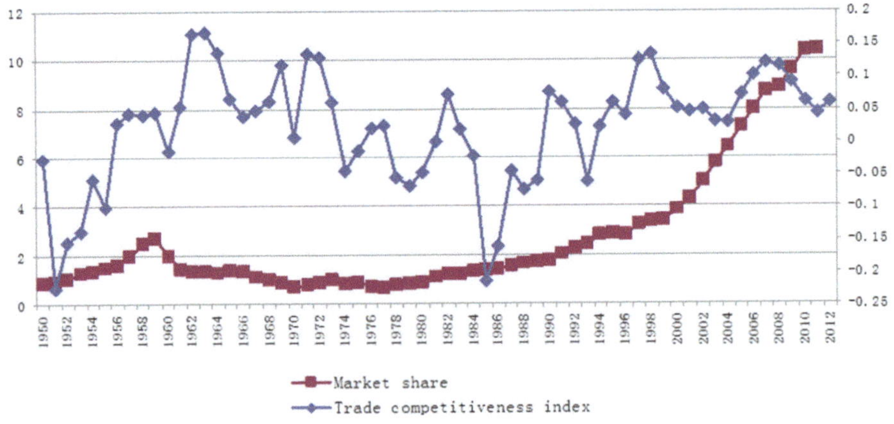


**Fig. 1.1** Trends in China's market share and trade competitiveness index

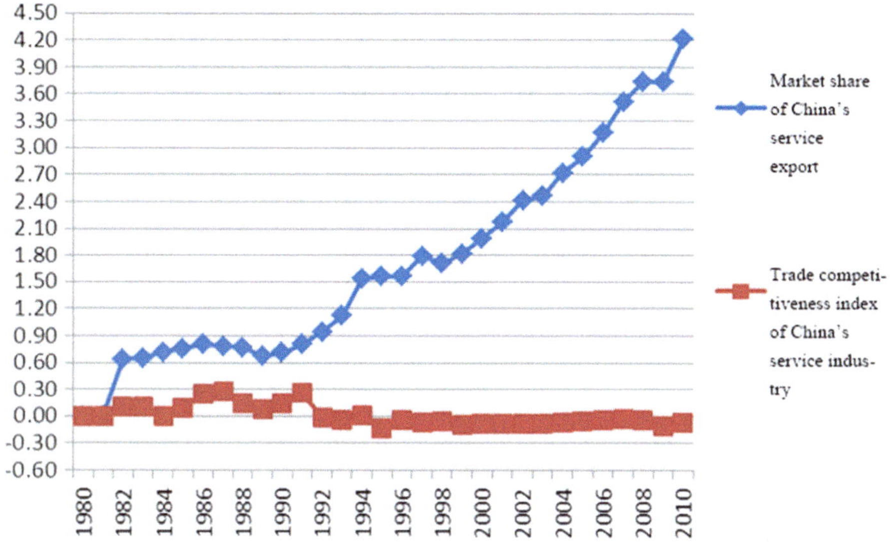


**Fig. 1.2** Changes in the share of China's service export and trade competitiveness index

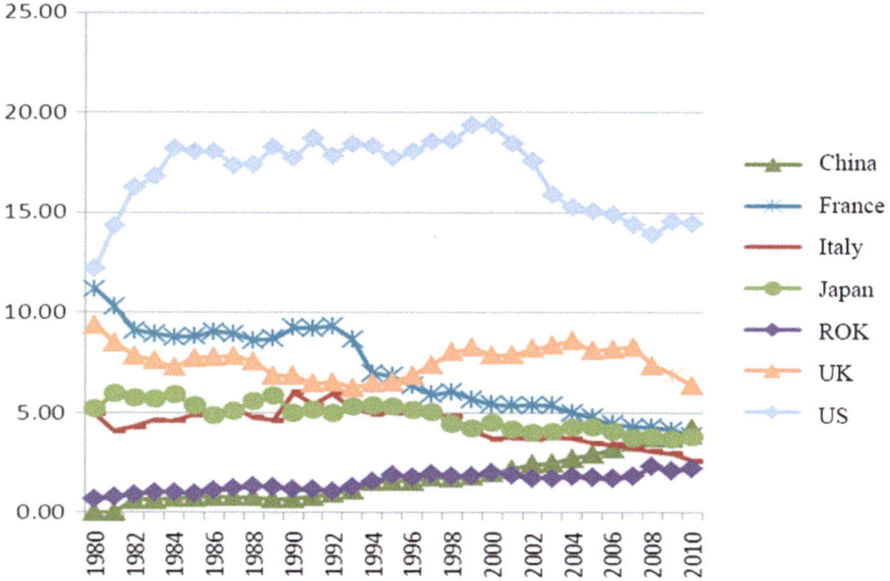


**Fig. 1.3** China's service exports as a proportion of global service exports: a comparison with some developed countries

**Table 1.1** China's service exports as a proportion of global service exports: a comparison with some developing countries

| | 1990 | 2000 | 2005 | 2007 | 2008 | 2009 | 2010 |
|---|---|---|---|---|---|---|---|
| Argentina | 0.295 | 0.322 | 0.258 | 0.298 | 0.309 | 0.318 | 0.349 |
| Brazil | 0.455 | 0.621 | 0.625 | 0.688 | 0.775 | 0.799 | 0.876 |
| China | 0.708 | 1.989 | 2.901 | 3.514 | 3.744 | 3.735 | 4.223 |
| Columbia | 0.193 | 0.133 | 0.104 | 0.104 | 0.105 | 0.121 | 0.119 |
| India | 0.559 | 1.091 | 2.048 | 2.501 | 2.652 | 2.612 | 3.105 |
| Malaysia | 0.466 | 0.911 | 0.763 | 0.847 | 0.771 | 0.829 | 0.868 |
| Mexico | 0.979 | 0.899 | 0.629 | 0.506 | 0.470 | 0.444 | 0.412 |
| Peru | 0.096 | 0.101 | 0.089 | 0.090 | 0.092 | 0.105 | 0.109 |
| The Philippines | 0.392 | 0.220 | 0.176 | 0.280 | 0.247 | 0.295 | 0.325 |
| South Africa | 0.412 | 0.329 | 0.440 | 0.397 | 0.325 | 0.346 | 0.373 |
| Thailand | 0.776 | 0.906 | 0.786 | 0.873 | 0.849 | 0.870 | 0.909 |
| Vietnam | 0.048 | 0.176 | 0.162 | 0.173 | 0.180 | 0.163 | 0.188 |

Transport, tourism, construction, and computing & information services account for a greater proportion in China's service exports, with the first two combined accounting for around 50%. However, these two are highly susceptible to international financial crises, and the trade competitiveness declined significantly. On the whole, trade competitiveness in construction services and computing & information services shows an upward trend but is also affected by international financial crises. The upward momentum of the trade in computing & information services wore out in 2009, and the construction service sector saw a downward trend. The trade competitiveness of the insurance and financial service sector, though grew slightly, is still very low (Fig. 1.4; Table 1.2).

3. **Competitiveness of creative and strategic emerging industries needs to improve**

In recent years, creative industries have received heightened attention from around the world. There is also much growth in the export of these industries, with greater momentum in developing countries than in developed ones. Between 2003 and 2008, the annual growth worldwide in creative industry exports was 11.53; 10.5% for developed countries, and 13.55% for developing countries. The growth in China's creative industry exports, 16.92%, was greater than that of developed and developing countries alike. The market share of its creative industry exports reached 20% in 2008, but there are acute structural problems: the competitiveness of the creative services is low, much lower than the competitiveness of creative products, of the creative products, books, newspapers, films and designs do not have large shares in the international market. The problem is even more acute for uncompetitive film products (Table 1.3; Fig. 1.5).

In order to transform its development pattern, China made huge efforts in strategic emerging industries such as new energy, new materials, new-generation

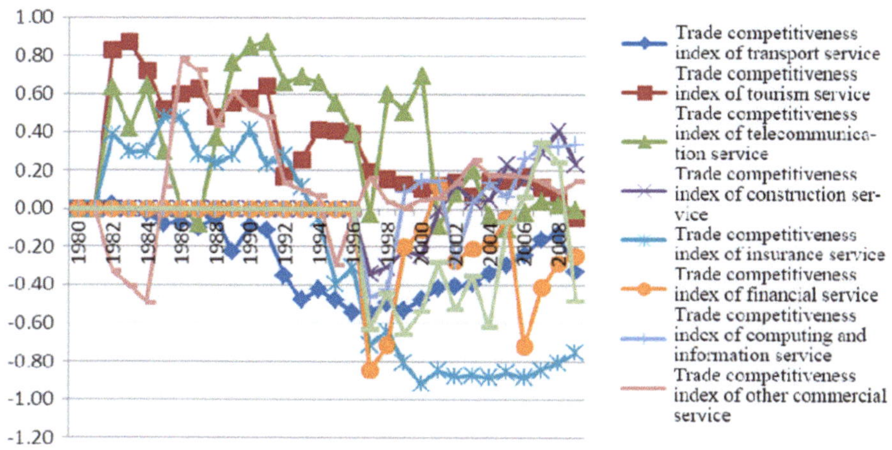


**Fig. 1.4** Changes in the trade competitiveness index of various services sectors

**Table 1.2** China's various service sectors as a proportion of the total (%)

| | 2000 | 2005 | 2006 | 2007 | 2008 | 2009 |
|---|---|---|---|---|---|---|
| Transport | 12.06 | 20.73 | 22.84 | 25.63 | 26.11 | 18.19 |
| Tourism | 53.33 | 39.37 | 36.90 | 30.46 | 27.76 | 30.62 |
| Communications | 4.42 | 0.65 | 0.80 | 0.96 | 1.06 | 0.92 |
| Construction | 1.97 | 3.48 | 2.99 | 4.40 | 7.02 | 7.30 |
| Insurance | 0.35 | 0.73 | 0.59 | 0.73 | 0.93 | 1.23 |
| Finance | 0.25 | 0.19 | 0.15 | 0.18 | 0.21 | 0.33 |
| Computing and information | 1.16 | 2.47 | 3.21 | 3.55 | 4.24 | 5.02 |
| Licensing fees | 0.26 | 0.21 | 0.22 | 0.28 | 0.38 | 0.33 |
| Other commercial services | 25.18 | 31.29 | 31.49 | 33.06 | 31.50 | 35.21 |
| Personal, cultural and entertainment services | 0.03 | 0.17 | 0.14 | 0.25 | 0.28 | 0.07 |
| Government services | 0.93 | 0.66 | 0.62 | 0.45 | 0.45 | 0.73 |

information technology, advanced equipment manufacturing, bio-tech, and energy-saving & new energy vehicles. The competitiveness of these industries is the key to successful transformation. There is a lack of data on the competitiveness of these industries and a systematic assessment is difficult at the moment. But what we can do is to carry out an initial analysis based on installed technologies.

Based on an assessment of the installed technologies of China's strategic emerging industries, it can be concluded that the competitiveness of China's strategic emerging industries is clearly inadequate. In terms of patents related to ICT, biotech, nanotech and new energy, China lags far behind developed countries (Table 1.4).

**Table 1.3** Changes in the trade competitiveness index of the creative industries

| Industry | 2002 | 2003 | 2004 | 2005 | 2006 | 2007 | 2008 | 2009 |
|---|---|---|---|---|---|---|---|---|
| Advertising, market research, opinion polls | −0.028 | 0.030 | 0.0971 | 0.201 | 0.204 | 0.177 | 0.063 | 0.083 |
| R&D services | −0.343 | – | – | – | – | – | – | – |
| Personal, cultural and entertainment services | −0.527 | −0.350 | −0.621 | −0.069 | 0.061 | 0.345 | 0.242 | −0.482 |
| Audio-visual and related services | −0.527 | −0.350 | −0.621 | −0.069 | 0.061 | 0.345 | 0.242 | −0.482 |
| All creative products | 0.833 | 0.840 | 0.855 | 0.866 | 0.871 | 0.856 | 0.866 | |
| Arts and crafts | 0.748 | 0.777 | 0.767 | 0.798 | 0.808 | 0.833 | 0.845 | |
| Films | −0.736 | −0.850 | −0.943 | −0.985 | −0.977 | −0.988 | −0.992 | |
| Designs | 0.905 | 0.913 | 0.924 | 0.928 | 0.929 | 0.922 | 0.915 | |
| Toy designs | 0.946 | 0.924 | 0.939 | 0.944 | 0.957 | 0.950 | 0.943 | |
| New media | 0.672 | 0.702 | 0.814 | 0.897 | 0.880 | 0.821 | 0.924 | |
| Recording media | −0.650 | −0.547 | −0.573 | −0.640 | −0.416 | – | – | |
| Music (CD, cassette tape) | −0.469 | −0.534 | −0.6894 | −0.771 | −0.783 | −0.371 | −0.387 | |
| Publishing | 0.279 | 0.259 | 0.429 | 0.424 | 0.541 | 0.610 | 0.637 | |
| Books | 0.616 | 0.656 | 0.733 | 0.742 | 0.766 | 0.795 | 0.830 | |
| Newspapers | −0.904 | −0.895 | −0.775 | −0.826 | 0.121 | 0.400 | 0.297 | |
| Antiques | 0.223 | 0.093 | 0.127 | −0.036 | 0.0354 | 0.208 | −0.502 | |
| Paintings | 0.918 | 0.921 | 0.889 | 0.946 | 0.944 | 0.882 | 0.854 | |
| Photography | 0.0350 | 0.217 | 0.071 | 0.209 | −0.052 | 0.415 | 0.516 | |
| Sculptures | 0.988 | 0.987 | 0.984 | 0.983 | 0.981 | 0.984 | 0.984 | |

*Source* calculations based on creative industry data from UNCTADstat

## 1.2 Technical Competitiveness of China's Industries

An important feature of the present division of labour in global industries is the division of labour along the industry chain. With the development in information technology, a drop in the cost of transport and collaboration, and the appearance of modular design, the manufacture of a product can be divided into a series of separate production processes and these production processes can then be further divided into different activities. In such a situation, it is difficult to report on a country's industrial competitiveness with only overall figures on the international market. An overall international market share cannot reflect a country's capability in creating added value in the industry chain. Neither can an overall trade competitiveness index give a complete picture of a country's trade competitiveness. For example, the overall trade competitiveness index of the USA is negative, which is

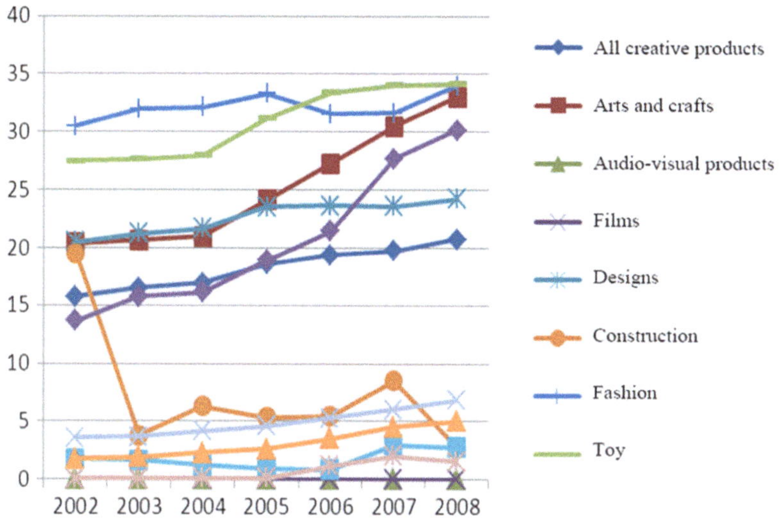


**Fig. 1.5** Trends in the market share of products from the creative industries. *Source* Chart drawn based on UNCTADstat data for the creative industries

lower than that of many countries, but its capability for creating added value is not as weak as its trade competitiveness index shows. Some countries.

Products may be manufactured through a number of separate processes, but value creation relies on transactions, which, in international trade, take two forms: One is the processing and assembling of imported products which are then re-exported; the other is to export products for further processing and assembly in the destination country. The trade competitiveness index does not actually cover the value created before the re-export in the first form of transactions. Also, a country will still have a high trade competitiveness index if it exports only a small amount of high-tech products but a very large amount of low-tech products. Therefore, the trade competitiveness index cannot give us an accurate understanding of how a country is doing in the global industrial division of labour.

To address the inadequacy of the overall international market share and the overall trade competitiveness index in showing a country's industrial competitiveness, some scholars and organisations began to use the added value method to calculate a country's share in the global total export. Calculated this way, China's market share, though grew fast, has not surpassed that of the USA. The level of industrial competitiveness revealed appears weaker than that revealed by the traditional overall market share index. This indicator measures the industrial competitiveness from another perspective. It can also be treated as another method for a country to increase its industrial competitiveness. At the moment there is constraint in the data that can be used in this method. Currently some calculations are still based on assumptions. As this method still needs further improvement, it has not been adopted in this research report. Instead, calculations of a product's technical

**Table 1.4** Patent applications by sector at the EU patent authority (as of 2009)

| | Proportion of ICT-related patents | | Proportion of bio-tech patents | | Proportion of nanotech patents | | Proportion of new energy patents |
|---|---|---|---|---|---|---|---|
| Sweden | 1.7 | Italy | 1.5 | France | 5.4 | UK | 4.53 |
| Finland | 1.8 | Belgium | 1.4 | Italy | 1.4 | France | 3.37 |
| Italy | 1.7 | Sweden | 1.5 | Korea | 3.2 | Japan | 9.59 |
| Canada | 1.7 | Korea | 1.1 | Germany | 11.7 | Denmark | 5.22 |
| Germany | 13.4 | Germany | 11.9 | Belgium | 1.2 | USA | 22.13 |
| France | 5.6 | France | 4.8 | Holland | 2.6 | Spain | 5.90 |
| | | Japan | 11.2 | Japan | 22.9 | Germany | 11.87 |
| Japan | 23.0 | Holland | 2.4 | Sweden | 1.3 | Korea | 4.13 |
| UK | 5.0 | UK | 5.7 | UK | 4.5 | China | 4.26 |
| Korea | 2.9 | Canada | 2.7 | Switzerland | 2.1 | | |
| Holland | 4.2 | USA | 42.5 | USA | 36.2 | | |
| USA | 30.2 | Australia | 1.8 | Canada | 1.3 | | |
| China | 0.5 | China | 0.6 | China | – | | |

*Source* OECD Science, Technology and Industry Scoreboard 2011 content, spatial distribution, detailed market share and refined trade competitiveness index are used to analyse China's position in the global system of industrial division of labour. Generally speaking, the higher the product technical content, the higher the capability to create added value. Therefore, as long as product classification is detailed enough, a country's capability to create added value can still be analysed by examining the product technical content, market share and trade competitiveness index, and the country's position in the global industrial division of labour will thus be revealed.

1. **Although the overall product technical content of China's exports is rising all the time, the overall level of technology is still ranked lower than 30th**

To quantify a product's added value and technical content and to a country's level of technology in its exports is key to understanding the country's current industrial competitiveness and studying its industrial upgrade and product restructuring. To this end, Hausmann and Klinger (2007) put forward the PRODY and EXPY indices. PRODY uses the weighted average of the per capita GDP of all countries that export a certain product to measure the added value or productivity of the product, while EXPY is the weighted average of a country's PRODY. Here, the weight is the share of the total export value of product $i$ in the country's total exports. These two indices are adopted in this report to estimate a country's product technical content.

To calculate the above indices, data of 1992–2010 are obtained from the UN Comtrade databank for products bearing a five-digit code in SITC rev.3.[1] For per capita GDP, data is taken from the World Bank World Development Indicators (WDI) database for annual GDP in constant 2000 US dollars. Given that per capita GDP changes with economic development and the number of countries covered in the UN Comtrade databank varies each year, we may fail to reveal the intrinsic characteristics of a product continuously and effectively if we simply use the data of different years to calculate *PRODY*, due to the influence of variations in national GDP and the changing proportions of countries of different development levels in the whole portfolio. In order to solve this problem, we first select data of the three years of 2008–2010 for countries fully covered in both the UN Comtrade and WDI databases, 139 in total, to calculate the PROXY values and then average them out to form a benchmark PRODY value for the product. In this way, we find China's EXPY to have grown to some extent, rising slightly above the world average and moving from below 40 before 2005 to one of the top 40 after 2005, However, China is still not within the top 30—higher than the rankings of India, Brazil, and South Africa, but far lower than those of the USA, Japan, Germany, France and Britain (see Figs. 1.6 and 1.7). Looking at the changing trends, after the international financial crisis, the product technical content in the exports from some countries reduced but this was not the case for China.

[1]SITC rev.3 contains more than 4000 kinds of products but we use data for only the 3118 kinds of products with a 5-digit code.

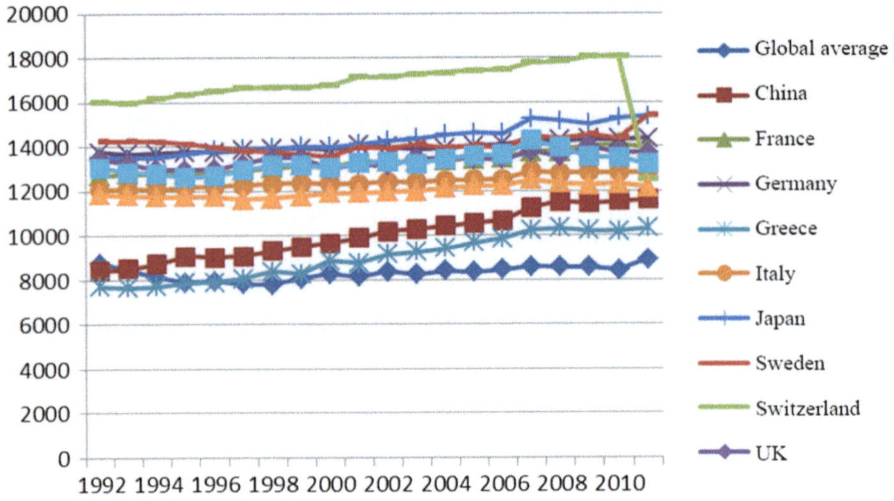


**Fig. 1.6** Changing trends in the product technical content of exports from China and some developed countries

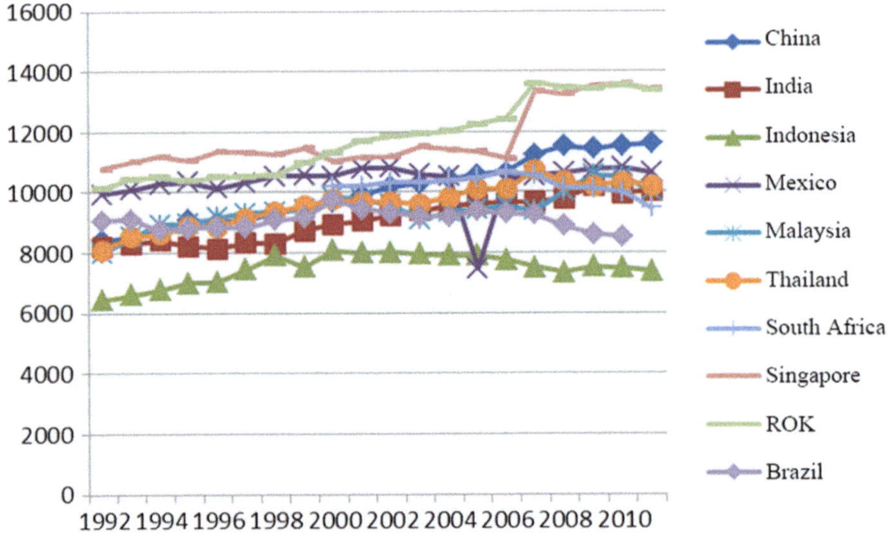


**Fig. 1.7** Changing trends in the product technical content of exports from China and some developing countries

2. **Among products of high, medium and low technical content, those of medium technical content are the least competitive on foreign markets**

According to the United Nations classification of industries by their technical content, there are four categories of industries: high, medium, low, and unclassified. China's industrial competitiveness is the strongest in the low-tech category and second strongest in the high-tech category. In the international market, China, as an important exporter of high-tech products, has seen its share in the global total high-tech exports approaching the share of its low-tech products in the world total since 2003. Although the gap between the two expanded briefly during 2006–2008, it began to shrink again during 2009–2010.

Even though China has a rather large share in international high-tech exports, it is also an important importer of high-tech products. Taking into consideration both the export and the import, China's competitiveness in the high-tech industry is still of medium level.

The international financial crisis had an impact on both the low-tech and high-tech industries. The low-tech industry suffered more but it was also clearly more resilient than the high-tech industry as well as other industries (for details see Figs. 1.8, 1.9 and 1.10).

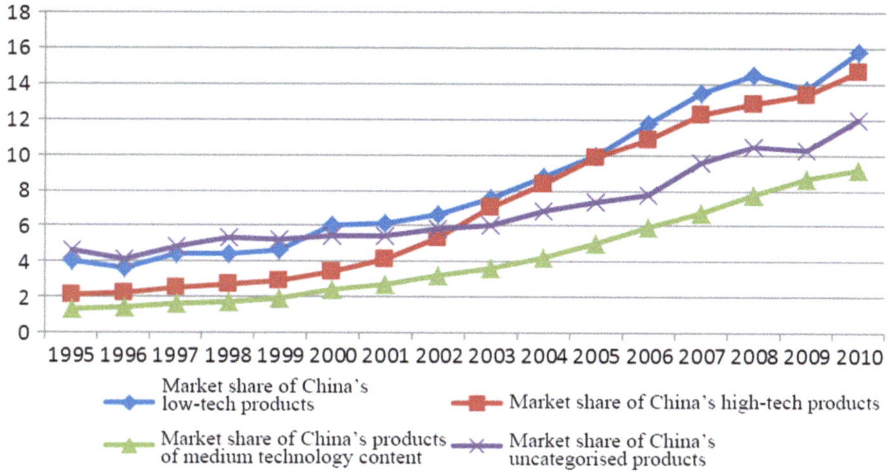


**Fig. 1.8** Changing market shares of China's products of different technical content

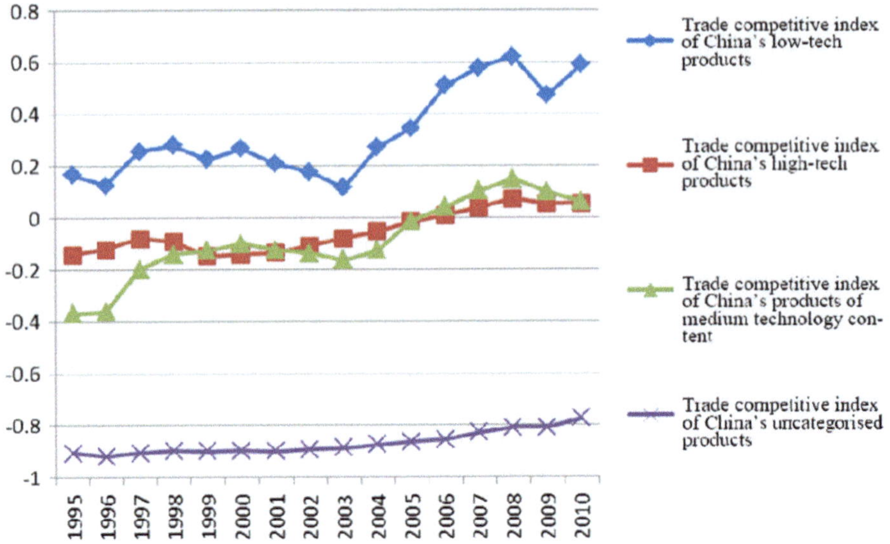


**Fig. 1.9** Changing trade competitiveness index of China's products of different technical content

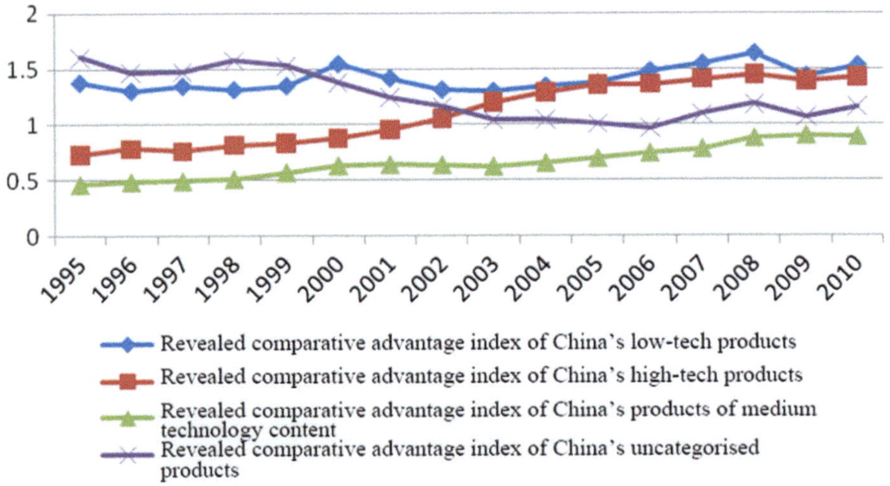


**Fig. 1.10** Changing revealed comparative advantage index of China's products of different technical content

## 1.3 Industrial Complexity of China

1. **Compared with developed countries, china needs to increase its product complexity**

Looking at the product diversity of China since the reform and opening up, we find that the diversity score of Chinese exports was 73 in 1985 and 282 in 2010—quite a sharp rise. In the 1980s, the rise in China's product diversity was mainly due to the 1987 exchange rate reform. Before this, China's product diversity score stood at 74 in 1986 and after it, the score surged to 212. Within a year, the number of product types for which China had comparative advantages increased by 138 and has been on the rise ever since, contributing greatly to China's continuous economic growth for nearly 30 years. However, the growth rate has not been high since 1987 with only 70 product categories added to the list up to 2010 to make a total that was less than 30% of the 1006 four-figure coded products of SITC. In contrast, this share for developed countries was over 50%. In 1985 China exported only 20 kinds of relatively complex products and the figure rose to 54 as the exchange rate was launched and pushed forward. However, despite the growth in product diversity, China's product complexity score dropped. In 2001 there were only 12 kinds of relatively high-complexity products in China's export portfolio. This may be because China's development had previously been extensive, the technical level of its manufacturing sector did not increase, and only low complexity products like toys and clothing were exported. Since 2001, with China's accession to the WTO and policies launch to change the extensive pattern of economic growth, China has been exporting more kinds of complex products and by 2008 the number rose to 26. Since the 11th Five-year Plan period, guided by the scientific outlook on development, the transformation of economic growth pattern progressed and the manufacturing and foreign trade sectors were steered towards a more technology-centred approach. By 2010, there number of complex export products increased further to 57. This was still far below the figures of developed countries. Therefore, we must continue to promote the complexity of our exported products in order to lay a solid foundation for further technological progress and higher international competitiveness of Chinese industries.

2. **In the global spatial distribution of products, Competitive Chinese products are moving from the periphery to the core markets and the comparative advantage of some labour-intensive products in the periphery appear to be weakening**

In recent years, an emerging method in industrial upgrade research is to use spatial structure diagrams to illustrate the spatial structure of global products and the distribution of a certain country's products. A country's position in the global industrial division of labour can be revealed by comparing the spatial distribution of the country's products with the global spatial structure of products. According relevant research, product spatial structure diagrams tend to show a core-periphery pattern. If a country's exports are all located in the periphery, it will be difficult for

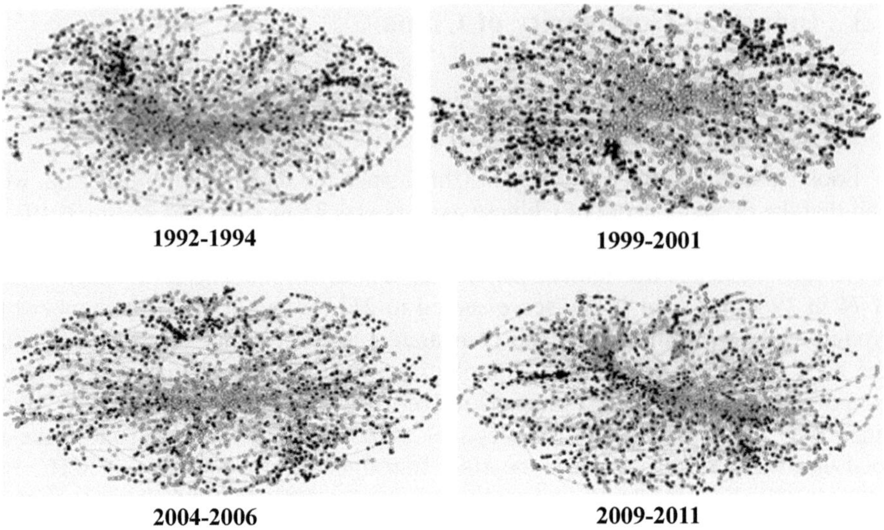


**Fig. 1.11** An evolution of China's comparative advantage

it to increase the technical content in its exports and to upgrade its industries; and it will probably remain at the lower end of the global industrial division of labour. By contrast, if most of its exports are in the core area, the technical content will is high, the potential for industrial upgrade will be great, and the country is more likely to move toward the high end in the industrial division of labour. Figure 1.11 compares the distribution of China's exports with comparative advantage the four periods of 1992–1994, 1999–2001, 2004–2006 and 2009–2011 (China's products with comparative advantage are marked in black). From the diagrams, we can see that firstly, China currently relies on traditional comparative edges in clothing and textile, and in electrical appliances and is moving towards the core; secondly, the move toward the centre is evident, especially after 2006 when electromechanical and chemical products rose at a growing speed to become pillar exports of China; thirdly, signs are clear that China's comparative edges in some labour-intensive products in the periphery is waning.

3. **China has the best comparative advantage in simple industries such as textile; in some complex industries with clear comparative advantage and high growth potential, it relies on import for some key components**

If we count industries with a comparative advantage index greater than 1 for the past ten years as industries with traditional comparative advantage, we will find 79 such industries out of the 256 bearing three-digit codes and the top ten are: 261 (silk), 666 (pottery), 752 (automatic data processing machines and unit thereof), 844 (women's or girls' coats, capes, jackets, etc. of textile fabrics, knitted or crocheted), 831 (trunks, camera cases, vanity cases, travel sets for personal toilet, sewing or shoe or clothes cleaning, etc.), 843 [men's or boys' coats, capes, jackets, suits, blazers, trousers, shorts, shirts, underwear, nightwear and similar articles of textile fabrics, knitted or crocheted (other than those of subgroup 845.2)], 658 (made-up articles, wholly or chiefly of textile materials, n.e.s.), 813 (lighting fixtures and fittings, n.e.s.), 697 (household equipment of base metal, n.e.s.), 846 (clothing accessories, of textile fabrics, whether or not knitted or crocheted (other than those for babies)). The competitiveness of these industries have been fairly stable (for details see Table 1.5). Most of these 10 industries are connected with textiles.

**Table 1.5** A comparative advantage index of the traditionally strong industries

| | 2002 | 2005 | 2006 | 2007 | 2008 | 2009 | 2010 | 2011 |
|---|---|---|---|---|---|---|---|---|
| 261 Silk | 15.53 | 10.56 | 8.46 | 9.43 | 9.35 | 8.05 | 6.21 | 6.83 |
| 666 Pottery | 5.71 | 5.18 | 5.10 | 4.12 | 4.03 | 4.68 | 4.98 | 5.24 |
| 752 Automatic data-processing machines and units thereof; magnetic or optical readers, machines for transcribing data onto data media in coded form and machines for processing such data, n.e.s. | 2.19 | 3.81 | 3.85 | 4.19 | 4.48 | 4.42 | 4.41 | 4.43 |
| 844 Textile fabrics either knitted or crocheted ladies wear or girls' coats, capes, jackets, suits, trousers, shorts, blouses/shirts, dresses and skirts, underwear, nightwear and similar articles (except for those of subgroup 845.2) | 3.65 | 3.32 | 4.32 | 4.62 | 4.26 | 3.99 | 4.21 | 4.38 |
| 831 Trunks, suitcases, vanity cases, executive cases, briefcases, school satchels, binocular cases, camera cases, musical instrument cases, spectacle cases, gun cases, holsters and similar containers; travelling bags, toilet bags, rucksacks, handbags, shopping bags, wallets, purses, map cases, cigarette cases, tobacco pouches, tool bags, sports bags, bottle cases, jewellery boxes, powder boxes, cutlery cases and similar containers, of leather or of composition leather, of sheeting of plastics, of textile materials, of vulcanized fibre or of paperboard, or wholly or mainly covered with such materials or with paper; travel sets for personal toilet, sewing or shoe or clothes cleaning | 5.42 | 4.29 | 4.06 | 3.93 | 4.25 | 4.06 | 4.28 | 4.37 |

(continued)

**Table 1.5** (continued)

| | 2002 | 2005 | 2006 | 2007 | 2008 | 2009 | 2010 | 2011 |
|---|---|---|---|---|---|---|---|---|
| 843 Men's or boys' coats, capes, jackets, suits, blazers, trousers, shorts, shirts, underwear, nightwear and similar articles of textile fabrics, knitted or crocheted (other than those of subgroup 845.2) | 3.57 | 3.63 | 4.45 | 5.28 | 4.89 | 4.30 | 4.24 | 4.21 |
| 658 Made-up articles, wholly or chiefly of textile materials, n.e.s. | 4.48 | 4.46 | 4.34 | 4.09 | 4.47 | 4.43 | 4.22 | 4.05 |
| 813 Lighting fixtures and fittings, n.e.s. | 4.26 | 3.73 | 3.66 | 3.58 | 3.82 | 3.65 | 3.89 | 3.95 |
| 697 Household equipment of base metal, n.e.s. | 3.90 | 3.79 | 3.71 | 3.56 | 3.52 | 3.51 | 3.70 | 3.87 |
| 846 Clothing accessories, of textile fabrics, whether or not knitted or crocheted (other than those for babies) | 3.22 | 3.40 | 3.44 | 3.51 | 3.92 | 3.78 | 3.73 | 3.86 |
| 652 Cotton fabrics, woven (except narrow fabrics or specially woven items) | 3.43 | 3.32 | 3.36 | 3.26 | 3.68 | 3.65 | 3.81 | 3.77 |
| 786 Trailers and semi-trailers; other vehicles not mechanically-propelled; specially designed and equipped transport containers | 4.57 | 4.24 | 3.54 | 3.39 | 3.27 | 2.07 | 3.50 | 3.70 |
| 894 Baby carriages, toys, games and sporting goods | 5.07 | 4.39 | 4.24 | 3.84 | 3.90 | 3.46 | 3.48 | 3.59 |
| 653 Fabrics, woven, of man-made textile materials (not including narrow or special fabrics) | 2.74 | 3.46 | 3.38 | 3.19 | 3.38 | 3.22 | 3.35 | 3.59 |
| 751 Office machines | 3.71 | 4.23 | 4.61 | 3.85 | 3.60 | 3.35 | 3.54 | 3.53 |
| 851 Footwear | 4.47 | 3.93 | 3.70 | 3.53 | 3.66 | 3.59 | 3.59 | 3.52 |
| 848 Articles of apparel and clothing accessories of other than textile fabrics; headgear of all materials | 6.41 | 5.39 | 4.09 | 3.54 | 3.40 | 3.42 | 3.40 | 3.40 |
| 655 Knitted or crocheted fabrics (including tubular knit fabrics, n.e.s., pile fabrics and openwork fabrics), n.e.s. | 2.46 | 2.53 | 2.64 | 2.71 | 2.87 | 3.06 | 3.18 | 3.25 |
| 696 Cutlery | 4.20 | 4.00 | 3.67 | 3.69 | 3.32 | 3.13 | 3.11 | 3.20 |
| 763 Sound recorders or reproducers; television image and sound recorders or reproducers; prepared unrecorded media | 3.88 | 4.52 | 4.28 | 3.67 | 3.84 | 3.79 | 3.23 | 3.13 |
| 845 Articles of apparel, of textile fabrics, whether or not knitted or crocheted, n.e.s. | 3.52 | 3.38 | 3.69 | 3.62 | 3.45 | 3.08 | 3.09 | 3.08 |

(continued)

**Table 1.5** (continued)

| | 2002 | 2005 | 2006 | 2007 | 2008 | 2009 | 2010 | 2011 |
|---|---|---|---|---|---|---|---|---|
| 764 Telecommunications equipment, n.e.s., and parts, n.e.s., and accessories of apparatus falling within division 76 | 1.92 | 2.38 | 2.46 | 2.82 | 2.91 | 2.91 | 2.86 | 3.06 |
| 775 Household-type electrical and non-electrical equipment, n.e.s. | 2.73 | 2.81 | 2.83 | 2.77 | 2.96 | 2.89 | 2.94 | 3.04 |
| 842 Women's or girls' coats, capes, jackets, suits, trousers, shorts, shirts, dresses and skirts, underwear, nightwear and similar articles of textile fabrics, not knitted or crocheted (other than those of subgroup 845.2) | 3.70 | 3.30 | 3.32 | 3.11 | 3.17 | 3.12 | 3.12 | 3.01 |
| 871 Optical instruments and apparatus, n.e.s. | 1.85 | 3.62 | 3.08 | 3.36 | 3.31 | 2.97 | 2.79 | 2.97 |
| 821 Furniture and parts thereof: bedding, mattresses, mattress supports, cushions and similar stuffed furnishings | 2.02 | 2.34 | 2.42 | 2.44 | 2.62 | 2.77 | 2.90 | 2.88 |
| 656 Tulle, lace, embroidery, ribbons, trimmings and other smallwares | 1.26 | 2.31 | 2.85 | 3.02 | 3.10 | 2.85 | 2.77 | 2.81 |
| 841 Men's or boys' coats, capes, jackets, suits, blazers, trousers, shorts, shirts, underwear, nightwear and similar articles of textile fabrics, not knitted or crocheted (other than those of subgroup 845.2) | 3.57 | 3.13 | 3.17 | 2.94 | 2.95 | 2.87 | 2.81 | 2.79 |
| 785 Motor cycles (including mopeds) and cycles, motorized and non-motorized; invalid carriages | 2.72 | 2.52 | 2.55 | 2.49 | 2.63 | 2.43 | 2.61 | 2.68 |
| 762 Radio-broadcast receivers, whether or not incorporating sound-recording or reproducing apparatus or a clock | 3.54 | 2.82 | 2.92 | 2.90 | 2.84 | 2.49 | 2.36 | 2.48 |
| 662 Clay construction materials and refractory construction materials | 1.08 | 1.58 | 1.71 | 1.61 | 1.93 | 2.14 | 2.36 | 2.43 |
| 654 Other textile fabrics, woven | 2.47 | 2.46 | 2.41 | 2.25 | 2.22 | 2.27 | 2.34 | 2.40 |
| 771 Electric power machinery (other than rotating electric plant of group 716), and parts thereof | 2.63 | 2.56 | 2.46 | 2.36 | 2.35 | 2.24 | 2.27 | 2.30 |
| 761 Television receivers (including video monitors and video projectors), whether or not incorporating radio-broadcast receivers or sound- or video-recording or reproducing apparatus | 1.44 | 2.02 | 2.08 | 2.27 | 2.11 | 2.00 | 2.11 | 2.19 |

(continued)

**Table 1.5** (continued)

| | 2002 | 2005 | 2006 | 2007 | 2008 | 2009 | 2010 | 2011 |
|---|---|---|---|---|---|---|---|---|
| 037 Fish, crustaceans, molluscs and other aquatic invertebrates, prepared or preserved, n.e.s. | 3.17 | 2.94 | 3.02 | 2.70 | 2.51 | 1.87 | 2.03 | 2.18 |
| 899 Miscellaneous manufactured articles, n.e.s. | 2.88 | 2.11 | 2.01 | 2.05 | 2.14 | 1.90 | 1.91 | 2.16 |
| 689 Miscellaneous non-ferrous base metals employed in metallurgy, and cements | 2.85 | 3.30 | 3.00 | 2.82 | 2.91 | 2.34 | 2.30 | 2.13 |
| 613 Furskins, tanned or dressed (including heads, tails, paws and other pieces or cuttings), unassembled, or assembled (without the addition of other materials), other than those of heading 848.31 | 2.33 | 2.23 | 2.24 | 1.74 | 1.77 | 2.31 | 1.85 | 2.12 |
| 657 Special yarns, special textile fabrics and related products | 0.89 | 1.17 | 1.20 | 1.29 | 1.59 | 1.76 | 1.88 | 2.07 |
| 593 Explosives and pyrotechnic products | 4.84 | 3.15 | 2.75 | 2.52 | 2.30 | 2.43 | 1.89 | 2.01 |
| 778 Electrical machinery and apparatus, n.e.s. | 1.64 | 1.53 | 1.56 | 1.72 | 1.90 | 1.82 | 1.84 | 1.98 |
| 291 Crude animal materials, n.e.s. | 3.57 | 2.69 | 2.31 | 2.07 | 2.09 | 1.92 | 1.83 | 1.95 |
| 523 Metal salts and peroxysalts, of inorganic acids | 2.65 | 2.35 | 2.18 | 2.07 | 2.27 | 2.12 | 1.81 | 1.95 |
| 612 Manufactures of leather or of composition leather, n.e.s.; saddlery and harness | 3.59 | 2.87 | 2.99 | 2.79 | 2.25 | 1.93 | 1.92 | 1.95 |
| 691 Structures and parts of structures, n.e.s., of iron, steel or aluminium | 1.40 | 1.54 | 1.70 | 1.95 | 2.21 | 1.94 | 1.98 | 1.94 |
| 661 Lime, cement and fabricated construction materials (except glass and clay materials) | 2.02 | 2.04 | 2.19 | 2.00 | 1.93 | 1.86 | 1.82 | 1.93 |
| 895 Office and stationery supplies, n.e.s. | 1.79 | 1.91 | 1.89 | 2.09 | 2.27 | 2.03 | 1.97 | 1.92 |
| 665 Glassware | 1.26 | 1.44 | 1.43 | 1.48 | 1.85 | 1.83 | 2.00 | 1.91 |
| 531 Synthetic organic colouring matter and colour lakes, and preparations based thereon | 1.94 | 1.72 | 1.68 | 1.83 | 2.01 | 1.84 | 1.84 | 1.88 |
| 759 Parts and accessories (other than covers, carrying cases and the like) suitable for use solely or principally with machines falling within groups 751 and 752 | 1.86 | 2.04 | 1.95 | 2.04 | 2.04 | 1.91 | 1.84 | 1.88 |
| 651 Textile yarn | 1.89 | 1.76 | 1.85 | 1.89 | 2.03 | 1.91 | 1.85 | 1.84 |

(continued)

**Table 1.5** (continued)

| | 2002 | 2005 | 2006 | 2007 | 2008 | 2009 | 2010 | 2011 |
|---|---|---|---|---|---|---|---|---|
| 056 Vegetables, roots and tubers, prepared or preserved, n.e.s. | 2.25 | 1.85 | 1.81 | 1.75 | 1.62 | 1.46 | 1.72 | 1.81 |
| 893 Articles, n.e.s., of plastics | 2.07 | 1.81 | 1.74 | 1.55 | 1.54 | 1.50 | 1.56 | 1.67 |
| 693 Wire products (excluding insulated electrical wiring) and fencing grills | 1.39 | 1.53 | 1.57 | 1.71 | 2.05 | 1.61 | 1.54 | 1.66 |
| 741 Heating and cooling equipment, and parts thereof, n.e.s. | 1.00 | 1.41 | 1.34 | 1.45 | 1.53 | 1.43 | 1.59 | 1.65 |
| 716 Rotating electric plant, and parts thereof, n.e.s. | 1.54 | 1.36 | 1.34 | 1.37 | 1.47 | 1.35 | 1.50 | 1.63 |
| 625 Rubber tyres, interchangeable tyre treads, tyre flaps and inner tubes for wheels of all kinds | 1.00 | 1.25 | 1.35 | 1.43 | 1.45 | 1.47 | 1.49 | 1.60 |
| 635 Wood manufactures, n.e.s. | 2.39 | 1.96 | 1.89 | 1.59 | 1.42 | 1.56 | 1.63 | 1.54 |
| 694 Nails, screws, nuts, bolts, rivets and the like, of iron, steel, copper or aluminium | 1.25 | 1.63 | 1.68 | 1.72 | 1.98 | 1.45 | 1.41 | 1.50 |
| 699 Manufactures of base metal, n.e.s. | 1.48 | 1.52 | 1.53 | 1.46 | 1.41 | 1.36 | 1.40 | 1.45 |
| 884 Optical goods, n.e.s. | 1.21 | 1.35 | 1.35 | 1.38 | 1.43 | 1.35 | 1.36 | 1.45 |
| 747 Taps, cocks, valves and similar appliances for pipes, boiler shells, tanks, vats or the like, including pressure-reducing valves and thermostatically controlled valves | 1.18 | 1.27 | 1.42 | 1.49 | 1.55 | 1.37 | 1.44 | 1.45 |
| 695 Tools for use in the hand or in machines | 1.31 | 1.36 | 1.30 | 1.28 | 1.22 | 1.29 | 1.33 | 1.42 |
| 325 Coke or semi-coke (including char) of coal, of lignite or of peat; whether or not agglomerated; retort carbon | 7.93 | 5.25 | 4.39 | 4.70 | 4.74 | 0.53 | 1.55 | 1.42 |
| 058 Fruit, preserved, and fruit preparations (excluding fruit juices) | 1.95 | 1.57 | 1.49 | 1.50 | 1.52 | 1.37 | 1.40 | 1.41 |
| 724 Textile and leather machinery, and parts thereof, n.e.s. | 0.90 | 1.05 | 1.16 | 1.15 | 1.25 | 1.28 | 1.31 | 1.40 |
| 278 Other crude minerals | 2.09 | 1.42 | 1.17 | 1.07 | 1.50 | 1.08 | 1.34 | 1.40 |
| 773 Equipment for distributing electricity, n.e.s. | 1.11 | 1.15 | 1.23 | 1.32 | 1.40 | 1.39 | 1.40 | 1.39 |
| 664 Glass | 0.98 | 1.14 | 1.15 | 1.21 | 1.26 | 1.20 | 1.29 | 1.36 |
| 268 Wool and other animal hair (including wool tops) | 1.42 | 1.48 | 1.50 | 1.31 | 1.27 | 1.23 | 1.27 | 1.34 |
| 659 Floor coverings, etc. | 1.29 | 1.10 | 1.05 | 1.07 | 1.25 | 1.29 | 1.36 | 1.33 |

(continued)

**Table 1.5** (continued)

| | 2002 | 2005 | 2006 | 2007 | 2008 | 2009 | 2010 | 2011 |
|---|---|---|---|---|---|---|---|---|
| 772 Electrical apparatus for switching or protecting electrical circuits or for making connections to or in electrical circuits (e.g., switches, relays, fuses, lightning arresters, voltage limiters, surge suppressors, plugs and sockets, lamp-holders and junct | 0.94 | 1.08 | 1.20 | 1.25 | 1.31 | 1.28 | 1.27 | 1.29 |
| 873 Meters and counters n.e.s. | 1.46 | 1.06 | 1.00 | 1.10 | 1.25 | 1.16 | 1.11 | 1.23 |
| 524 Other inorganic chemicals; organic and inorganic compounds of precious metals | 1.32 | 2.92 | 1.60 | 1.41 | 1.40 | 1.06 | 1.23 | 1.21 |
| 522 Inorganic chemical elements, oxides and halogen salts | 1.70 | 1.47 | 1.41 | 1.42 | 1.32 | 1.05 | 1.19 | 1.20 |
| 074 Tea and mat | 2.15 | 1.66 | 1.53 | 1.36 | 1.23 | 1.21 | 1.08 | 1.17 |
| 034 Fish, fresh (live or dead), chilled or frozen. | 1.44 | 1.20 | 1.14 | 0.98 | 0.97 | 1.06 | 1.07 | 1.12 |
| 075 Spices | 1.57 | 1.92 | 1.46 | 1.14 | 1.22 | 1.30 | 1.25 | 0.92 |
| 671 Pig-iron, spiegeleisen, sponge iron, iron or steel granules, iron or steel powders and ferro-alloys | 1.85 | 1.77 | 1.32 | 1.36 | 1.38 | 0.62 | 0.69 | 0.90 |

Since 2002 there has been some obvious change in China's comparative advantage; some traditionally strong industries have seen diminishing edges, whereas new strong points have emerged. Eighteen industries are no longer advantageous with a competitive advantage index lower than 1 in the past five years. Among them are agricultural products, and energy-, pollution-, and resource-intensive products. The latter, in particular, saw a big drop in its export and became a disadvantaged industry. This is the result of China's effort to transform its development pattern and to reduce the export of such products. If we take industries whose comparative advantage index was 1 before but have become greater than 1 in the past three years as emerging industries with comparative advantage, then we will see China has 26 such industries, mainly those related to mechanical installations and the chemical industry (for details see Table 1.6).

In some traditionally strong industries of China, high-end products remain largely uncompetitive. For instance, the motorcycle industry has quite a strong comparative advantage on the whole, but a closer look will reveal that the advantage mainly comes from low-power models while high-power ones are obviously disadvantaged. In some emerging advantaged industries, some key

**Table 1.6** Comparative advantage index shown for emerging strong industries and disappearing strong industries

| | 2002 | 2003 | 2004 | 2005 | 2006 | 2007 | 2008 | 2009 | 2010 | 2011 |
|---|---|---|---|---|---|---|---|---|---|---|
| 711 Steam or other vapour-generating boilers, superheated water boilers, and auxiliary plant for use therewith; parts thereof | 0.89 | 0.65 | 0.85 | 0.86 | 1.31 | 1.89 | 3.24 | 3.29 | 3.08 | 3.52 |
| 793 Ships, boats (including hovercraft) and floating structures | 0.81 | 0.96 | 0.75 | 0.90 | 1.15 | 1.31 | 1.54 | 2.07 | 2.28 | 2.26 |
| 897 Jewellery, goldsmiths' and silversmiths' wares, and other articles of precious or semiprecious materials, n.e.s. | 1.25 | 1.04 | 0.97 | 0.95 | 0.82 | 0.76 | 0.68 | 0.61 | 1.12 | 1.97 |
| 712 Steam turbines and other vapour turbines and parts thereof, n.e.s. | 0.22 | 0.26 | 0.29 | 0.38 | 0.50 | 0.70 | 1.38 | 1.50 | 1.55 | 1.70 |
| 266 Synthetic fibres suitable for spinning | 0.44 | 0.56 | 0.56 | 0.75 | 0.90 | 1.07 | 1.33 | 1.08 | 1.22 | 1.66 |
| 811 Prefabricated buildings | 0.16 | 0.24 | 0.42 | 0.77 | 1.20 | 1.51 | 1.64 | 1.67 | 1.60 | 1.66 |
| 674 Flat-rolled products of iron or non-alloy steel, clad, plated or coated | 0.13 | 0.11 | 0.24 | 0.29 | 0.79 | 1.00 | 1.32 | 0.78 | 1.26 | 1.65 |
| 678 Wire of iron or steel | 0.75 | 0.74 | 0.92 | 0.96 | 1.18 | 1.25 | 1.67 | 1.44 | 1.43 | 1.49 |
| 679 Tubes, pipes and hollow profiles, and tube or pipe fittings, of iron or steel | 0.72 | 0.77 | 0.86 | 1.03 | 1.28 | 1.48 | 1.78 | 1.40 | 1.30 | 1.48 |
| 724 Textile and leather machinery, and parts thereof, n.e.s. | 0.90 | 0.92 | 0.94 | 1.05 | 1.16 | 1.15 | 1.25 | 1.28 | 1.31 | 1.40 |
| 675 Flat-rolled products of alloy steel | 0.08 | 0.09 | 0.19 | 0.20 | 0.42 | 0.65 | 0.91 | 0.41 | 0.72 | 1.40 |
| 749 Non electrical parts and accessories of machinery, n.e.s. | 0.47 | 0.50 | 0.54 | 0.62 | 0.70 | 0.81 | 1.14 | 1.27 | 1.18 | 1.23 |
| 744 Mechanical handling equipment, and parts thereof, n.e.s. | 0.75 | 0.71 | 0.82 | 0.88 | 0.93 | 0.99 | 1.25 | 1.36 | 1.23 | 1.22 |
| 737 Metalworking machinery (other than machine tools), and parts thereof, n.e.s. | 0.43 | 0.49 | 0.57 | 0.68 | 0.78 | 0.89 | 1.29 | 1.38 | 1.15 | 1.21 |

(continued)

**Table 1.6** (continued)

| | 2002 | 2003 | 2004 | 2005 | 2006 | 2007 | 2008 | 2009 | 2010 | 2011 |
|---|---|---|---|---|---|---|---|---|---|---|
| 776 Thermionic, cold cathode or photo-cathode valves and tubes (e.g., vacuum or vapour or gas-filled valves and tubes, mercury arc rectifying valves and tubes, cathode-ray tubes, television camera tubes); diodes, transistors and similar semiconductor devices; | 0.56 | 0.61 | 0.72 | 0.76 | 0.85 | 0.89 | 1.08 | 1.03 | 1.10 | 1.19 |
| 881 Photographic apparatus and equipment, n.e.s. | 1.36 | 1.15 | 0.78 | 0.55 | 0.40 | 0.68 | 0.85 | 0.94 | 0.89 | 1.16 |
| 746 Ball- or roller bearings | 1.13 | 0.93 | 0.96 | 0.95 | 0.90 | 0.92 | 1.04 | 0.92 | 1.05 | 1.15 |
| 898 Musical instruments and parts and accessories thereof; records, tapes and other sound or similar recordings (excluding goods of groups 763 and 883) | 0.67 | 0.70 | 0.81 | 0.76 | 0.74 | 1.30 | 1.52 | 1.32 | 1.20 | 1.13 |
| 514 Nitrogen-function compounds | 0.88 | 0.75 | 0.78 | 0.87 | 0.99 | 0.95 | 1.16 | 1.11 | 1.05 | 1.13 |
| 745 Non-electrical machinery, tools and mechanical apparatus, and parts thereof, n.e.s. | 0.57 | 0.62 | 0.69 | 0.74 | 0.77 | 0.82 | 0.89 | 0.97 | 1.06 | 1.08 |
| 513 Carboxylic acids and their anhydrides, halides, peroxides and peroxyacids and their halogenated, sulfonated, nitrated or nitrosated derivatives | 0.79 | 0.72 | 0.74 | 0.75 | 0.76 | 0.84 | 1.00 | 0.95 | 1.05 | 1.07 |
| 663 Mineral manufactures not otherwise specified | 0.50 | 0.51 | 0.51 | 0.56 | 0.59 | 0.59 | 0.76 | 0.73 | 0.89 | 1.06 |
| 525 Radioactive and associated materials | 0.97 | 0.69 | 0.68 | 0.49 | 0.43 | 0.34 | 0.39 | 0.18 | 0.47 | 1.02 |
| 677 Pearls and precious or semiprecious stones, unworked or worked | 0.39 | 0.35 | 0.32 | 0.29 | 0.67 | 0.82 | 1.25 | 1.40 | 0.93 | 1.02 |
| 562 Fertilizers (other than those of group 272) | 0.52 | 0.85 | 0.99 | 0.55 | 0.56 | 1.15 | 0.64 | 0.65 | 0.93 | 1.01 |

(continued)

**Table 1.6** (continued)

| | 2002 | 2003 | 2004 | 2005 | 2006 | 2007 | 2008 | 2009 | 2010 | 2011 |
|---|---|---|---|---|---|---|---|---|---|---|
| 743 Pumps (except liquid pump), air or other gas compressors and fans; ventilating or recycling hoods incorporating a fan, whether or not fitted with filters; centrifuges; filtration or purification devices; and their components | 0.72 | 0.76 | 0.81 | 0.88 | 0.86 | 0.86 | 0.91 | 0.95 | 1.00 | 1.00 |
| 515 Organo-inorganic compounds, heterocyclic compounds, nucleic acids and their salts and sulfonamides | 0.42 | 0.42 | 0.41 | 0.47 | 0.56 | 0.68 | 1.12 | 0.83 | 0.90 | 1.00 |
| 036 Crustaceans, molluscs and other aquatic invertebrates, whether in shell or not, fresh (live or dead), chilled, frozen, dried, salted or in brine; crustaceans, in shell, cooked by steaming or boiling in water, whether or not chilled, frozen, dried, salted or in brine; flours, meals and pellets of crustaceans or of aquatic invertebrates, fit for human consumption | 1.13 | 1.04 | 1.05 | 0.76 | 0.60 | 0.50 | 0.49 | 0.96 | 1.00 | 0.99 |
| 054 Vegetables, fresh, chilled, frozen or simply preserved (including dried leguminous vegetables); roots, tubers and other edible vegetable products, n.e.s., fresh or dried | 1.37 | 1.17 | 1.08 | 1.04 | 1.01 | 0.86 | 0.82 | 0.89 | 1.03 | 0.96 |
| 671 Pig iron, spiegeleisen, sponge iron, iron or steel granules, iron or steel powders and ferro-alloy | 1.85 | 1.90 | 2.24 | 1.77 | 1.32 | 1.36 | 1.38 | 0.62 | 0.69 | 0.90 |

(continued)

**Table 1.6** (continued)

| | 2002 | 2003 | 2004 | 2005 | 2006 | 2007 | 2008 | 2009 | 2010 | 2011 |
|---|---|---|---|---|---|---|---|---|---|---|
| 591 Insecticides, rodenticides, fungicides, herbicides, anti-sprouting products and plant-growth regulators, disinfectants and similar products, put up in forms or packings for retail sale or as preparations or articles (e.g., sulphur-treated bands, wicks and candles, and fly-papers) | 1.06 | 0.98 | 1.21 | 1.18 | 0.78 | 0.81 | 0.89 | 0.66 | 0.71 | 0.81 |
| 676 Iron and steel bars, rods, angles and sections (including sheet piling) | 0.39 | 0.45 | 0.72 | 0.84 | 1.15 | 1.45 | 1.45 | 0.49 | 0.70 | 0.79 |
| 885 Watches and clocks | 1.68 | 1.54 | 1.30 | 1.09 | 0.91 | 0.89 | 0.86 | 0.88 | 0.80 | 0.73 |
| 673 Flat-rolled products of iron or non-alloy steel, not clad, plated or coated | 0.26 | 0.20 | 0.65 | 0.79 | 1.29 | 1.50 | 1.63 | 0.70 | 0.95 | 0.39 |
| 272 Fertilizers, crude, other than those of division 56 | 1.93 | 1.79 | 1.38 | 1.05 | 0.66 | 0.67 | 0.84 | 0.37 | 0.42 | 0.31 |
| 245 Fuel wood (except wood waste) and wood charcoal | 3.17 | 2.18 | 1.16 | 0.57 | 0.49 | 0.30 | 0.29 | 0.26 | 0.32 | 0.28 |
| 685 Lead | 3.30 | 2.75 | 2.76 | 2.30 | 2.33 | 1.22 | 0.50 | 0.27 | 0.28 | 0.21 |
| 321 Coal, whether or not pulverised, but not agglomerated | 2.40 | 2.08 | 1.82 | 1.25 | 0.91 | 0.70 | 0.61 | 0.30 | 0.21 | 0.19 |
| 042 Rice | 1.11 | 1.16 | 0.41 | 0.30 | 0.47 | 0.41 | 0.25 | 0.28 | 0.19 | 0.17 |
| 611 Leather | 1.11 | 1.05 | 1.05 | 1.04 | 0.96 | 0.54 | 0.19 | 0.15 | 0.18 | 0.17 |
| 687 Tin | 2.37 | 2.00 | 1.68 | 0.89 | 0.73 | 0.81 | 0.07 | 0.06 | 0.07 | 0.09 |
| 686 Zinc | 1.85 | 1.47 | 0.78 | 0.49 | 0.98 | 0.69 | 0.18 | 0.09 | 0.09 | 0.09 |
| 044 Maize (not including sweet corn), unmilled | 2.30 | 2.70 | 0.42 | 1.32 | 0.38 | 0.48 | 0.03 | 0.02 | 0.01 | 0.01 |
| 672 Ingots and other primary forms, of iron or steel; semi-finished products of iron or steel | 0.48 | 0.42 | 1.36 | 1.30 | 1.36 | 0.84 | 0.27 | 0.01 | 0.02 | 0.00 |

products actually remain uncompetitive. Shipbuilding is an emerging industry with comparative advantage in China, but the related power devices are not very competitive.

## Reference

Hausmann, R., and B. Klinger. 2007. The structure of the product space and the evolution of comparative advantage.

# Chapter 2 Transforming the Growth Model and the Choice of China's Spearhead Industries

**Qizi Zhang, Chaoxian Guo and Mei Bai**

## 2.1 Transforming the Model of Economic Growth and the Selection Criteria for Spearhead Industries

Economic growth is made up of growth in different industries. Different industries will make different contributions to economic growth at different stages of economic development. For a country to quicken its economic growth, it needs to find the spearhead industries that will play a significant role in economic growth. Here and abroad, there are two methods for identifying the spearhead industries. One method is based on input-output using the forward correlation coefficient and the backward correlation coefficient, i.e. the degree of correlation as a benchmark in selecting the spearhead industries. The other method is the elastic approach, which we may call the elasticity benchmark. For example, in 1957 the Japanese economist Miyohei Shinohara in his *Industrial Structure* (*Sangyo Kozo*) introduced two important criteria for selecting spearhead industries. These are the "income elasticity criterion" and the "productivity increase criterion", which together referred to as the "Shinohara criteria". Under the income elasticity criterion, the income elasticity of product demand is the criteria for industrial structure planning, and the growth in industrial demand is related to national income growth and structure. For products with high income elasticity, when per capita income grows, the rise in demand for that product will exceed the rise in income. This means that the market for that product is promising, and the industry with high income elasticity, should be selected as the spearhead industry. The productivity increase criterion starts from the supply in society in order to select the spearhead industries. Shinohara believes

Q. Zhang (✉) · C. Guo · M. Bai
Chinese Academy of Social Sciences, Beijing, China
e-mail: zhangqizi65@126.com



Q. Zhang (ed.), *Transforming Economic Growth and China's Industrial Upgrading*, Research Series on the Chinese Dream and China's Development Path,
https://doi.org/10.1007/978-981-13-0962-5_2

that priority should be given to the development in improving technology to quicken the pace of change; industries with high total factor productivity become the spearhead industries. The United Nations Industrial Development Organization (UNIDO) suggests that the criteria of growth elasticity and size elasticity be used to select spearhead industries (Liu Yong 2006, p. 148).

As different industries play different roles in economic growth, different industrial development will also play different roles in transforming the mode for economic growth. To quicken growth model transformation, it is also necessary to find those industries that are most conducive to achieving the transformation. Although the aforementioned industrial correlation and elasticity are different criteria, what they have in common is the emphasis on the role of the spearhead industries in providing impetus to economic growth, which is for the industry to drive economic growth. The spearhead industries selected by this kind of criteria probably may not fit the requirement for growth model transformation, which has different spearhead industry selecting criteria from economic growth (Guo Kesha 2003; Liu Yazheng 2008; Lin Sujiao, Jiang Bing 2008). The criteria under China's current circumstance of growth model transformation include: the employment—whether it is conducive to expanding employment; expanding domestic demands—whether it is conducive to expanding domestic demands; environmental friendliness and resources conservation—whether it is conducive to conserving resources and protecting the environment; making progress in science and technology—whether it is conducive to making progress in science and technology, etc. (refer to Table 3.1 for details).

The spearhead industries selected by the criteria emphasizing on economic growth can hardly satisfy the requirement of growth model transformation. Therefore, in accordance with China's need, scholars propose new criteria, among which a more representative work is Guo Kesha's paper published in 2003 entitled "Selecting Spearhead Industries in the New Era of Industrialization". In this paper, Guo Kesha points out that many areas should be taken into account in selecting emerging spearhead industries in the new era of industrialization, including the industry's growth potential, employment function, driving effect, productivity increase rate, technology intensity, sustainability of growth, etc. This set of selection criteria for spearhead industries is relatively comprehensive in reflecting the requirement for the mode of transformation but it is still incomplete. For instance, it does not include the criterion for expanding domestic demands. When applying these criteria in selecting the spearhead industries to practice, the author employed different criteria. As for the driving effect, the author gave consideration to the correlation between industries, but the other indicators completely disregard this. When using the sustainable development criterion to determine the spearhead industries, the author employed the indicator for economic efficiency. This indicator cannot fully reflect the impact the industry has on resources conservation and environmental protection.

The impact of an industry on growth model transformation is not solely dependent on its direct effect, but also on the impact of this industry has on other industries, i.e. its indirect effect. In selecting industries to transform the growth model, it is necessary to consider both their direct and indirect impact. A better tool for achieving this task is based on the analysis of the input-output table. The input-output analysis describes and explains the productivity in different industrial sectors of the national economy and their relationship with other sectors; it is an indispensable basic tool for assessing key sectors and analysing the industrial structure. It helps us understand the relationship between the industries, and then concentrate on the key industrial sector to achieve industrial upgrade. Therefore, here we employ a new industry correlation criterion in the discussion of selecting spearhead industries for achieving quicker economic growth and transforming the mode for economic growth. To achieve this aim, we have added some new content to the existing input-output table, such as energy consumption, emission of waste gas and discharge of waste water and residue, labour force occupancy, investment in R&D, resident income, etc. Table 3.1 lists different measurements for different criteria. For the effect on employment, we use the direct employment occupancy coefficient and the complete occupancy coefficient to measure. For the criterion to expand domestic demands, we use the production inducement coefficient or the resident income multiplier to measure. For the resource conservation and environmental friendliness criterion, we use the direct energy consumption and the complete consumption coefficients to measure, etc. (see details in Table 2.1). The last row in Table 3.1 is an example with reference to the industry selection criteria to protect growth.

**Table 2.1** Industry selection criteria for growth model transformation

| Selection criteria | Measurement | Type of indicator |
|---|---|---|
| Employment: whether it is conducive to expanding employment | Direct employment occupancy coefficient and complete occupancy coefficient | Positive indicator |
| Expanding domestic demands: whether it is conducive to the contribution for growth by raising demands; whether it is conducive to expanding domestic demands | The production inducement coefficient of final demand and resident income multiplier | Positive indicator |
| Resource conservation and environmental friendliness: whether it is conducive to energy conservation and environmental protection | Resources complete consumption coefficient and complete emissions coefficient of "three wastes" | Negative indicator |
| Progress in science and technology: whether it is conducive to scientific and technological progress | The effect of R&D spillovers | Positive indicator |
| Promoting economic growth: whether it is conducive to economic growth | Impact coefficient and reaction coefficient | Positive indicator |

## 2.2 Selecting Spearhead Industries Under the Context of Different Criteria

1. **The employment criterion in selecting spearhead industries**

To analyse the selection of spearhead industries from the perspective of employment, we need to start from the input-output table, using the number of the direct and complete labour force occupancy coefficients as indicators for measuring the impact of the various industries on employment. The direct labour force occupancy coefficient of an industry is:

$$l_j = \frac{L_j}{X_j} \tag{2.1}$$

of which, j = 1, 2, …, n.

Marking $l = (l_j)_{1\times n}$ as a row vector, then the row vector formed by the complete labour force occupancy coefficient of an industry is:

$$\bar{l} = (\bar{l}_j)_{1\times n} = l \times (I - A)^{-1} \tag{2.2}$$

Before calculating the direct and complete labour force occupancy coefficients, we need to estimate the figures of employment by sector. There are employment figures of the whole society in the *2007 China Statistical Yearbook* and *China Labour Statistical Yearbook*. However, sectors in these yearbooks are quite roughly divided and do not correspond well with the 42 sectors in the input-output table. Therefore, it is necessary to undertake estimation and adjustment of the actual employment figures in the industries according to the 42 sectors in the input-output table. The following are the methods to estimate and adjust: (1) the figure can be used directly where the sector employment figure is in the yearbook, and where the definition of the sector is in agreement between the table and the yearbook; (2) the data of the various industrial sectors should be divided into the three categories of mining, manufacturing, and the production and supply of electricity, gas & water, and then adjustment is carried out with reference to the number of workers in the various sectors as proportions of the total number of employed personnel. The *2007 China Statistical Yearbook*, contains figures of employment by sector, but the total is much smaller than the total number of employed in society. However, these figures can be put to use. Let us assume that the employment figures by sector is structured in the same way as that of the total number of employed in society, then a ratio can be reached by dividing the total number of industrial employment in society with the total of employment by industry sector, which can be used to estimate the total number of employed in society by industry sector; (3) in the tertiary industry, if there is no direct statistical data, then labour remuneration in the input-output table and the number of related employment in the statistical yearbook can be combined to estimate and determine the employment figure in the various sectors of the tertiary industry.

Using formulae (2.1) and (2.2), the direct and complete labour occupancy coefficients are calculated; by sifting through the industries that come top in employment figure, direct and complete labour occupancy coefficients, we can come up with results.

2. **The energy conservation and environment protection criteria in selecting spearhead industries**

To strengthen energy conservation and ecological protection, and to bolster sustainable development are urgent tasks facing China's economic and social development. These important tasks need to be fulfilled in growth model transformation. Therefore, the selection criteria based on energy conservation and environmental protection are important content in achieving the transformation.

This is the method for calculating the direct energy consumption coefficient and the complete consumption coefficient of an industry: condensing the five industries of coal mining and washing, oil and gas extraction, petroleum coking and nuclear fuel processing, electricity and heating production supply, and fuel gas production and supply into a large sector of energy production and supply. The sum of direct consumption coefficient by the various sectors for these five industries, as well as the sum of complete consumption, gives us the direct energy consumption coefficient and the complete consumption coefficient.

Production activities will consume a certain amount of environment's resources and pollute the environment. Therefore, the emission of pollutants is treated as consumption of the environment's resources, i.e. the 'three wastes' (waste gas, waste water and solid waste) emission volume (physical quantity) is treated as an input of environmental resource. In order to calculate the direct consumption coefficient and the complete consumption coefficient of the waste emissions, it is necessary to extend the input-output table, including the waste emissions added to the input-output table as in the format of Table 2.2.

**Table 2.2** Format of the extended output table

| Input | | Output | | | | Total use | Total output |
|---|---|---|---|---|---|---|---|
| | | Intermediate use | | | | | |
| | | Sector 1 | Sector 2 | … | Sector n | | |
| Intermediate inputs | Sector 1 | | | | | | |
| | … | | | | | | |
| | Sector n | | | | | | |
| Initial input | | | | | | | |
| Total input | | $X_1$ | $X_2$ | … | $X_n$ | | |
| Emission of pollutants (physical quantity) | Waste water discharge | $FS_1$ | $FS_2$ | … | $FS_n$ | | |
| | Waste gases emission | $FQ_1$ | $FQ_2$ | … | $FQ_n$ | | |
| | Solid waste | $GF_1$ | $GF_2$ | … | $GF_n$ | | |

The direct emission coefficients of wastes in liquid, gas and solids by the various sectors are:

$$fs_j = \frac{FS_j}{X_j} \tag{2.3}$$

$$fq_j = \frac{FQ_j}{X_j} \tag{2.4}$$

$$gf_j = \frac{QF_j}{X_j} \tag{2.5}$$

of which, j = 1, 2, …, n. Marking $P = \begin{pmatrix} fs \\ fq \\ gf \end{pmatrix}_{3\times n}$ as the direct emission coefficient matrix of the 'three wastes' emission, then the complete emission coefficient matrix of the wastes from the various industries is:

$$\overline{P} = P \times (I - A)^{-1} \tag{2.6}$$

It is necessary to first estimate the total volume of emitted pollutants in order to calculate the direct emission coefficient and the complete emission coefficient of wastes. There is complete data on China's total wastes emission (but the industrial categories are not the same as those in the input-output table and require adjustment). However, there lacks data on the total wastes emission from agriculture and the tertiary industry. Therefore, we need to estimate the data from agriculture and the tertiary industry. This is the specific method: (1) Re-categorise the industries in accordance with the categories in the input-output table. Industrial sectors are divided into four categories of emission scales, to calculate the corresponding emission levels for every $10,000 of intermediate inputs. (2) Consider the characteristics of emission from primary and tertiary industries. These emissions will be graded with reference to the standards of the various industrial sectors. (3) Based on the assumption of emission levels and the intermediate inputs data, to estimate the emission data of the various industries in the primary and tertiary industries.

3. **The production inducement coefficient criterion in the selection of spearhead industries**

Products from all sectors are either to satisfy intermediate demand or final demand, but ultimately the production level is determined by the final demand; intermediate demand is only a derived requirement. Therefore, to reveal the link between production level and final demand, we need to calculate production inducement coefficient.

The production inducement coefficient indicates the output of the all sectors as induced by final demand in a certain unit. The greater the production inducement coefficient, the greater the production ripple and effect. Since imports of intermediary input do not induce domestic production in the process, in order to accurately analyse the inducement effect of the final demand on the national economy, we need to eliminate the effect of the import factor when calculating the inducement effect and the degree of dependency. A simple method is to deduct according to the share of the sector's imports in that sector's overall domestic consumption. The assumption for such a method is: The same intermediate inputs consumed by all sectors during production is proportionally the same in the production within the country (region). As there is an identity relation as follows in the input-output table: overall domestic consumption = total output + imports-exports = intermediate products + domestic final consumption, we can assume $\alpha$ = (total output-exports)/total consumption, to indicate the share of domestically produced products in overall domestic consumption, marking $\hat{\alpha}$ as a diagonal matrix of the ratio of domestic consumption to domestic production. Then, the formula finally used for the production inducement coefficient is expressed as:

$$\mathrm{R} = (I - \hat{\alpha}A)^{-1} \times S \tag{2.7}$$

of which, R is the column vector of the production inducement coefficient used in the end, $(I - \hat{\alpha}A)^{-1}$ is the Leontief inverse matrix after eliminating the effect of import (input), S is the end-use structural coefficients in the column vector. When S represents the column vector for final consumption, capital formation or exports respectively, R represents the corresponding column vector for production inducement coefficient triggered by final consumption, capital formation or exports.

According to the above formula, production inducement coefficient for final consumption, capital formation and exports can be calculated. It can be seen from the figures calculated that between the three inducement coefficients, apart from agriculture and the majority of the tertiary industry having the final consumption inducement coefficient as the largest, almost all the sectors in secondary industries either have the capital formation inducement coefficient or the export inducement coefficient as the largest. Given that consumer demand is the original driving force of economic growth, its pace of growth has a significant effect on GDP. Growth model transformation requires to drive development by boosting domestic demand, especially consumer demand, so as to transform growth model from relying on investment and exports to driven by consumption and investment, with domestic demand working in tandem with foreign demand. Therefore, in revising the relationship between investment, exports and consumption, growth model transformation requires boosting domestic demand. As such, in selecting industries, those sectors accounting for a large share in the consumption structure and with large consumption inducement coefficient should be developed.

4. **The income multiplier criterion in selecting spearhead industries**

Production is not just a process in the consumption of raw materials, energy and services. It is also a process in the consumption of living labour. The consumption of living labour is shown as remuneration in the input-output table. Thus, the process of living labour consumption is the process that enables personal income growth, which is the basis for boosting domestic demand. The income multiplier can be used to measure an industry's impact on income growth. The income multiplier refers to the increment in the income of people in all sectors induced directly or indirectly by one unit of increase in the final product of a certain sector. In a sense, fostering industries that have a large income multiplier enables people to gain more from economic development.

Measuring the income multiplier requires an appropriate revision of the original input-output table. Households should be separately listed, as n + 1, in the intermediate consumption matrix. It means subsuming households of the second quadrant as well as the remuneration in the third quadrant into the first quadrant. Thus, the first quadrant forms the (n + 1) × (n + 1) flow matrix. The new model becomes:

$$(I - A^*)X^* = Y^* \tag{2.8}$$

in the formula, $A^* = \begin{pmatrix} A & h_c \\ \beta h_r & 0 \end{pmatrix}$, $X^* = \begin{pmatrix} X \\ X_c \end{pmatrix}$, $Y^* = \begin{pmatrix} Y - Y_c \\ 0 \end{pmatrix}$

Of which, A, X, and Y are the direct consumption coefficient matrix, the total output column vector, and the final product column vector in the ordinary input-output model respectively. $X_c$ indicates the total resident income (total remuneration), $Y_c$ is the total resident consumption column vector, $h_r$ is the worker remuneration coefficient row vector, $h_c$ indicates the column vector for household consumption structure, $\beta$ indicates the average propensity to consume, and $\beta = \sum_{i=1}^{n} Y_c^i / X_c$ are adjustments to balance the total resident income and total consumption.

According to formula (2.8), we have:

$$X^* = (I - A^*)^{-1} Y^* \tag{2.9}$$

The new Leontief inverse matrix $B^* = (I - A^*)^{-1}$ not only reflects direct and indirect demands arising from intermediate inputs, but also includes direct and indirect demands for products as a result of increased household demands caused by rising remuneration. Therefore, it describes the correlation between the sectors given the effect from the households, and in this way, it is possible to estimate increment in the income of all households induced by one unit of increase in the final product of a certain sector, i.e. the household income multiplier.

The formula for calculating the household income multiplier is:

$$M_{vj} = \sum_{i=1}^{n} a_{vi} b_{ij}^* \quad (j = 1, 2, \ldots, n) \tag{2.10}$$

Of which, $M_{vj}$ is the household income multiplier for sector j, $a_{vi}$ is the remuneration coefficient for sector i, $b_{ij}^{*}$ is the element in the new Leontief inverse matrix $B^{*} = (I - A^{*})^{-1}$.

The household income multiplier is calculated according to formula (2.10). It can be seen that the effect of the household multiplier is greater on labour intensive industries, such as agriculture, education, public administration and social organizations, health, social security and social welfare, the postal service, scientific research, coal mining and washing, other social services and textile. Compared with capital intensive industries, these labour intensive industries have a larger share of remuneration in their unit production cost. The large amount of remuneration turns into more consumption demand, which then induce higher household income, and so the household income multiplier in these industries is rather higher (Table 3.3).

5. **The criterion for scientific and technological progress in selecting spearhead industries**

The crux of China's growth model transformation is to drive economic growth that relies on capital and materials towards growth by progress in science and technology and human resources. The fundamental idea in the technology for input and output is that a sector's input in technology not only spurs on that sector's technological progress, but, with enhanced productivity, it can also raise productivity in other sectors, having a role in the progress in science and technology in other sectors. Thus, by calculating the spillover effect in scientific and technological progress, we can identify key sectors that can stimulate a country's progress in science and technology.

Axuel During put forward an R&D flow matrix that measures the knowledge and innovation spillover effect from input/output technologies.

$$X_{R\&D} = \langle R\&D \rangle \langle X \rangle^{-1} (I - A)^{-1} \langle Y \rangle$$

Here, $X_{R\&D}$ is the flow matrix for R&D (hypothetical). ⟨R&D⟩, ⟨X⟩ and ⟨Y⟩ indicate the diagonal matrix formed respectively by the R&D expenditure column vector, total output column vector, and final output column vector. $X_{R\&D}$ Row i shows the figure of sector i's input in research and development funds 'apportioned' among other sectors in their final production process—it is the measurement of sector i as a contributor in technology. $X_{R\&D}$ Row j shows research and development funding obtained by sector j's product via the economic system—it is the measurement of j sector as a beneficiary of technology (Zhang Hongxia 2004, pp. 165–170).

Instructed by this, we start by constructing a 'hypothetical' technology resources flow coefficient matrix as the basis for calculating the spillover effect in scientific and technological progress from the various sectors.

In input/output technologies, a distribution coefficient matrix is generally used to analyse inter-sectoral forward connection. As such, the definition of the forward technological flow coefficient matrix is as follows:

$D_{KJ} = \langle KJ \rangle \langle X \rangle^{-1} (I - A_C)^{-1}$, of which, $A_C$ is the input-output distribution coefficient.

$D_{KJ}$ Row i shows the spillover effect of sector i's technological activities during production on all sectors of the national economy. It measures the spillover effect of sector i as a contributor to the science and technology resources. The sum of this row measures the overall spillover effect of sector i's science and technology on all sectors of the national economy. The formula is:

$$MD_{KJ} = \sum_{j=1}^{n} \mathrm{d}_{\mathrm{kj}}^{\mathrm{ij}}$$

The technology resources index uses figures from internal expenditure of funded science and technology activities. The specific data contain three parts: figures from research and development organizations, large and medium sized industrial corporations, and higher education institutions in corresponding year. Of these, the internal expenditure of funded science and technology activities in universities all comes under the education sector.

According to the formula and data above, we calculate the spillover effect of science and technology in all sectors. The top ten in science and technology spillover are: scientific research, transport facilities manufacturing, education, smelting and flat-roll processing, electrical, mechanical and equipment manufacturing, coal mining and washing, communications facilities, manufacture of computing and other electronic devices, the chemical industry, oil and gas extraction, general purpose or special equipment manufacturing. As can be seen, sectors in scientific research, education, some heavy industry sectors, the equipment manufacturing sector and the new high-tech manufacturing sector have a big science and technology spillover effect on the national economy. Therefore, from the perspective of promoting progress in science and technology, strengthening independent innovation capability and giving science and technology a leading role in the national economy, it is of strategic importance to increase scientific and technological input.

## 2.3 Maintaining Economic Growth and Growth Model Transformation—A Dichotomy

1. **The growth criterion in selecting spearhead industries**

The national economy is a complex entity, with extensive and close economic and technological links between sectors. Therefore, any changes in the production process of a sector will ripple through to other sectors via this industrial connectivity. With the input-output method, we can carry out a quantitative analysis on the national economy in a given period, of the economic and technological connection that has formed, as a result of social reproduction, among the industry sectors, in direct and indirect mutual reliance and mutual constraint. In input-output analysis, the induction coefficient is used to reflect the degree of influence of one industry by other industries; and the impact coefficient is used to reflect the extent that an industry influences other industries. Generally speaking, Industries with a higher impact coefficient have a greater diffusion on production in the society. Industries with a higher induction coefficient have a greater constraint on economic development. In particular, when economic growth is too fast, these industry sectors will first face huge pressure for demand, which leads to a state of demand outstripping supply. When both the impact and induction coefficients of an industry sector are high, this industry sector plays a decisive role in economic development.

We calculated the impact coefficient and induction coefficient of industries with the aforementioned formulae, and selected twelve industries with both coefficients exceeding the median value. They are: food production and tobacco processing, textile, paper making, printing and stationery manufacturing, petroleum processing, coking and nuclear fuel processing, chemical industry, smelting and flat-roll processing, fabricated metal products, general purpose or special equipment manufacturing, transport facilities manufacturing, electrical, mechanical and equipment manufacturing, communications devices, the manufacture of computing and other electronic devices, construction. These industries have a substantial forward and backward correlation with the national economy. Their rapid development will play a bigger role in driving forward the national economy, and their sluggish development will place a big constraint on the development of the national economy. The growth of their final demand will have a substantial ripple effect on production in other sectors. If we use the impact and induction coefficients that exceed the median as a selection criterion for spearhead industries, from the perspective of the economic growth rate, these industries can become spearhead industries in China's national economy and be given priority development.

2. **A sub-optimal scheme in selecting spearhead industries**

Transforming the mode for economic growth demands different criteria from industries, and with regards these criteria they are inconsistent with those required of industries for maintaining growth. However, whether the two can be reconciled is not entirely determined by the difference in the criteria but by the difference in the industry cluster selected. If they are consistent, then reconciling the two will be very easy; if partly consistent, then there is great difficulty; and if completely inconsistent, then concessions are needed to choose a sub-optimal scheme.

Tables 2.3 and 2.4 contain comprehensive lists of spearhead industries selected based on the various criteria. We can easily see from the tables that there are no such industries currently in China that can promote economic growth as well as drive the growth model transformation. Therefore, currently we cannot promote economic growth by implementing the transformation of the mode for economic growth. We have no choice but to make concessions between promoting economic growth on the one hand, and transforming the growth model on the other hand. To

**Table 2.3** Multi criteria in the selection of spearhead industries (positive indicator)

| Impact coefficient | Induction coefficient | Labour fully utilised coefficient | Final consumption inducement coefficient | Final use inducement coefficient | Household income multiplier | Science and technology spillover effect |
|---|---|---|---|---|---|---|
| Communications devices, the manufacture of computing and other electronic devices (3) | The chemical industry (4) | Agriculture | Agriculture | Construction industry | Agriculture | Scientific research |
| Transport equipment manufacturing | Agriculture (8) | Food production and tobacco processing (5) | Food production and tobacco processing | Agriculture | Education | Transport equipment manufacturing |
| Electrical, mechanical and equipment manufacturing (2) | Smelting and flat-rolling processing | Textile industry (3) | Public administration and social organisations | Wholesale and retail trade | Public administration and social organisations | Education |
| Instrumentation and office machinery manufacturing (1) | Wholesale and retail trade (4) | Education (5) | Wholesale and retail trade | The chemical industry | Health, social security and social welfare | Smelting and flat-rolling processing |
| Leather and down feather garments and products | Transport and warehousing | Leather and down feather garments and products | The chemical industry | Transport and warehousing | Postal service | Electrical, mechanical and equipment manufacturing |
| Fabricated metal products (1) | Construction industry | Accommodation and catering industry (3) | Education | Food production and tobacco processing | Scientific research | Coal mining and washing |
| General purpose or special equipment manufacturing (4) | Production and supply of | Public administration | The property industry | Smelting and flat-rolling processing | Coal mining and washing | Communications devices, the manufacture of |

(continued)

**Table 2.3** (continued)

| Impact coefficient | Induction coefficient | Labour fully utilised coefficient | Final consumption inducement coefficient | Final use inducement coefficient | Household income multiplier | Science and technology spillover effect |
|---|---|---|---|---|---|---|
| | electricity and heating (1) | and social organisations (7) | | | | computing and other electronic devices |
| Textile industry (3) | General purpose or special equipment manufacturing | Health, social security and social welfare (2) | Transport and warehousing | General purpose or special equipment manufacturing | Other social services | Chemical industry |
| Construction industry (3) | Paper making, printing and stationery manufacturing (1) | Post service (1) | Construction industry | Communications devices, the manufacture of computing and other electronic devices | Textile industry | Oil and gas extraction (1) |
| Smelting and flat-rolling processing (2) | Transport equipment manufacturing | Other social services | Accommodation and catering industry | Transport equipment | Other manufacturing industries | General purpose and special equipment manufacturing |

*Note* The figures in parentheses indicate the quantity of fulfilled criteria

**Table 2.4** Multi criteria in the selection of spearhead industries (negative indicator)

| Energy total consumption coefficient | Waste water complete discharge coefficient | Waste gas total emission coefficient | Solid wastes total discharge coefficient | Capital formation inducement coefficient | Export inducement coefficient |
|---|---|---|---|---|---|
| Scrap and waste | Scrap and waste | Scrap and waste | Scrap and waste | Tourist industry | Fuel production and supply |
| The property industry | The property industry | Finance and insurance industry | Tourist industry | Postal service | Scientific research |
| Finance and insurance industry | Tourist industry | The property industry | Agriculture | Fuel production and supply | Water production and supply |
| Tourist industry | Finance and insurance industry | Agriculture | Finance and insurance industry | Water production and supply | Postal service |
| Public administration and social organisations | Integrated technical services | Public administration and social organisations | Public administration and social organisations | Scientific research | Tourist industry |
| Agriculture | Oil and gas extraction | Wholesale and retail trade | The property industry | Instrumentation and office machinery manufacturing | Scrap and waste |
| Food production and tobacco processing | Public administration and social organisations | Accommodation and catering | Wholesale and retail trade | Cultural, sports and entertainment industries | Integrated technical services |
| Integrated technical services | Transport and warehousing | Tourist industry | Cultural, sports and entertainment industries | Scrap and waste | Mining and ore dressing |
| Accommodation and catering | Wholesale and retail trade | Integrated technical services | Food production and tobacco processing | Health, social security and social welfare | Health, social security and social welfare |
| Cultural, sports and entertainment industries | Education | Cultural, sports and entertainment industries | Accommodation and catering | Mining and ore dressing | Public administration and social organisations |

wholeheartedly aim for maintaining growth by driving the transformation is not entirely practical in China's current stage.

Growth model transformation is necessary for China to maintain sustained economic growth. However, we should not sacrifice economic growth as a price for the transformation. Different industries will have different roles to play in economic growth and in the transformation. Although we cannot find an industry that can completely fulfil the criteria to maintain growth and transform the growth model, there is, however, a sub-optimal choice of industries. Compared with others, these industries are more conducive to achieving these two goals at the same time. Currently, with a heavy economic slowdown risk, a downturn in growth rate will affect household income and employment, which will then affect the size and capacity of the market. Therefore, key industries should be selected on the basis of maintaining growth. In drawing up industries for revitalisation in order to maintain growth, the emphasis should be on choosing those with greater impact and at the same time can better fulfil other criteria. With this as the criteria, the industries to be prioritised in China include: communications devices and the manufacture of computing and other electronic devices, general purpose and special equipment manufacturing, the manufacture of transport equipment, the textile industry, and the construction industry. Apart from fulfilling the requirement for impact, these industries also can better fulfil other selection criteria (in Table 2.3 the figures in parentheses indicate the number of fulfilled criteria).

Since 2008 when China's growth rate started to slow down, unemployment has gradually become a prominent problem. To maintain growth is without doubt important for employment, but maintaining growth and promoting employment is not at all the same thing. From the perspective of promoting employment, the industries to be prioritised for development include: agriculture, public administration and services, food production and tobacco processing, education, textile, and accommodation and catering. The industries currently drawn up for revitalisation in China include: textile, automotive, steel, ship building, equipment manufacture, petrochemical, electronics, non-ferrous metals, light industry, etc. These industries fulfil the criterion for maintaining growth in the selection of spearhead industries. The reason for maintaining growth is to ensure employment. From this perspective, other industries such as construction, and the tertiary industry, should also be incorporated into this combination.

The pressure for energy conservation and emission reduction has slightly eased, but the work on these must not relax. From a long-term perspective, the biggest conflict in maintaining growth and achieving growth model transformation will manifest as favouring those industries that promote economic growth, and causing disadvantage to resources and environmental protection. Therefore, in the current circumstances, reconciling economic growth with protecting resources and the environment is critical. The key in reconciling economic growth and transforming growth model is to maintain a fairly high rate in growth, while raising the efficiency in the use of resources and the environment. The route to achieving this goal is to promote progress in technology, in particular using new high-tech to enhance industrial upgrade, including inter- and intra-industrial upgrade.

# Chapter 3
# Assessment on the Impact of Development Pattern Transformation on Industries

**Gang Li and Keting Shen**

## 3.1 An Analysis of the Evolution in Industrial Structure

To assess the impact of development pattern transformation on industries, it is necessary to forecast industrial development trend. Most of the industrial structure forecasts in China are on the future of the primary, secondary and tertiary industries. In compiling the relevant forecast results, we found that the proportion of those concerning the primary industry in 2020 range from 5.8–7.0%, 38–67.3% for the secondary industry, and 19.7–55% for the tertiary industry.

There is not a lot of relevant literature on forecasting the development of the industrial structure. There are broadly two approaches used. The first is the CGE approach. The second is the time series analysis approach, such as the grey model (GM). Generally, when using the time series analysis approach to forecast changes in the industrial structure, the first step is to reduce the dimensionality of the raw data. There are quite a number of ways to reduce the dimensionality, such as using logarithms or square roots.

On the whole, the CGE approach is more complicated. However, it is better than simply using the time series analysis approach for forecasting the long-term industrial structure. This is because the time series analysis approach does not take into consideration other factors that affect the variables, but is premised on the assumption that the development of the industrial structure will follow the same trend as before. This approach can only be applied on short-term forecast. In China, there is a lot of momentum coming from the government for industrial restructuring. If the role and impact of these 'external forces' are not taken into consideration, it is difficult to accurately take stock of changes in the long-term industrial structure (Table 3.1).

G. Li (✉)
Chinese Academy of Social Sciences, Beijing, China

K. Shen
Zhejiang Gongshang University, Hangzhou, China



Q. Zhang (ed.), *Transforming Economic Growth and China's Industrial Upgrading*,
Research Series on the Chinese Dream and China's Development Path,
https://doi.org/10.1007/978-981-13-0962-5_3

**Table 3.1** Forecasts by different organisations on the future of China's industrial structure

| Forecast by organisation | Forecast method | Forecast details |
|---|---|---|
| Development Research Centre of the State Council (1999) | CGE | In 2020, the percentages of the primary, secondary and tertiary industries are 5.8, 67.3 and 19.7% respectively |
| Development Research Centre of the State Council (2003) | CGE | The percentages of the primary, secondary and tertiary industries are respectively: 10.6, 54.2 and 35.2% in 2010; 7.0, 52.6 and 40.4% in 2020 |
| World Bank (2007) | DRG-CGE | There are two scenarios—the proportion of the secondary industry is: 44 or 49% during 2005–15, 40 or 48% during 2015–25, and 36 or 47% during 2025–35 |
| The Institute of Quantitative and Technical Economics of the Chinese Academy of Social Sciences (2010) | – | The percentages of the primary, secondary and tertiary industries are respectively: 9.7, 44 and 46% in 2010; 7.7, 41 and 51% in 2015; 6.3, 38 and 55% in 2020 |
| The National Development and Reform Commission's Energy Research Institute Task Force (2009) | – | There are three scenarios, and with the scenario for energy conservation, there is some optimization of the economic structure. By 2030 the tertiary industry will be the main component of the economic structure. The characteristic in a society of secondary industry is high consumption of materials, with heavy industry still occupying an important position. In low carbon scenario and enforced low carbon scenario, the economic structure is further optimized, which is similar to the configuration in developed countries now: the percentages of the primary, secondary and tertiary industries are respectively: 10.1, 49.2 and 40.8% in 2010; 6.8, 48.7 and 44.5% in 2020; 4.3, 45.5 and 50.2% in 2030; 3.1, 40.6 and 56.2% in 2040; 2.5, 36.4 and 61.2% in 2050 |

(continued)

**Table 3.1** (continued)

| Forecast by organisation | Forecast method | Forecast details |
|---|---|---|
| Wang (2005) | Following a non-linear dimensionality reduction, a forecast of the compositional data is carried out using spherical projection | Development trend of primary, secondary and tertiary industries in Beijing |
| Shi (2007) | Start by reducing the dimensionality of the compositional data using logarithmic transformation. After dimensionality reduction, a forecast is carried out using the GM (1, 1) model | The proportions of the three industries forecasts for 2005–2007 |
| Yang (2009) | Forecast based on differential evolution algorithm of the support vector machines (SVM) | In 2010 the resource-based industries, and industries in low technology, medium technology and high technology as a proportion of the total manufacturing industry are 0.16, 0.06, 0.41 and 0.37 respectively |

The Institute of Industrial Economics at the Chinese Academy of Social Sciences applied the Markov matrix to forecast China's industrial structure up to 2050. Since the industrial structure evolves, to a degree, similarly to a Markov process, the Markov chain can be used to describe the changing process of the industrial structure, the key in which is to construct a transition probability matrix. There are many ways to construct a Markov transition probability matrix. Common methods include subjective probability and survey. The Institute of Economic Research Task Force constructed an industry transition probability matrix using historical survey, technology correlation and target search. Basic steps are:

Step one: Based on the growth by year of added value, labour and fixed assets investment, the preliminary elements on the main diagonal of the transition matrix are determined. The basic rule is that industries having historically fast growth rate also have elements of relatively large values on the main diagonal, whereas industries having slow growth rate have elements of relatively small values on the main diagonal. Elements on the main diagonal should have the basic properties of a Markov matrix, i.e. $0 \leq a_{ii} \leq 1$. It is a fact there is greater intra-industry movement than inter-industry, and also on the whole the ratio between the industries in the short term is stable. As such, the elements on the main diagonal are generally of bigger value—they are not smaller than 0.8, with most of the elements changing around 0.9. This study adopts the following formula to determine the elements on the main diagonal of the Markov transition matrix: $a_{ii} = 0.8 + 0.2 * y_i$, of which $y_i$ is the standardized average growth rate in added value by industry for the past five years. Standardization is based on $y_i = (g_i - \min(g))/(\max(g))$, in which g is the original vector (average growth rate in added value by industry for the past five years), $g_i$ is the element value of the original vector, and $y_i$ is the corresponding element value after standardization.

Step two: Based on the degree of technology correlation between the various industries (a broad definition of technology correlation includes the possibility for technology connection between the industries, personnel or capital movement), an initial step is taken to determine the various off-diagonal elements. The degree of technology correlation between industries is made with reference to relevant data of the input-output table or the similarity degree coefficient of product space. Off-diagonal elements should have the basic properties of a Markov matrix, i.e. $0 \leq a_{ij} \leq 1 (i \neq j)$, and also $\sum_{i \neq j} a_{ij} = 1 - a_{ii}$. In using the input-output table, this study uses the intermediate inputs of the ratios from the various industries for an initial determination of the off-diagonal elements of the Markov transition matrix. The formula for calculation is: $a_{ij} = (1 - a_{ii}) * \frac{x_{ij}}{\sum_{j(j \neq i)} x_{ij}}$, of which $x_{ij}$ is the corresponding element in the input-output table of China in 2002.

Step three: Calculation is carried out by using the initial time numerical value of all industries (added-value structure) and the transition matrix initially constructed. Consideration is given to industrial structures formed under a stable state. The computations from these are then compared to the rules of industrial structures evolution under industrialization, to see whether they fit the basic direction and objective for an industrial structure within the process of industrialization.[1] Then the elements of the transition matrix are calibrated in turn. In the calibration of the various elements, values of the corresponding elements on the main diagonal will first be adjusted (industries with a big deviation will first be adjusted, with proportions on the low side being adjusted up, and those on the high side being adjusted down; the step size should not be too big). Then the off-diagonal elements are adjusted. This adjustment should still follow the rules set out in step two above. Calibration is a dynamic process of adjustment until the objective is achieved. The whole process can be undertaken by relevant calculation tools used in computers. The target industrial structure under stable conditions as determined by this study is the current average value of the USA, UK, Germany, Japan and Korea (calculated based on the normalised data of the 2005 input-output table as supplied by the OECD website).

The industrial structure evolution trend reached through the above steps is shown in Table 3.2. In this chapter, the forecast of industrial structure is based on the dynamic CGE forecast of 42 sectors, as seen in Table 3.3. It can be seen from a comparison of Tables 3.2 and 3.3 that forecasts using the Markov chain and the

[1]Major directions of industrial structure optimization and upgrading include more service-based, heavy-industrialized, more process-based, and greater intensification of knowledge and technology.

**Table 3.2** A forecast of China's evolving industrial structure using the Markov chain

| | 2007 (actual) | 2010 | 2015 | 2020 | 2025 | 2030 |
|---|---|---|---|---|---|---|
| Agriculture, forestry, animal husbandry and fishery | 11.13 | 9.62 | 8.07 | 7.22 | 6.75 | 6.49 |
| Coal mining and washing | 1.72 | 1.49 | 1.23 | 1.07 | 0.96 | 0.90 |
| Oil and gas extraction | 2.37 | 2.43 | 2.55 | 2.67 | 2.78 | 2.87 |
| Ferrous metals mining and ore dressing | 0.34 | 0.31 | 0.27 | 0.25 | 0.23 | 0.22 |
| Non-ferrous metals mining and ore dressing | 0.36 | 0.29 | 0.23 | 0.19 | 0.17 | 0.15 |
| Non-metallic mineral mining and dressing | 0.19 | 0.17 | 0.16 | 0.15 | 0.14 | 0.14 |
| Other types of mining | 0.00 | 0.06 | 0.05 | 0.04 | 0.04 | 0.04 |
| Agricultural foodstuff processing | 1.70 | 1.45 | 1.15 | 0.95 | 0.81 | 0.72 |
| Food production | 0.68 | 0.67 | 0.63 | 0.57 | 0.52 | 0.47 |
| Beverage manufacturing | 0.69 | 0.61 | 0.51 | 0.45 | 0.41 | 0.37 |
| Tobacco products | 1.07 | 0.88 | 0.67 | 0.54 | 0.45 | 0.40 |
| Textile industry | 1.80 | 1.57 | 1.29 | 1.09 | 0.96 | 0.87 |
| Textile garments, footwear, hat manufacturing | 0.83 | 0.77 | 0.69 | 0.62 | 0.56 | 0.52 |
| Leather, fur, down feather and other products | 0.54 | 0.49 | 0.43 | 0.39 | 0.36 | 0.33 |
| Wood processing, timber, bamboo, palm fibre and straw products | 0.38 | 0.32 | 0.27 | 0.24 | 0.22 | 0.21 |
| Furniture manufacturing | 0.24 | 0.23 | 0.21 | 0.20 | 0.18 | 0.17 |
| Paper making and paper products | 0.64 | 0.55 | 0.46 | 0.39 | 0.35 | 0.32 |
| Printing and reproduction of recorded media | 0.25 | 0.24 | 0.22 | 0.20 | 0.19 | 0.18 |
| Stationery and sports equipment manufacturing | 0.20 | 0.18 | 0.16 | 0.15 | 0.13 | 0.12 |
| Petroleum processing, coking and nuclear fuel processing | 1.14 | 1.05 | 0.90 | 0.77 | 0.68 | 0.61 |
| Chemical raw materials and chemical products manufacturing | 2.69 | 2.13 | 1.56 | 1.25 | 1.08 | 0.98 |
| Pharmaceutical manufacturing | 0.84 | 0.79 | 0.72 | 0.66 | 0.60 | 0.55 |
| Chemical fibre manufacturing industry | 0.30 | 0.45 | 0.54 | 0.53 | 0.49 | 0.45 |
| Rubber products industry | 0.35 | 0.39 | 0.39 | 0.37 | 0.34 | 0.31 |
| Plastic products industry | 0.78 | 0.79 | 0.77 | 0.73 | 0.68 | 0.63 |
| Non-metallic mineral products | 1.78 | 1.52 | 1.20 | 0.98 | 0.83 | 0.72 |
| Ferrous metals smelting and flat-rolling processing | 3.31 | 3.03 | 2.62 | 2.28 | 2.00 | 1.78 |
| Non-ferrous metals smelting and flat-rolling processing | 1.64 | 1.29 | 0.92 | 0.71 | 0.59 | 0.51 |

(continued)

**Table 3.2** (continued)

| | 2007 (actual) | 2010 | 2015 | 2020 | 2025 | 2030 |
|---|---|---|---|---|---|---|
| Fabricated metal products | 1.10 | 1.08 | 1.00 | 0.90 | 0.81 | 0.73 |
| General purpose equipment manufacturing | 1.87 | 1.82 | 1.64 | 1.45 | 1.28 | 1.14 |
| Special equipment manufacturing | 1.13 | 1.54 | 1.84 | 1.85 | 1.74 | 1.60 |
| Transport equipment manufacturing | 2.56 | 2.33 | 1.98 | 1.69 | 1.45 | 1.28 |
| Electrical, mechanical and equipment manufacturing | 2.22 | 1.78 | 1.31 | 1.03 | 0.86 | 0.75 |
| Communications devices, the manufacture of computing and other electronic devices | 2.91 | 2.16 | 1.46 | 1.09 | 0.88 | 0.74 |
| Instrumentation, cultural and office machinery manufacturing | 0.43 | 0.59 | 0.57 | 0.48 | 0.40 | 0.35 |
| Crafts and other manufacturing industries | 0.34 | 0.32 | 0.29 | 0.26 | 0.24 | 0.23 |
| Discarded and waste materials recycling and processing | 0.06 | 0.28 | 0.35 | 0.33 | 0.30 | 0.28 |
| Production and supply of electricity and heating | 3.24 | 3.49 | 3.92 | 4.27 | 4.51 | 4.68 |
| Fuel production and supply | 0.11 | 0.25 | 0.35 | 0.40 | 0.43 | 0.45 |
| Water production and supply | 0.13 | 0.20 | 0.25 | 0.26 | 0.26 | 0.25 |
| Construction industry | 5.54 | 5.87 | 6.28 | 6.56 | 6.73 | 6.82 |
| Transport, warehousing and postal service | 5.75 | 6.20 | 6.75 | 7.08 | 7.27 | 7.35 |
| Wholesale and retail industry | 7.33 | 7.42 | 7.62 | 7.82 | 8.00 | 8.15 |
| Accommodation and catering industry | 2.16 | 2.37 | 2.71 | 3.01 | 3.26 | 3.45 |
| Financial services industry | 5.18 | 6.30 | 7.87 | 9.15 | 10.18 | 11.02 |
| The property industry | 4.77 | 5.48 | 6.41 | 7.08 | 7.56 | 7.89 |
| Other services | 15.18 | 16.73 | 18.53 | 19.65 | 20.36 | 20.81 |
| Total | 100 | 100 | 100 | 100 | 100 | 100 |

dynamic CGE model yield different results. The general trend is a reduced ratio for agriculture, an increased ratio for the tertiary industry, and in the industrial sectors a reduced ratio for heavy industries, but the rate of change is not the same, for example the falling trend as forecast using the Markov chain is slower than that using the dynamic CGE model.

**Table 3.3** Forecast of China's industrial structure using the dynamic CGE of the 41 sectors

| | 2002 | 2010 | 2015 | 2020 | 2025 | 2030 |
|---|---|---|---|---|---|---|
| Agriculture | 8.772848 | 7.653041 | 6.920885 | 6.120324 | 5.265971 | 4.377019 |
| Coal mining and washing | 1.211336 | 1.984293 | 1.617982 | 1.315551 | 1.113116 | 0.977092 |
| Oil and gas extraction | 1.055502 | 1.049132 | 1.133412 | 1.233786 | 1.343115 | 1.458834 |
| Mining and ore dressing | 0.444945 | 0.393682 | 0.373479 | 0.35043 | 0.322832 | 0.291402 |
| Non-metallic mineral mining and dressing | 0.450734 | 0.395067 | 0.360796 | 0.321731 | 0.278312 | 0.23261 |
| Food production and tobacco processing | 4.609407 | 4.237087 | 4.056649 | 3.839195 | 3.596723 | 3.34981 |
| Textile industry | 3.034879 | 2.089102 | 1.798335 | 1.562247 | 1.363839 | 1.199072 |
| Leather and down feather garments and products | 2.186825 | 1.870245 | 1.724962 | 1.579376 | 1.446836 | 1.335127 |
| Timber processing and furniture manufacturing | 1.291895 | 1.238881 | 1.216061 | 1.189919 | 1.164268 | 1.142083 |
| Paper making, printing and stationery manufacturing | 2.407232 | 2.070135 | 1.989656 | 1.92434 | 1.856071 | 1.779661 |
| Petroleum processing, coking and nuclear fuel processing | 1.869653 | 2.210544 | 2.47787 | 2.871692 | 3.424314 | 4.165089 |
| The chemical industry | 6.971525 | 6.359187 | 6.268666 | 6.166765 | 5.999703 | 5.764525 |
| Non-metallic mineral products | 1.656058 | 1.804424 | 1.844102 | 1.878352 | 1.914224 | 1.952465 |
| Smelting and flat-rolling processing | 4.471322 | 4.463389 | 4.46391 | 4.462877 | 4.454705 | 4.438095 |
| Fabricated metal products | 1.954789 | 1.891737 | 1.890837 | 1.884228 | 1.869181 | 1.847655 |
| General purpose or special equipment manufacturing | 3.685867 | 3.696901 | 3.671866 | 3.642145 | 3.609587 | 3.573052 |
| Transport equipment manufacturing | 2.794457 | 2.79393 | 2.808402 | 2.825865 | 2.843845 | 2.859858 |
| Electrical, mechanical and equipment manufacturing | 2.346157 | 2.174138 | 2.170445 | 2.157428 | 2.121314 | 2.062941 |
| Communications devices, the manufacture of computing and other electronic devices | 4.26955 | 4.900018 | 5.28301 | 5.485589 | 5.483925 | 5.285852 |
| Instrumentation, cultural and office machinery manufacturing | 0.626375 | 0.477527 | 0.419057 | 0.352493 | 0.280197 | 0.21139 |
| Other manufacturing industries and scrap and waste | 0.642695 | 0.574863 | 0.549645 | 0.526943 | 0.506177 | 0.487214 |
| Production and supply of electricity and heating | 2.596508 | 2.687788 | 2.7815 | 2.902587 | 3.033804 | 3.161091 |
| Fuel production and supply | 0.115764 | 0.119504 | 0.122254 | 0.12841 | 0.137387 | 0.147946 |

(continued)

**Table 3.3** (continued)

| | 2002 | 2010 | 2015 | 2020 | 2025 | 2030 |
|---|---|---|---|---|---|---|
| Water production and supply | 0.200724 | 0.190112 | 0.187071 | 0.186135 | 0.186558 | 0.187653 |
| Construction industry | 6.711933 | 8.954218 | 9.638949 | 10.22505 | 10.84377 | 11.5377 |
| Transport and warehousing | 4.51138 | 4.456552 | 4.530557 | 4.649842 | 4.787335 | 4.924409 |
| Postal service | 0.182298 | 0.165215 | 0.158688 | 0.15319 | 0.147883 | 0.142238 |
| Information transmission, computing services and software industry | 1.722734 | 1.823956 | 1.965027 | 2.144109 | 2.346385 | 2.551317 |
| Wholesale and retail trade | 5.335058 | 5.109731 | 5.037402 | 4.96793 | 4.89607 | 4.82358 |
| Accommodation and catering industry | 2.390286 | 2.662055 | 2.716673 | 2.709092 | 2.669246 | 2.616629 |
| Finance and insurance industry | 2.577677 | 3.239047 | 3.590826 | 3.918181 | 4.226659 | 4.505693 |
| The property industry | 2.429351 | 2.306807 | 2.426348 | 2.672003 | 3.024428 | 3.467212 |
| Leasing and business services industry | 1.44141 | 1.908734 | 2.128322 | 2.265361 | 2.312308 | 2.27281 |
| Tourist industry | 0.247102 | 0.390578 | 0.474904 | 0.549198 | 0.612163 | 0.661819 |
| Scientific research | 0.307257 | 0.33547 | 0.342282 | 0.344817 | 0.345276 | 0.344515 |
| Integrated technical services | 0.841266 | 0.845743 | 0.864754 | 0.8917 | 0.923325 | 0.957061 |
| Other social services | 1.830032 | 1.573825 | 1.495436 | 1.438912 | 1.39027 | 1.342568 |
| Education | 2.628382 | 2.355316 | 2.22518 | 2.110663 | 2.005326 | 1.904064 |
| Health, social security and social welfare | 1.67596 | 1.580813 | 1.547805 | 1.521793 | 1.497386 | 1.470711 |
| Cultural, sports and entertainment industries | 0.664918 | 0.629738 | 0.62381 | 0.617439 | 0.60887 | 0.59774 |
| Public administration and social organisations | 4.835908 | 4.337476 | 4.102184 | 3.912314 | 3.74729 | 3.592399 |

## 3.2 Single Region Dynamic CGE Model

There are two types of CGE models: static and dynamic. A static model cannot be used to study and simulate the policy effect of multiple periods of time. In addition, a basic static model cannot depict the interaction between capital formation and consumption, neither can it take full account of changes in capital accumulation, growth in labour force, technological progress and enhanced labour productivity as a result of an extended time dimension. Therefore, when evaluating the macroeconomic effects of various policies, a basic static model has obvious limitation. The theoretic basis of dynamic model is designed as a dynamic macroeconomic model. Most of the dynamic models in the literature of the CGE model are based on the analysis framework of the neo-classical economic growth theory. Similar to the construction of the static basic model, the fundamental work in designing a dynamic model is still to collect data and construct a corresponding database. A pragmatic dynamic CGE model is commonly of the recursive dynamic structure. It is by nature a static CGE model calculating one period at a time via an iterative process. The effect of the interconnection between periods is described by an exogenous function. Together with the necessary dynamics of exogenous variables and parameters, the subsequent period of the outcome in the model is arrived at via an iterative process. Since the dynamic model is mainly based on the static basic model with an added module, the other modules in the model is basically the same as the static model. Therefore, for brevity, only the core equation of the dynamic module will be described.

1. **Dynamic changes in total labour supply**

In a dynamic model, changes in future supply of labour are usually set with reference to external data. This is because population and working age change with their own momentum. Studies in the fields of demographics and population statistics usually provide more direct and reliable data and forecasts.

Let us assume that the forecast for the annual increases in period t for the future of labour supply is $popgw_t$, then total labour supply $popgw_t$ has the following recursive relationship across periods:

$$\overline{LS}(t+1) = (1 + popgw_t) \cdot \overline{LS}(t)$$

In any given period, the assumption still adopts the dynamic model, i.e. labour can move between sectors, with the total supply of labour being determined exogenously. Labour for all sectors follows the standard measures, with the rate of pay being equal.

2. **Dynamic changes in the supply of capital**

The supply of capital for each period can be treated as a dynamic endogenous variable. This is because in any given period the capital stock is connected with capital formation in the previous period. Let us assume that for period t the investment of sector i is $DK_i(t)$, the capital depreciation rate is $deprate_{it}$, then for period t sector i's capital stock $\overline{K_i}(t)$ has the following recursive relationship across periods:

$$\overline{K_i}(t+1) = (1 - deprate_{it})\overline{K_i}(t) + DK_i(t)$$

i.e. the capital stock for the following period equals to the capital stock of the current period less depreciation, plus this period's investment or capital formation.

We can obtain the capital stock $\overline{K_i}(t)$ and the depreciation $DEP_i(t)$ of the initial period based on relevant statics, from which we can project the depreciation rate $deprate_{it}$:

$$deprate_t = DEP_i(t)/\overline{K_i}(t)$$

3. **Dynamic changes in technological progress or labour productivity**

Similar to the neo-classical model for economic growth, there is a corresponding method in the dynamic CGE model for describing how technological progress contribute to economic growth, e.g. total factor productivity, or capital-embodied technology and labour-embodied technology.

Our model uses the nested CES (constant elasticity of substitution) production function. Taking (I-3) as an example, the function's scale factor $A_{vi}$, i.e. the total factor productivity (TFP) rate includes contributions from all productive elements, and by determining the rate of growth for the total factor productivity $d_{A_{vi}}$ we can arrive at the recursive relationship across periods for the total factor productivity $A_{vi}$:

$$A_{vi}(t+1) = (1 + d_{A_{vi}}) \cdot A_{vi}(t)$$

According to the nested structure of the production function, we can also determine and simulate the impact of technological progress from energy or capital-energy combined.

## 3.3 The Impact of Wage Increase

An important aspect of development pattern transformation is to boost domestic demand. An important initiative in boosting domestic demand is to increase wages in the GDP ratio. In 2004 the central government required local governments to raise the lowest wage levels at least once every two years. As a result, wages on the lowest level were increased. Amongst these, wage rises are more frequent and by a bigger margin in economically developed eastern coastal areas. For many years Beijing and Shanghai have revised the levels of the lowest wages. Beijing has been raising the levels for the lowest wage since 2004, and between 2004 and 2008, the lowest monthly wage was RMB545, RMB580, RMB640 and RMB800 respective, a total rise of 46.8%. For Shanghai the lowest monthly wage between 2004 and 2008 was RMB635, RMB690, RMB750, RMB840 and RMB960 respectively, a total rise of 51.2%. During the 4 years since 2005, the lowest wage level in Shenzhen has increased by over 80%, way ahead of the consumer price index. In 2011 the national per capita income in urban areas was 15,412 yuan, an increase of 12.4%. This was mainly due to rises in the lowest wage levels in most places, with some areas implementing paying subsidies, while some enterprises raised salaries and bonuses (Table 3.4).

Increasing wages is conducive to enhancing the current structure in income distribution, but will have different impact for the development in different industries. This study, based on the matrix for the 2002 social accounting and audit, simulates the impact of increased wages. Assuming that an enterprise takes 5% of its profit to pays its workers' wages, the impact from a dynamic simulation of the 41 sectors is shown in Table 3.5.

## 3.4 The Impact of Revising Export Tax Rebates

In 1985, China implemented the export tax rebate policy. The initial goal was simply to boost exports. The 1994 taxation reform established the principle of zero-rating on exports of goods, i.e. the rebate is the tax rate at the time of levying the two-tier value added tax at 13 and 17%. This policy increased exports by a large margin, but also left the central coffers with a heavy burden. The government revised down the rate for tax rebate in 1995 and again in 1996. Following the 1997 financial crisis in South-east Asia, the export tax rebate was revised up again to drive growth in exports.

After the 1990s, when the opening up of China entered a period of rapid development,[2] the 'export oriented' policy for foreign investment and trade played a positive role in boosting the scale of exports, strengthening the international competitiveness of exports, increasing employment, and maintaining a sustainable rapid development for the economy. From our perspective of 'growth model

[2]In 1992 China's actual use of FDI exceeded foreign loans for the first time, and it became the main source of foreign investment. In 1993 the trade deficit was gradually stabilised and became a surplus.

**Table 3.4** Changes to employee wages

| Year region | Average wage (dollars) | | | | | Average wage index (last year = 100) | | | | | Actual average wage index (last year = 100) | | | | |
|---|---|---|---|---|---|---|---|---|---|---|---|---|---|---|---|
| | Total | | State-owned | Urban collective | Other | Total | | State-owned | Urban collective | Other | Total | | State-owned | Urban collective | Other |
| | | #Employee in post | Units | Units | Units | | #Employee in post | Units | Units | Units | | #Employee in post | Units | Units | Units |
| 1995 | 5348 | 5500 | 5553 | 3934 | 7728 | 118.9 | 121.2 | 117.3 | 121.1 | 119.9 | 101.8 | 103.8 | 100.4 | 103.7 | 102.6 |
| 1996 | 5980 | 6210 | 6207 | 4312 | 8521 | 111.8 | 112.9 | 111.8 | 109.6 | 110.3 | 102.8 | 103.8 | 102.7 | 100.7 | 101.3 |
| 1997 | 6444 | 6470 | 6679 | 4516 | 9092 | 107.8 | 104.2 | 107.6 | 104.7 | 106.7 | 104.5 | 101.1 | 104.4 | 101.6 | 103.5 |
| 1998 | 7446 | 7479 | 7579 | 5314 | 9241 | 115.5 | 106.6 | 113.5 | 117.7 | 101.6 | 116.2 | 107.2 | 114.2 | 118.4 | 102.3 |
| 1999 | 8319 | 8346 | 8443 | 5758 | 10,142 | 111.7 | 111.6 | 111.4 | 108.4 | 109.8 | 113.2 | 113.1 | 112.9 | 109.8 | 111.2 |
| 2000 | 9333 | 9371 | 9441 | 6241 | 11,238 | 112.2 | 112.3 | 111.8 | 108.4 | 110.8 | 111.3 | 111.4 | 110.9 | 107.5 | 109.9 |
| 2001 | 10,834 | 10,870 | 11,045 | 6851 | 12,437 | 116.1 | 116.0 | 117.0 | 109.8 | 110.7 | 115.3 | 115.2 | 116.2 | 109.0 | 109.9 |
| 2002 | 12,373 | 12,422 | 12,701 | 7636 | 13,486 | 114.2 | 114.3 | 115.0 | 111.5 | 108.4 | 115.4 | 115.5 | 116.2 | 112.6 | 109.5 |
| 2003 | 13,969 | 14,040 | 14,358 | 8627 | 14,843 | 112.9 | 113.0 | 113.0 | 113.0 | 110.1 | 111.9 | 112.0 | 112.0 | 112.0 | 109.1 |
| 2004 | 15,920 | 16,024 | 16,445 | 9723 | 16,519 | 114.0 | 114.1 | 114.5 | 112.7 | 111.3 | 110.3 | 110.5 | 110.9 | 109.1 | 107.7 |
| 2005 | 18,200 | 18,364 | 18,978 | 11,176 | 18,362 | 114.3 | 114.6 | 115.4 | 114.9 | 111.2 | 112.5 | 112.8 | 113.6 | 113.1 | 109.4 |
| 2006 | 20,856 | 21,001 | 21,706 | 12,866 | 21,004 | 114.6 | 114.4 | 114.4 | 115.1 | 114.4 | 112.9 | 112.7 | 112.7 | 113.4 | 112.7 |
| 2007 | 24,721 | 24,932 | 26,100 | 15,444 | 24,271 | 118.5 | 118.7 | 120.2 | 120.0 | 115.6 | 113.4 | 113.6 | 115.0 | 114.8 | 110.6 |
| 2008 | 28,898 | 29,229 | 30,287 | 18,103 | 28,552 | 116.9 | 117.2 | 116.0 | 117.2 | 117.6 | 110.7 | 111.0 | 109.8 | 111.0 | 111.4 |
| 2009 | 32,244 | 32,736 | 34,130 | 20,607 | 31,350 | 111.6 | 112.0 | 112.7 | 113.8 | 109.8 | 112.6 | 113.0 | 113.7 | 114.8 | 110.8 |
| 2010 | 36,539 | 37,147 | 38,359 | 24,010 | 35,801 | 113.3 | 113.5 | 112.4 | 116.5 | 114.2 | 109.8 | 110.0 | 108.9 | 112.9 | 110.7 |

*Note* Information source: The 2011 China Statistical Yearbook

**Table 3.5** The impact of raising remuneration

| Year | 2010 (%) | 2011 (%) | 2012 (%) | 2013 (%) | 2014 (%) | 2015 (%) | 2020 (%) |
|---|---|---|---|---|---|---|---|
| **Total output** | −0.71 | −0.73 | −0.73 | −0.74 | −0.74 | −0.74 | −0.71 |
| **Price** | 0.71 | 0.73 | 0.74 | 0.75 | 0.75 | 0.74 | 0.70 |
| Output by sector | | | | | | | |
| Agriculture | −0.08 | −0.11 | −0.13 | −0.14 | −0.16 | −0.17 | −0.23 |
| Coal mining and washing | −2.22 | −2.15 | −2.08 | −1.99 | −1.90 | −1.81 | −1.40 |
| Oil and gas extraction | −1.49 | −1.52 | −1.53 | −1.54 | −1.54 | −1.53 | −1.44 |
| Mining and ore dressing | −1.77 | −1.78 | −1.77 | −1.76 | −1.74 | −1.71 | −1.54 |
| Non-metallic mineral mining and dressing | −1.56 | −1.55 | −1.54 | −1.52 | −1.51 | −1.48 | −1.35 |
| Food production and tobacco processing | −0.01 | −0.02 | −0.03 | −0.03 | −0.03 | −0.03 | −0.03 |
| Textile industry | −1.10 | −1.08 | −1.06 | −1.02 | −0.98 | −0.93 | −0.69 |
| Leather and down feather garments and products | −1.09 | −1.06 | −1.03 | −0.98 | −0.93 | −0.88 | −0.63 |
| Timber processing and furniture manufacturing | −1.03 | −1.02 | −1.00 | −0.99 | −0.97 | −0.94 | −0.81 |
| Paper making, printing and stationery manufacturing | −0.80 | −0.81 | −0.83 | −0.83 | −0.83 | −0.83 | −0.76 |
| Petroleum processing, coking and nuclear fuel processing | −1.29 | −1.33 | −1.35 | −1.38 | −1.39 | −1.41 | −1.44 |
| The chemical industry | −1.14 | −1.16 | −1.17 | −1.17 | −1.17 | −1.16 | −1.05 |
| Non-metallic mineral products | −1.29 | −1.27 | −1.25 | −1.23 | −1.21 | −1.19 | −1.06 |
| Smelting and flat-rolling processing | −1.60 | −1.58 | −1.57 | −1.54 | −1.52 | −1.49 | −1.32 |
| Fabricated metal products | −1.46 | −1.45 | −1.44 | −1.42 | −1.40 | −1.38 | −1.22 |
| General purpose or special equipment manufacturing | −1.60 | −1.58 | −1.55 | −1.53 | −1.50 | −1.47 | −1.30 |
| Transport equipment manufacturing | −1.14 | −1.13 | −1.12 | −1.11 | −1.10 | −1.09 | −0.99 |
| Electrical, mechanical and equipment manufacturing | −1.60 | −1.61 | −1.61 | −1.60 | −1.58 | −1.56 | −1.39 |
| Communications devices, the manufacture of computing and other electronic devices | −2.07 | −2.09 | −2.09 | −2.09 | −2.07 | −2.05 | −1.89 |
| Instrumentation, cultural and office machinery manufacturing | −2.90 | −2.96 | −2.99 | −3.00 | −3.00 | −2.98 | −2.75 |
| Other manufacturing industries and scrap and waste | −0.79 | −0.79 | −0.78 | −0.77 | −0.76 | −0.74 | −0.66 |
| Production and supply of electricity and heating | −0.86 | −0.87 | −0.87 | −0.86 | −0.85 | −0.83 | −0.74 |
| Fuel production and supply | −0.22 | −0.27 | −0.31 | −0.35 | −0.38 | −0.41 | −0.48 |
| Water production and supply | −0.46 | −0.49 | −0.51 | −0.53 | −0.54 | −0.55 | −0.55 |

(continued)

**Table 3.5** (continued)

| Year | 2010 (%) | 2011 (%) | 2012 (%) | 2013 (%) | 2014 (%) | 2015 (%) | 2020 (%) |
|---|---|---|---|---|---|---|---|
| Construction industry | −1.62 | −1.55 | −1.50 | −1.45 | −1.41 | −1.37 | −1.17 |
| Transport and warehousing | −0.86 | −0.87 | −0.88 | −0.88 | −0.88 | −0.88 | −0.82 |
| Postal service | 0.05 | 0.02 | −0.01 | −0.03 | −0.04 | −0.06 | −0.10 |
| Information transmission, computing services and software industry | −0.84 | −0.86 | −0.87 | −0.88 | −0.88 | −0.88 | −0.84 |
| Wholesale and retail trade | −0.80 | −0.81 | −0.80 | −0.80 | −0.79 | −0.78 | −0.70 |
| Accommodation and catering industry | −0.32 | −0.32 | −0.31 | −0.30 | −0.29 | −0.28 | −0.22 |
| Finance and insurance industry | − 0.89 | −0.89 | −0.88 | −0.87 | −0.86 | −0.85 | −0.78 |
| The property industry | −0.49 | −0.54 | −0.58 | −0.61 | −0.64 | −0.66 | −0.71 |
| Leasing and business services industry | −1.78 | −1.80 | −1.80 | −1.80 | −1.80 | −1.78 | −1.65 |
| Tourist industry | −1.31 | −1.33 | −1.34 | −1.35 | −1.35 | −1.34 | −1.26 |
| Scientific research | 0.40 | 0.40 | 0.40 | 0.40 | 0.40 | 0.40 | 0.41 |
| Integrated technical services | −0.08 | −0.09 | −0.10 | −0.11 | −0.11 | −0.10 | −0.06 |
| Other social services | 0.02 | −0.01 | −0.03 | −0.04 | −0.06 | −0.07 | −0.09 |
| Education | 0.80 | 0.77 | 0.74 | 0.72 | 0.69 | 0.67 | 0.59 |
| Health, social security and social welfare | 0.68 | 0.64 | 0.61 | 0.59 | 0.56 | 0.54 | 0.46 |
| Cultural, sports and entertainment industries | −0.02 | −0.03 | −0.04 | −0.05 | −0.06 | −0.06 | −0.04 |
| Public administration and social organisations | 0.77 | 0.75 | 0.74 | 0.72 | 0.71 | 0.70 | 0.67 |

transformation', the 'export-oriented' policy for foreign investment and trade enhanced the overall social benefit. With increased employment, some workers' rights were protected, so that to a degree, the social objective as required by 'growth model transformation' was achieved. However, as the volume of international trade grew steadily, and with the annual rise in foreign direct investment (FDI), the negative aspect of the 'export-oriented' policy was also emerging. Firstly, China rapidly entered into a period of sustained 'double surpluses' in the balance of payments current and capital accounts, with its foreign exchange reserves rising from US$73.6 billion in 1995 to US$1.202 trillion in 2006. Whilst a sustained period of 'double surpluses' increased international payments, it also caused a series of problems that must not be overlooked: greater trade conflict, rising value of the RMB, value maintenance and increment of foreign reserves, inflation at home, greater pressure for structural adjustment, etc. Secondly, the 'export-oriented' policy encouraged a lot of exports of polluting products that are high on resource and energy consumption and of low added value, which are not conducive to industrial upgrade, suppressed wages, and seriously damaged China's resources and environment, and had a direct impact on the economy's sustainable development. After a long period of implementing the 'export oriented' policy for foreign investment and trade, the negative effects began to exceed the positive. It no longer fulfilled the economic and environmental resources goals in the 'growth model transformation', and to a degree damaged the social objective.

After 2003 China's 'export oriented' foreign trade policy underwent some adjustment. The emphasis of the foreign trade policy began to shift towards industrial restructuring and resources and environmental protection. As export continued to grow, the government again revised down the rate for export tax rebate in 2003. In this tax rebate revision, different tiers of tax rebate were introduced for different products. The rate of tax rebate remained unchanged or even increased for some agricultural processing enterprises supported by the state. For mechanical and electrical products of relatively high technical content and closely related products the rate of tax rebate remained unchanged. For textile and garment products that can lead to potential trade friction the rate of tax rebate was appropriately revised down. Export tax rebate was reduced or abolished for some resources including concentrates, crude oil, timber, softwood, non-renewable resources, and where there is a shortage of a product in the country.

After 2006 China's 'export-oriented' foreign investment and trade policy witnessed rapid changes. In foreign trade policy, there were frequent revisions to the export tax rebate policy and processing trade policy. From 2006 to the onset of the international financial crisis, the export tax rebate policy had been revised for 7 times. Fiscal and Tax [208] No. 111 issued on 30th July 2008 increased the export tax rebate for some textile and garments, from 11 to 13%, and for some bamboo products to 11%. Apart from this, other revisions basically abolished or reduced the rate of export tax rebate. The export tax rebate had been abolished for most of the 'two high' resource type products (polluting products that are high on resource and energy consumption), and an extra tariff had even levied on some such key products.

Development pattern transformation requires to balance investment, consumption and export. In its implementation, the export tax rebate can be lowered and even abolished altogether. However, it is bound to have an impact on industrial development and economic growth. This study used the dynamic CGE model of the 41 sectors to simulate the effect of a reduction in the export tax rebate (equivalent to 3%). Table 3.6 shows the results. The results demonstrate that overall, a revision of the export tax rebate has a negative impact on the manufacturing industry, but a positive impact on the development of the service industries.

**Table 3.6** The impact of revising export tax rebates

| Year | 2010 (%) | 2011 (%) | 2012 (%) | 2013 (%) | 2014 (%) | 2015 (%) | 2020 (%) |
|---|---|---|---|---|---|---|---|
| **Total output** | −0.22 | −0.23 | −0.25 | −0.27 | −0.29 | −0.31 | −0.42 |
| **Price** | −0.20 | −0.18 | −0.16 | −0.13 | −0.11 | −0.09 | 0.05 |
| Output by sector | | | | | | | |
| Agriculture | 0.19 | 0.18 | 0.18 | 0.17 | 0.16 | 0.15 | 0.11 |
| Coal mining and washing | −4.42 | −4.47 | −4.47 | −4.41 | −4.32 | −4.20 | −3.51 |
| Oil and gas extraction | 0.50 | 0.46 | 0.41 | 0.36 | 0.30 | 0.24 | −0.10 |
| Mining and ore dressing | 0.35 | 0.34 | 0.33 | 0.31 | 0.28 | 0.25 | 0.11 |
| Non-metallic mineral mining and dressing | 0.34 | 0.37 | 0.39 | 0.40 | 0.40 | 0.40 | 0.34 |
| Food production and tobacco processing | 0.13 | 0.14 | 0.13 | 0.13 | 0.12 | 0.12 | 0.07 |
| Textile industry | −2.42 | −2.32 | −2.22 | −2.13 | −2.04 | −1.96 | −1.53 |
| Leather and down feather garments and products | −3.13 | −3.07 | −3.01 | −2.94 | −2.87 | −2.80 | −2.35 |
| Timber processing and furniture manufacturing | −0.21 | −0.20 | −0.20 | −0.20 | −0.20 | −0.20 | −0.19 |
| Paper making, printing and stationery manufacturing | −0.12 | −0.10 | -0.08 | −0.08 | −0.08 | −0.09 | −0.14 |
| Petroleum processing, coking and nuclear fuel processing | −0.61 | −0.72 | −0.84 | −0.97 | −1.11 | −1.26 | −2.13 |
| The chemical industry | −0.63 | −0.65 | −0.68 | −0.72 | −0.75 | −0.80 | −1.02 |
| Non-metallic mineral products | 0.07 | 0.05 | 0.03 | 0.01 | −0.02 | −0.05 | −0.18 |
| Smelting and flat-rolling processing | −0.25 | −0.26 | −0.28 | −0.29 | −0.31 | −0.33 | −0.44 |
| Fabricated metal products | −0.85 | −0.84 | −0.85 | −0.86 | −0.87 | −0.89 | −0.96 |
| General purpose or special equipment manufacturing | 0.13 | 0.12 | 0.11 | 0.10 | 0.09 | 0.07 | −0.02 |
| Transport equipment manufacturing | 0.31 | 0.30 | 0.28 | 0.27 | 0.25 | 0.23 | 0.13 |
| Electrical, mechanical and equipment manufacturing | −1.73 | −1.74 | −1.75 | −1.76 | −1.79 | −1.81 | −1.93 |
| Communications devices, the manufacture of computing and other electronic devices | −3.41 | −3.55 | −3.70 | −3.86 | −4.01 | −4.16 | −4.92 |
| Instrumentation, cultural and office machinery manufacturing | −9.52 | −9.74 | −9.96 | −10.18 | −10.39 | −10.61 | −11.59 |
| Other manufacturing industries and scrap and waste | −0.87 | −0.83 | −0.79 | −0.76 | −0.73 | −0.70 | −0.59 |
| Production and supply of electricity and heating | 0.07 | 0.07 | 0.07 | 0.06 | 0.05 | 0.04 | −0.05 |

(continued)

**Table 3.6** (continued)

| Year | 2010 (%) | 2011 (%) | 2012 (%) | 2013 (%) | 2014 (%) | 2015 (%) | 2020 (%) |
|---|---|---|---|---|---|---|---|
| Fuel production and supply | 0.39 | 0.39 | 0.39 | 0.38 | 0.38 | 0.37 | 0.30 |
| Water production and supply | 0.18 | 0.16 | 0.15 | 0.13 | 0.11 | 0.09 | −0.03 |
| Construction industry | 1.03 | 0.96 | 0.90 | 0.84 | 0.79 | 0.74 | 0.53 |
| Transport and warehousing | 0.39 | 0.37 | 0.36 | 0.34 | 0.32 | 0.29 | 0.16 |
| Postal service | 0.94 | 0.92 | 0.90 | 0.87 | 0.85 | 0.82 | 0.70 |
| Information transmission, computing services and software industry | 0.64 | 0.63 | 0.61 | 0.60 | 0.58 | 0.56 | 0.44 |
| Wholesale and retail trade | 0.13 | 0.10 | 0.07 | 0.04 | 0.01 | −0.02 | −0.18 |
| Accommodation and catering industry | 0.80 | 0.77 | 0.74 | 0.70 | 0.67 | 0.64 | 0.47 |
| Finance and insurance industry | 0.62 | 0.60 | 0.57 | 0.54 | 0.51 | 0.49 | 0.34 |
| The property industry | 0.73 | 0.74 | 0.74 | 0.73 | 0.72 | 0.71 | 0.61 |
| Leasing and business services industry | 1.15 | 1.13 | 1.11 | 1.08 | 1.04 | 1.01 | 0.76 |
| Tourist industry | 1.38 | 1.35 | 1.32 | 1.28 | 1.24 | 1.20 | 0.99 |
| Scientific research | 0.85 | 0.81 | 0.76 | 0.72 | 0.68 | 0.65 | 0.46 |
| Integrated technical services | 0.67 | 0.65 | 0.64 | 0.62 | 0.59 | 0.57 | 0.45 |
| Other social services | 0.49 | 0.48 | 0.46 | 0.44 | 0.41 | 0.39 | 0.27 |
| Education | 0.59 | 0.57 | 0.55 | 0.53 | 0.51 | 0.49 | 0.38 |
| Health, social security and social welfare | 0.63 | 0.61 | 0.59 | 0.57 | 0.55 | 0.53 | 0.41 |
| Cultural, sports and entertainment industries | 0.75 | 0.73 | 0.70 | 0.67 | 0.64 | 0.61 | 0.46 |
| Public administration and social organisations | 3.81 | 3.77 | 3.74 | 3.71 | 3.67 | 3.64 | 3.48 |

## Bibliography


Development Research Centre of the State Council. 1999. *An analysis of China's economic development outlook in the next 20 years*.

Development Research Centre of the State Council. 2003. *A forecast of economic growth and development in China in 2021–2050*.

Shi, Jiuyu. 2007. Application of the grey compositional data model in the analysis and forecast of China's industrial structure. *Statistics and Information Forum* (1).

Wang, Yini. 2005. A forecast of automotive demands in China: An analysis based on the Gompertz model. *Research on Financial and Economic Issues* (11).

Yang, Hongjiao, and Linyan, Sun. 2009. An analysis of the characteristics in the evolution of China's industrial structure and its future forecast. *Science Research Management* (9).

# Chapter 4
# The Implications of Reducing Greenhouse Gas Emissions

**Liu Yu**

## 4.1 Calibrating the Baseline for 9 Regions and 17 Sectors for 2004–2050

In order to analyse the impact of reducing emission, we use the GTAP-E model to carry out the assessment. When using the dynamic GTAP-E model, we need to construct a baseline. In other words, we need to describe what path will be taken by the world's economy if there was no policy impact. A policy scenario refers to a certain point when a policy is brought out, causing the whole economy to veer from its original trajectory. Within this, the magnitude of deviation is the effect of the policy.

Since the policy scenario effect is the magnitude of its deviation from the baseline, how the baseline is set will have a major influence on the policy effect. For instance, the proportion of an industry to the economy may be quite high at the moment, but with changing technological progress, industrial division of labour and comparative advantage, the proportion of that industry in the economy will decline in the future. Thus, if the study looks at the effect of reducing the import tariff for that product at a point in time, the result will be completely different. The reason is that if the proportion of that industry to the economy is high, the effect of reducing the import tariff will be relatively high; by contrast the effect will be relatively low. Therefore, to determine how that industry will change has particular significance.

1. **Setting/Constructing the baseline**

Given the significance of the baseline, in addition to calibrating the macro variables, the output of some energy products are also controlled in this study. In calibrating the macro variables, the model needs to ensure the assumptions made for

L. Yu (✉)
Chinese Academy of Sciences, Beijing, China

 
Q. Zhang (ed.), *Transforming Economic Growth and China's Industrial Upgrading*, Research Series on the Chinese Dream and China's Development Path,
https://doi.org/10.1007/978-981-13-0962-5_4

economics and balance. The following are conditions for a dynamic GTAP-E model in equilibrium:

1. **The region's income equals expenditure (in balance)**

$$Y = \text{Real GDP} + \text{NFY} = C + G + S$$

Y represents total income; Real GDP represents actual GDP; NFY represents net foreign income; C, G and S represent total personal consumption, total government consumption and savings respectively. In this balanced equation, we can find the data for Real GDP, C, G and NF, therefore we calibrated these macro variables; by contrast S is determined endogenously by the model and the equation.

2. **The region's current account is in balance**

$$X - M + \text{NFY} = S - I$$

X and M represent the region's exports and imports respectively; I represents the region's investments. Since we have controlled the two variables of NFY and S, we only need to control I or X − M here. We chose to calibrate investments (I) so that the equation determines endogenously the changes in the trade balance (X − M).

3. **Total global investment equals global savings**
Since global investment must equal global savings, we cannot control the investment of every country, but have to leave the investment of one country for the model to decide (in a Walrasian equilibrium, if there are N markets, then when N − 1 is in equilibrium, N will automatically be in equilibrium). As we mainly focus on other eight separate regions, this study will not contain rest of the world (ROW).
4. **Income equals expenditure on global foreign assets**
There are many restrictions on the income of foreign assets. We finally chose to calibrate the income of Chinese assets held abroad (YQTF).

2. **Calibrating the main macroeconomic variables**

In this study the macro variables calibrated include economic growth, population, private consumption, government consumption and investment. The historical and predicted data of the macroeconomic variables are research outcomes from the task force of the Chinese Academy of Social Sciences Industrial Economic Research Institute.

Table 4.1 shows that China's GDP growth slows down after 2010. By 2050 the annual average of China's GDP will slow to 3.3%. Like China, the GDP of other developing countries such as India and Brazil also slow down after 2010 and 2015 respectively. The GDP of South Africa also appears to slow down from 2015 onwards.

Compared with developing countries, future changes to the GDP of developed countries are milder. The annual GDP growth rate of the USA between 2010 and

**Table 4.1** Cumulative growth rates for nine regions, 2004–2050 (%)

| Economic growth | 2010 | 2015 | 2020 | 2025 | 2030 | 2035 | 2040 | 2045 | 2050 |
|---|---|---|---|---|---|---|---|---|---|
| China | 73.8 | 54.4 | 46.2 | 40.9 | 34.5 | 28.2 | 23.5 | 20.2 | 17.7 |
| EU | 3.1 | 7.9 | 9.5 | 8.8 | 8.3 | 8.5 | 7.9 | 6.2 | 3.6 |
| USA | 3.1 | 12.2 | 14.9 | 13.3 | 11.9 | 11.7 | 11.5 | 11.1 | 10.6 |
| Japan | −2.1 | 3.7 | 6.4 | 6.1 | 5.3 | 4.6 | 4.2 | 4.0 | 4.0 |
| Australia | 14.3 | 15.5 | 15.5 | 14.7 | 13.1 | 11.1 | 9.5 | 8.5 | 8.0 |
| India | 47.7 | 43.5 | 40.7 | 38.3 | 36.5 | 34.9 | 33.4 | 31.8 | 30.2 |
| Brazil | 15.5 | 20.0 | 19.8 | 17.3 | 15.3 | 14.0 | 12.8 | 11.4 | 10.0 |
| South Africa | 19.6 | 21.9 | 21.6 | 20.1 | 18.2 | 16.5 | 15.7 | 15.7 | 16.0 |
| Other countries | 8.0 | 17.1 | 16.6 | 11.6 | 10.5 | 13.8 | 15.6 | 14.7 | 12.3 |

*Data source* Task force of the Chinese Academy of Social Sciences Industrial Economic Research Institute
*Note* The figure for 2010 is the cumulative growth rate during 2004–2010, the figures for other years are five-year cumulative growth rates

2050 basically remains between 2 and 3%. The annual GDP growth rate of the EU before 2045 is basically between 1.2 and 1.8%, slowing to below 1% during 2045–2050. The annual GDP growth rate for Japan will remain between 0.8 and 1.0% during 2010–2050. Australia is the exception: during 2010–2030 the annual GDP growth rate is 2–3%, slowing to below 2% after 2030.

As shown in Table 4.2, China's population will peak around 2035 and then begins to drop. Brazil's population will peak around 2045. Japan's population growth will remain relatively low for a long period and will enter a period of zero growth from around 2040. The population of other countries and regions will continue to grow before 2050.

In China, the growth of private consumption will exceed the growth of GDP around 2015, and it will become the main contributor to GDP. However, as economic growth slacks in China, the growth in private consumption will also start to decline after 2015. India, Brazil and South Africa will follow a similar trend. By contrast, developed countries will witness little change in the growth rate of private consumption. The main reason is that their economic structure and consumption structure are basically stable, with a steady economic growth rate. See Table 4.3 for details. A comparison of Tables 4.3 and 4.4 shows that the trend in government consumption is similar to that in private consumption. The difference is that the former is more stable, due mainly to the stability of government consumption itself.

Investment is an important driver for a country's economic development. Therefore, changes in investment has a strong correlation with changes to the GDP

**Table 4.2** Cumulative population growth rates for nine regions, 2004–2050 (%)

| Population | 2010 | 2015 | 2020 | 2025 | 2030 | 2035 | 2040 | 2045 | 2050 |
|---|---|---|---|---|---|---|---|---|---|
| China | 0.5 | 1.9 | 2.3 | 1.8 | 1.1 | 0.5 | −0.1 | −0.5 | −1.0 |
| EU | 2.8 | 2.7 | 2.5 | 2.2 | 1.9 | 1.7 | 1.4 | 1.2 | 0.9 |
| USA | 3.7 | 5.4 | 5.7 | 5.0 | 4.4 | 4.2 | 4.0 | 3.8 | 3.5 |
| Japan | −0.2 | 0.0 | 0.2 | 0.2 | 0.1 | 0.1 | 0.0 | 0.0 | 0.0 |
| Australia | 5.7 | 5.2 | 5.1 | 5.2 | 5.1 | 4.4 | 3.9 | 3.9 | 4.1 |
| India | 6.1 | 6.4 | 6.0 | 4.9 | 3.9 | 3.1 | 2.5 | 1.9 | 1.4 |
| Brazil | 4.2 | 3.9 | 3.3 | 2.4 | 1.7 | 1.1 | 0.5 | 0.0 | −0.5 |
| South Africa | 4.6 | 3.1 | 2.5 | 2.4 | 2.3 | 1.9 | 1.4 | 1.1 | 1.0 |
| Other countries | 2.6 | 7.6 | 9.6 | 9.0 | 6.6 | 3.2 | 0.9 | 0.2 | 1.0 |

*Data source* Task force of the Chinese Academy of Social Sciences Industrial Economic Research Institute
*Note* The figure for 2010 is the cumulative growth rate during 2004–2010, the figures for other years are 5-year cumulative growth rates

**Table 4.3** Cumulative private consumption growth rates for nine regions, 2004–2050 (%)

| Personal consumption | 2010 | 2015 | 2020 | 2025 | 2030 | 2035 | 2040 | 2045 | 2050 |
|---|---|---|---|---|---|---|---|---|---|
| China | 53.9 | 62.6 | 57.3 | 49.5 | 42.6 | 36.5 | 29.6 | 22.8 | 16.7 |
| EU | 2.8 | 7.8 | 9.5 | 8.8 | 8.3 | 8.5 | 7.9 | 6.2 | 3.6 |
| USA | 5.6 | 9.2 | 11.3 | 12.3 | 12.4 | 11.9 | 11.4 | 11.0 | 10.6 |
| Japan | −1.6 | 2.0 | 5.1 | 7.4 | 7.4 | 5.4 | 3.8 | 3.5 | 4.2 |
| Australia | 15.0 | 15.6 | 15.4 | 14.7 | 13.1 | 11.1 | 9.5 | 8.5 | 8.0 |
| India | 49.6 | 43.8 | 40.6 | 38.3 | 36.5 | 34.9 | 33.4 | 31.8 | 30.2 |
| Brazil | 24.6 | 21.5 | 19.1 | 17.1 | 15.4 | 14.1 | 12.7 | 11.4 | 10.0 |
| South Africa | 20.3 | 22.1 | 21.5 | 19.8 | 18.3 | 17.2 | 15.4 | 12.8 | 9.9 |
| Other countries | 7.5 | 10.7 | 12.2 | 12.8 | 13.9 | 15.6 | 15.7 | 14.3 | 12.0 |

*Data source* Task force of the Chinese Academy of Social Sciences Industrial Economic Research Institute
*Note* The figure for 2010 is the cumulative growth rate during 2004–2010, the figures for other years are 5-year cumulative growth rates

of a country. As shown in Table 4.5, the financial crises had a negative impact on investments in the USA and Japan during 2004–2010.

3. **Calibrating main energy-related products**

The emission of carbon dioxide is mainly produced by burning fuel. Therefore, an increase in the output of energy-related products is a significant factor in the forecast of emissions. As such, we also calibrated the growth of energy-related products in the nine regions during 2004–2050 of the countries can fall into three categories by coal production. The first contains countries with positive but slowly

**Table 4.4** Cumulative government consumption growth rates for regions, 2004–2050 (%)

| Government spending | 2010 | 2015 | 2020 | 2025 | 2030 | 2035 | 2040 | 2045 | 2050 |
|---|---|---|---|---|---|---|---|---|---|
| China | 60.6 | 60.7 | 57.1 | 51.7 | 45.4 | 39.0 | 31.2 | 23.4 | 16.4 |
| EU | 7.9 | 8.9 | 9.0 | 8.5 | 8.4 | 8.6 | 7.9 | 6.2 | 3.6 |
| USA | 5.4 | 13.5 | 15.4 | 13.4 | 11.9 | 11.6 | 11.5 | 11.1 | 10.6 |
| Japan | 7.1 | 5.8 | 5.4 | 5.7 | 5.5 | 4.7 | 4.1 | 3.9 | 4.0 |
| Australia | 16.0 | 14.0 | 13.7 | 14.2 | 13.4 | 11.2 | 9.4 | 8.5 | 8.0 |
| India | 60.4 | 44.9 | 40.2 | 38.1 | 36.5 | 34.9 | 33.4 | 31.8 | 30.2 |
| Brazil | −0.5 | 16.6 | 21.4 | 18.0 | 15.0 | 13.9 | 12.8 | 11.5 | 10.0 |
| South Africa | 19.7 | 21.9 | 21.6 | 20.1 | 18.2 | 16.5 | 15.7 | 15.7 | 16.0 |
| Other countries | 10.1 | 12.7 | 13.3 | 13.0 | 14.0 | 16.0 | 16.1 | 14.1 | 11.2 |

*Data source* Task force of the Chinese Academy of Social Sciences Industrial Economic Research Institute

*Note* The figure for 2010 is the cumulative growth rate during 2004–2010, the figures for other years are 5-year cumulative growth rates

**Table 4.5** Cumulative investment growth rates for nine regions, 2004–2050 (%)

| Investment | 2010 | 2015 | 2020 | 2025 | 2030 | 2035 | 2040 | 2045 | 2050 |
|---|---|---|---|---|---|---|---|---|---|
| China | 71.5 | 45.4 | 36.3 | 31.5 | 24.1 | 16.0 | 13.1 | 15.2 | 19.9 |
| EU | 0.0 | 7.2 | 9.8 | 8.9 | 8.2 | 8.5 | 7.9 | 6.2 | 3.6 |
| USA | −26.8 | 19.5 | 33.3 | 18.0 | 9.8 | 10.6 | 12.0 | 11.7 | 10.3 |
| Japan | −7.3 | 11.8 | 13.1 | 2.5 | −2.7 | 1.3 | 5.8 | 6.2 | 3.1 |
| Australia | 32.4 | 6.9 | 3.2 | 10.9 | 15.0 | 12.0 | 9.1 | 8.0 | 8.2 |
| India | 45.6 | 43.3 | 40.9 | 38.3 | 36.5 | 34.9 | 33.4 | 31.8 | 30.2 |
| Brazil | 22.8 | 21.2 | 19.2 | 17.1 | 15.4 | 14.1 | 12.7 | 11.4 | 10.0 |
| South Africa | 14.1 | 20.9 | 22.1 | 20.2 | 18.1 | 16.5 | 15.7 | 15.7 | 16.0 |
| Other countries | 2.9 | 18.2 | 20.2 | 15.1 | 12.2 | 12.7 | 13.7 | 14.3 | 14.5 |

*Data source* Task force of the Chinese Academy of Social Sciences Industrial Economic Research Institute

*Note* The figure for 2010 is the cumulative growth rate during 2004–2010, the figures for other years are 5-year cumulative growth rates

declining growth by 2050—this includes Japan, India, South Africa and other countries. The second category those countries entering negative growth earlier—this includes the EU and Brazil. The third category is those undergoing a transition from positive growth to negative growth—this includes China, the USA and Australia (Table 4.6).

Unlike coal, oil production in most countries remains in positive growth. Oil production in Japan, Australia, India, Brazil, South Africa and other countries will continue to grow before 2050, and in particular, in Brazil the output of oil will remain at a relatively high level of growth. However, the trend for China and the USA is a slowly declining growth rate changing to negative growth (Table 4.7).

**Table 4.6** Cumulative coal production growth rates for nine regions, 2004–2050 (%)

| Coal production | 2010 | 2015 | 2020 | 2025 | 2030 | 2035 | 2040 | 2045 | 2050 |
|---|---|---|---|---|---|---|---|---|---|
| China | 57.8 | 14.2 | 10.9 | 7.7 | 5.0 | 4.0 | 3.2 | −1.7 | −3.6 |
| EU | −4.3 | −5.0 | −7.0 | −9.0 | −11.0 | −13.0 | −15.0 | −17.0 | −19.0 |
| USA | 0.8 | 6.8 | 5.4 | 4.0 | 3.5 | 1.6 | 0.4 | −0.1 | −0.3 |
| Japan | 37.1 | 8.0 | 6.5 | 5.0 | 3.5 | 2.6 | 1.4 | 1.2 | 0.8 |
| Australia | 20.7 | 13.2 | 10.8 | 8.6 | 6.5 | 4.5 | 2.4 | 0.7 | −1.0 |
| India | 74.0 | 10.0 | 9.8 | 9.6 | 9.4 | 9.2 | 9.0 | 8.8 | 8.6 |
| Brazil | 16.1 | −18.0 | −16.0 | −14.0 | −12.0 | −10.0 | −8.0 | −6.0 | −4.0 |
| South Africa | 45.6 | 6.3 | 5.4 | 4.7 | 4.1 | 3.5 | 3.0 | 2.5 | 2.1 |
| Other countries | 25.3 | 3.8 | 3.1 | 3.0 | 3.0 | 2.0 | 2.0 | 2.0 | 2.0 |

*Data source* Task force of the Chinese Academy of Social Sciences Industrial Economic Research Institute
*Note* The figure for 2010 is the cumulative growth rate during 2004–2010, the figures for other years are 5-year cumulative growth rates

**Table 4.7** Cumulative growth rates in oil production for nine regions, 2004–2050 (%)

| Oil production | 2010 | 2015 | 2020 | 2025 | 2030 | 2035 | 2040 | 2045 | 2050 |
|---|---|---|---|---|---|---|---|---|---|
| China | 7.5 | 6.6 | 6.3 | 6.1 | 2.1 | −0.4 | −1.5 | −2.7 | −5.7 |
| EU | −19.1 | 9.4 | 8.5 | 7.6 | 6.7 | 5.8 | 4.9 | 4.0 | 3.1 |
| USA | 6.3 | 5.5 | 4.7 | 3.9 | 3.1 | 2.3 | 1.5 | 0.7 | −0.1 |
| Japan | 6.0 | 6.0 | 5.9 | 5.9 | 5.8 | 5.8 | 5.7 | 5.7 | 5.6 |
| Australia | 0.2 | 7.4 | 6.8 | 6.2 | 5.6 | 5.0 | 4.4 | 3.8 | 3.2 |
| India | 5.7 | 6.1 | 5.6 | 5.0 | 4.5 | 3.9 | 3.2 | 2.5 | 1.7 |
| Brazil | 25.5 | 19.6 | 19.1 | 18.6 | 18.1 | 17.6 | 17.1 | 16.6 | 16.1 |
| South Africa | 6.0 | 6.0 | 5.5 | 5.0 | 4.5 | 4.0 | 3.5 | 3.0 | 2.0 |
| Other countries | 5.3 | 8.8 | 8.4 | 8.1 | 7.5 | 6.5 | 6.1 | 5.7 | 5.4 |

*Data source* Task force of the Chinese Academy of Social Sciences Industrial Economic Research Institute
*Note* The figure for 2010 is the cumulative growth rate during 2004–2010, the figures for other years are 5-year cumulative growth rates

Compared with coal and oil, natural gas emits less carbon dioxide. Therefore, the production of natural gas will remain at a relatively high growth rate in all countries, especially China, Japan, India, Brazil and South Africa (Table 4.8).

The output of refined oil in all countries is affected by oil production, but is also closely related to a country's own imports in oil and refined oil products. Table 4.9 shows that the output of refined oil products in developing countries will remain at a relatively high growth rate, whereas that of developed countries will remain at a relatively low growth rate and will likely decline.

**Table 4.8** Cumulative growth rates in natural gas production for 9 regions, 2004–2050 (%)

| Natural gas production | 2010 | 2015 | 2020 | 2025 | 2030 | 2035 | 2040 | 2045 | 2050 |
|---|---|---|---|---|---|---|---|---|---|
| China | 86.3 | 24.9 | 20.5 | 16.3 | 12.8 | 8.3 | 4.2 | −2.7 | −8.2 |
| EU | −5.7 | 10.0 | 7.2 | 6.4 | 5.6 | 3.8 | 2.0 | 1.2 | 0.4 |
| USA | 27.4 | 19.7 | 18.6 | 15.2 | 13.0 | 12.8 | 10.6 | 8.4 | 6.2 |
| Japan | 42.0 | 16.0 | 14.8 | 12.6 | 10.4 | 8.2 | 6.0 | 3.8 | 2.6 |
| Australia | 35.2 | 33.8 | 29.0 | 28.0 | 27.0 | 26.5 | 25.0 | 23.5 | 22.0 |
| India | 89.3 | 51.3 | 47.3 | 43.3 | 39.3 | 35.3 | 31.3 | 27.3 | 23.3 |
| Brazil | 38.2 | 5.7 | 4.9 | 3.1 | 1.8 | 1.2 | 1.0 | 0.6 | 0.1 |
| South Africa | 48.0 | 14.0 | 13.8 | 13.6 | 13.4 | 13.2 | 13.0 | 12.8 | 12.6 |
| Other countries | 28.2 | 21.3 | 19.8 | 18.7 | 18.0 | 17.3 | 16.5 | 15.8 | 15.0 |

*Data source* Task force of the Chinese Academy of Social Sciences Industrial Economic Research Institute

*Note* The figure for 2010 is the cumulative growth rate during 2004–2010, the figures for other years are 5-year cumulative growth rates

**Table 4.9** Cumulative growth rates in finished petroleum products for 9 regions, 2004–2050 (%)

| Natural gas production | 2010 | 2015 | 2020 | 2025 | 2030 | 2035 | 2040 | 2045 | 2050 |
|---|---|---|---|---|---|---|---|---|---|
| China | 44.8 | 32.1 | 26.4 | 21.8 | 16.4 | 11.1 | 7.4 | 1.7 | −5.6 |
| EU | −3.1 | −1.3 | −0.5 | 0.1 | 0.6 | 0.8 | 1.3 | 1.5 | 1.6 |
| USA | −5.2 | 0.6 | 1.8 | 1.9 | 2.0 | 2.1 | 2.2 | 2.3 | 2.3 |
| Japan | 16.2 | −1.2 | −1.2 | −1.1 | −1.1 | −1.1 | −1.1 | −1.1 | −1.1 |
| Australia | 3.9 | 5.0 | 3.8 | 3.2 | 3.0 | 2.9 | 2.4 | 2.0 | 1.7 |
| India | 79.8 | 21.6 | 20.7 | 20.4 | 19.0 | 18.1 | 17.5 | 17.1 | 16.3 |
| Brazil | 35.8 | 10.3 | 9.5 | 8.9 | 8.1 | 7.5 | 7.0 | 6.6 | 6.2 |
| South Africa | 35.1 | 7.2 | 7.0 | 7.0 | 5.7 | 4.5 | 2.9 | 0.0 | −1.0 |
| Other countries | 17.0 | 11.3 | 9.0 | 8.0 | 7.4 | 6.3 | 5.0 | 4.0 | 3.0 |

*Data source* Task force of the Chinese Academy of Social Sciences Industrial Economic Research Institute

*Note* The figure for 2010 is the cumulative growth rate during 2004–2010, the figures for other years are 5-year cumulative growth rates

## 4.2 BAU Emission Forecast for 9 Regions During 2004–2050

1. **Simulation scenarios**

This paper uses the latest dynamic GTAP model and V7 database. The database is constructed from matrices in social accounting and audit of all countries for 2004, covering 113 countries and 57 products. For the research, we total up the data of these countries into 17 product sectors and nine countries and regions.

Given the objectives of this study, we designed detailed baseline scenarios.

**Baseline scenarios**: this paper uses the dynamic method to simulate the baseline scenarios for 2004–2015. The baseline scenarios assume that all the countries will continue with their current policies. In addition, consideration is given to the fact that China will continue to revise its tariff policy during 2001–2010 in accordance with the WTO agreement, to the termination of the Multi-Fibre Agreement (MFA) in January 2005, and to the enlargement of the EU, etc.

2. **Forecast outcome**

With the dynamic GTAP-E model calibrated by macro variables and energy-related products output, we forecast the carbon dioxide emission of the 9 countries as follows:

Table 4.10 shows that, firstly, there is a fast increase of carbon dioxide emission in developing countries, especially China and India; secondly, carbon dioxide emission of each country peaks at different times, and only Japan will peak before 2050. Emission by other countries will not peak before 2050, especially China, India and Brazil, which have greater potential for increase; thirdly, global carbon dioxide emission still has a high growth rate and large growth potential. As shown in Table 4.10, global carbon dioxide emission will increase from 32.95 billion tons in 2010, to 73.72 billion tons in 2050, an increase of 123%.[1] Therefore, if $CO_2$ emission is not further controlled, global temperature will rise by nearly 6° by 2050. This is far from our aim to restrict global climate change to within 2°[2] by 2050.

The table below is an estimate by this research on the historic emission from the eight major global economies and a forecast of a BAU scenario during 2010–2050. As shown in the table, China's annual increase of carbon dioxide emission during 2001–2008 is 10.5%, decreases to 2.8% during 2010–2030, and decreases further to 0.7% during 2030–2050. India's annual increase of carbon dioxide emission will also reduce from 5.4% during 2001–2008, to 4.1% during 2010–2030, and to 3.6% during 2030–2050. The annual increase of carbon dioxide emission by other developing countries will also continue to fall during 2010–2050.

Compared with developing countries, the increase in carbon dioxide emission in developed countries is slower and will fall, and in particular Japan's annual increase will become negative by 2045–5050. Some developed countries will still witness a slight rise in carbon dioxide emission. For example, the emission of the USA will increase by 0.18% during 2001–2008, rise to 1.23% during 2010–2030, but maintain at 0.86% during 2030–2050. Some developed countries achieve results in the control of carbon dioxide emission, such as the EU, which achieves a fall during 2001–2008 through the establishment of a carbon market. During 2010–2050, emission in the EU will still continue to increase but will remain at a relatively low

[1] This is quite close to the IEA study Energy Technology Perspectives 2008, completed by the International Energy Agency (IEA), which warned that if policy change and major supply constraints are eliminated, then by 2050 global oil needs will increase by 70%, and $CO_2$ emission by 130%.

[2] This is the threshold for preventing the dangers of climate change.

**Table 4.10** $CO_2$ emission in 9 regions during 2010–2050 (hundred million tons)

| Carbon dioxide | 2010 | 2015 | 2020 | 2025 | 2030 | 2035 | 2040 | 2045 | 2050 |
|---|---|---|---|---|---|---|---|---|---|
| China | 72.5 | 85.5 | 98.4 | 113.7 | 126.6 | 135.1 | 140.3 | 143.6 | 144.9 |
| EU | 34.8 | 36.1 | 37.7 | 39.4 | 41.3 | 43.9 | 47.0 | 49.4 | 51.2 |
| USA | 64.8 | 69.0 | 73.4 | 77.9 | 82.7 | 87.6 | 92.0 | 95.9 | 98.2 |
| Japan | 12.7 | 13.0 | 13.4 | 13.7 | 14.0 | 14.3 | 14.5 | 14.6 | 14.3 |
| Australia | 4.6 | 5.4 | 6.3 | 7.2 | 8.1 | 8.9 | 9.7 | 10.3 | 10.8 |
| India | 18.5 | 22.8 | 28.3 | 34.3 | 41.6 | 50.0 | 59.7 | 71.9 | 84.0 |
| Brazil | 3.9 | 4.3 | 4.6 | 5.0 | 5.5 | 5.9 | 6.4 | 6.8 | 7.0 |
| South Africa | 5.2 | 5.8 | 6.5 | 7.3 | 8.1 | 8.8 | 9.3 | 9.6 | 9.7 |
| Other countries | 112.6 | 132.9 | 154.0 | 174.2 | 196.0 | 223.6 | 255.7 | 286.6 | 317.1 |
| Summary | 329.5 | 374.9 | 422.7 | 472.6 | 523.9 | 578.0 | 634.6 | 688.8 | 737.2 |

*Data source* Dynamic GTAP-E simulation

rate. On the whole, compared with historic emissions, countries under the BAU scenario shows a marked fall. Countries that continue the rise in emission are close to or have reached a peak (Table 4.11).

Around the Copenhagen Summit, countries made conditional or unconditional commitments to their emission reduction targets for 2020. The table below shows that there are two main differences in the pledges made. Firstly, the methods for commitment are different, including absolute or relative reduction in emission; secondly, the benchmark years are different, with the countries pledging to different years for comparison. These two aspects are important factors that affect the 2020 emission reduction targets.

In addition, carbon dioxide emission under the BAU scenarios are also important indicators for measuring how well the countries have achieved their emission reduction pledges. This study carried out an estimate of emission by the countries in 2020 against the targets they had pledged. Compared with the emission levels

**Table 4.11** $CO_2$ emission in 9 regions during 2010–2050 (hundred million tons)

| Carbon dioxide | Annual increase rate 2001–2008 (%) | Annual increase rate 2010–2030 (%) | Annual increase rate 2030–2050 (%) |
|---|---|---|---|
| China | 10.52 | 2.83 | 0.68 |
| EU | −0.22 | 0.85 | 1.08 |
| USA | 0.18 | 1.23 | 0.86 |
| Japan | 0.12 | 0.49 | 0.10 |
| Australia | 3.24 | 2.92 | 1.45 |
| India | 5.45 | 4.14 | 3.57 |
| Brazil | 1.98 | 1.71 | 1.27 |
| South Africa | 2.91 | 2.25 | 0.92 |
| Other countries | 3.25 | 2.81 | 2.43 |

*Data source* Worldbank WDI databank, Dynamic GTAP-E simulation arrived at by this study under the BAU scenario, the table shows that South Africa has the highest level of reduction at 74%, followed by Australia, Brazil, Japan, the USA, India, at 60, 44, 40, 35 and 18% respectively. The levels of reduction by China and the EU are 8 and 14% respectively. As shown, it is easier to achieve relative reduction than absolute reduction.

3. **Distribution of carbon dioxide emission by industry**

The following two tables are carbon dioxide emission by industry in all countries. As shown in the tables, from a long-range perspective, the electricity sector will still emit the highest level of carbon dioxide. Apart from electricity, the ranking of other sectors may change. This indicates changes in industrial structure of all countries in the future. As an example, China's agricultural sector will continue to need more energy to satisfy modern agricultural development; emissions from the services and transport industries will also increase. However, emissions from the construction, manufacturing and metal mining industries will reduce by 2050 (Table 4.12).

## 4.3 The Effect of Emission Reduction by China

I. **Setting emission scenarios**

Different scenario assumptions will lead to different results even given the same impact. Therefore, before the simulation, we will briefly introduce the baseline used and the assumed scenario, especially the carbon dioxide trends in different years and peak times.

Under the baseline (S00) scenario, China's carbon dioxide emission will continue to rise but will gradually slow down. It will reach 14.49 billion tons in 2050, i.e. it has doubled from the 2010 emission of 7.25 billion tons. At the same time, under the baseline scenario, the emission will not peak in China. Over the nine points during 2010–2050 China's aggregate carbon dioxide emission totals 106.09 billion tons, averaging 11.79 billion tons at each point in time.

Under the very stringent energy conservation scenario (S25) China's carbon dioxide emission will peak in 2025 (absolute value, not growth rate), and thereafter will fall. Emission reaches 9.69 billion tons when it peaks in 2025, and falls back to 7.78 billion tons by 2050, equivalent to the emission level in 2013. Over the nine points during 2010–2050 China's aggregate carbon dioxide emission totals 78.32 billion tons, averaging 8.7 billion tons at each point. Also, we believe this to be the most likely scenario.

Under stringent energy conservation scenario (S30) China's carbon dioxide emission will peak in 2030, and thereafter will fall. Emission reaches 10.63 billion tons when it peaks in 2030, and falls to 9.29 billion tons by 2050, equivalent to the emission level in 2020. Over the nine points during 2010–2050 China's aggregate carbon dioxide emission totals 85.94 billion tons, averaging 9.55 billion tons at each point.

**Table 4.12** Carbon dioxide changes in the various countries during 2010–2050 (in million tons)

| | China | | | USA | | | EU | | | Japan | | |
|---|---|---|---|---|---|---|---|---|---|---|---|---|
| | 2010 | 2030 | 2050 | 2010 | 2030 | 2050 | 2010 | 2030 | 2050 | 2010 | 2030 | 2050 |
| Agriculture | 163 | 396 | 641 | 59 | 82 | 87 | 71 | 91 | 88 | 32 | 32 | 26 |
| Food | 72 | 88 | 73 | 81 | 118 | 144 | 61 | 79 | 96 | 12 | 12 | 10 |
| Coal production | 140 | 844 | 2546 | 1 | 2 | 3 | 1 | 1 | 1 | 0 | 0 | 0 |
| Oil production | 56 | 175 | 246 | 26 | 41 | 60 | 9 | 13 | 17 | 0 | 0 | 0 |
| Natural gas production | 49 | 59 | 14 | 40 | 70 | 112 | 4 | 5 | 5 | 0 | 0 | 0 |
| Finished petroleum products | 6 | 14 | 21 | 173 | 181 | 181 | 41 | 41 | 41 | 11 | 11 | 11 |
| Electricity | 3962 | 5598 | 4535 | 2738 | 3468 | 3997 | 1076 | 1386 | 1968 | 466 | 551 | 608 |
| Construction | 46 | 64 | 46 | 13 | 18 | 22 | 19 | 21 | 24 | 15 | 21 | 23 |
| Wholesale and retail | 73 | 172 | 152 | 86 | 138 | 186 | 58 | 67 | 80 | 19 | 21 | 20 |
| Steel | 362 | 585 | 496 | 67 | 101 | 153 | 68 | 75 | 92 | 51 | 47 | 49 |
| Manufacturing industry | 374 | 489 | 359 | 216 | 324 | 458 | 122 | 141 | 166 | 38 | 35 | 32 |
| Other types of transport | 184 | 382 | 307 | 765 | 805 | 837 | 553 | 554 | 585 | 202 | 219 | 201 |
| Water transport | 181 | 367 | 277 | 40 | 49 | 64 | 112 | 157 | 233 | 24 | 38 | 58 |
| Air transport | 25 | 64 | 67 | 433 | 470 | 509 | 141 | 145 | 153 | 15 | 17 | 18 |
| Chemical industry | 336 | 609 | 603 | 235 | 426 | 736 | 98 | 145 | 213 | 73 | 78 | 87 |
| Metal mining | 603 | 597 | 358 | 79 | 119 | 157 | 96 | 117 | 148 | 27 | 26 | 24 |
| Services industry | 115 | 242 | 240 | 231 | 377 | 538 | 115 | 143 | 174 | 95 | 100 | 93 |
| | India | | | Australia | | | Brazil | | | South Africa | | |
| | 2010 | 2030 | 2050 | 2010 | 2030 | 2050 | 2010 | 2030 | 2050 | 2010 | 2030 | 2050 |
| Agriculture | 1 | 2 | 3 | 6 | 7 | 6 | 22 | 29 | 24 | 6 | 15 | 13 |
| Food | 42 | 67 | 95 | 3 | 7 | 11 | 6 | 7 | 7 | 1 | 2 | 2 |
| Coal production | 3 | 11 | 34 | 2 | 4 | 5 | 0 | 0 | 0 | 0 | 0 | 0 |
| Oil production | 4 | 13 | 34 | 4 | 5 | 6 | 9 | 18 | 26 | 0 | 0 | 0 |

(continued)

**Table 4.12** (continued)

| | India | | | Australia | | | Brazil | | | South Africa | | |
|---|---|---|---|---|---|---|---|---|---|---|---|---|
| | 2010 | 2030 | 2050 | 2010 | 2030 | 2050 | 2010 | 2030 | 2050 | 2010 | 2030 | 2050 |
| Natural gas production | 7 | 36 | 127 | 4 | 12 | 53 | 2 | 1 | 1 | 0 | 0 | 0 |
| Finished petroleum products | 13 | 26 | 44 | 3 | 3 | 3 | 5 | 7 | 9 | 5 | 12 | 29 |
| Electricity | 1093 | 2378 | 4710 | 270 | 516 | 557 | 34 | 55 | 90 | 330 | 461 | 497 |
| Construction | 1 | 3 | 6 | 3 | 4 | 6 | 0 | 0 | 0 | 1 | 2 | 3 |
| Wholesale and retail | 11 | 15 | 21 | 3 | 7 | 17 | 4 | 5 | 8 | 2 | 3 | 4 |
| Steel | 73 | 179 | 415 | 6 | 16 | 44 | 28 | 31 | 40 | 26 | 39 | 37 |
| Manufacturing industry | 51 | 108 | 211 | 25 | 49 | 99 | 25 | 29 | 35 | 14 | 22 | 22 |
| Other types of transport | 109 | 211 | 342 | 31 | 38 | 47 | 101 | 133 | 155 | 28 | 54 | 83 |
| Water transport | 28 | 51 | 83 | 2 | 3 | 4 | 15 | 17 | 23 | 2 | 4 | 7 |
| Air transport | 7 | 14 | 23 | 35 | 43 | 49 | 16 | 20 | 23 | 6 | 14 | 24 |
| Chemical industry | 79 | 295 | 822 | 5 | 14 | 35 | 21 | 32 | 43 | 30 | 48 | 46 |
| Metal mining | 67 | 133 | 262 | 8 | 16 | 32 | 14 | 20 | 27 | 16 | 24 | 26 |
| Services industry | 9 | 17 | 32 | 3 | 6 | 17 | 3 | 5 | 7 | 10 | 16 | 24 |

**Table 4.13** Scenario setting—China's emission peaking at different years (unit: billion tons)

| Peak year | 2010 | 2015 | 2020 | 2025 | 2030 | 2035 | 2040 | 2045 | 2050 |
|---|---|---|---|---|---|---|---|---|---|
| Baseline | 72.5 | 85.8 | 98.3 | 113.8 | 126.7 | 135.0 | 140.3 | 143.6 | 144.9 |
| 2025 | 72.5 | 81.0 | 89.4 | **96.9** | 95.8 | 94.2 | 90.3 | 85.3 | 77.8 |
| 2030 | 72.5 | 83.4 | 92.3 | 100.9 | **106.3** | 106.2 | 104.8 | 100.1 | 92.9 |
| 2040 | 72.5 | 85.0 | 96.1 | 107.8 | 115.6 | 118.7 | **118.9** | 115.9 | 111.4 |

*Data source* Task force of the Chinese Academy of Social Sciences Industrial Economic Research Institute

Under the S40 energy conservation scenario, China's carbon dioxide emission will peak in 2040, and thereafter will fall. Emission reaches 11.89 billion tons when it peaks in 2040, and falls back to 11.14 billion tons by 2050, equivalent to the emission level in 2028. Over the nine points during 2010–2050 China's aggregate carbon dioxide emission totals 94.19 billion tons, averaging 10.47 billion tons at each point (Table 4.13).

II. **Macroeconomic effects**

1. **Overall economic impact**

Compared with the baseline scenario, there is a fall in China's GDP growth under the S25, S30 and S40 policy scenarios, with cumulative falls of 20.9, 14.8 and 8.7% respectively. Therefore, China's carbon tax for emission reduction will have a negative effect on the economy. Clearly, the later the economy peaks, the less the effect on China, whereas an early peak will have a greater impact. There are two explanations for this. Firstly, aggregate emissions are different. The reason is that in setting the scenarios, the earlier emission peaks China's total carbon dioxide emission will be less during 2010–2050, and therefore the impact on the whole economy will be greater. Under scenario S25, China's aggregate emission over the nine points is 78.32 billion tons, whereas under the S40 scenario, it is 94.19 billion tons. Secondly, economic structures are different. The reason is that if it peaks earlier it means that China's absolute volume of carbon dioxide emission will fall earlier. The sooner it peaks, the greater the proportion of China's secondary industry, the smaller the proportion of the tertiary industry, and therefore the impact on the whole economy will be greater. According to the model, China's economy slips back because of a fall in domestic capital stocks. Carbon tax leads to reduced rates of return for domestic enterprises as well as a decline in domestic investment. Therefore, in the long run, declining investment will reduce capital stocks,[3] making China's GDP contract. Because the earlier the carbon dioxide emission peaks, the higher the investment, and therefore the effect on the economy is greater. In

[3]In the dynamic GTAP model, from a long-range perspective, assuming that the labour force and total territory of a country (region) are fixed whereas the capital stock can change, and therefore the change in long-range economic growth is caused entirely by changes in capital stocks.

addition, economic slowdown will indirectly reduce tax revenue, which also has a negative effect on the growth of the whole of the economy.

2. **Effects on exports**

In terms of demand, a decline in the overall economy in China will result in shrinking domestic consumption. The model shows that under the three policy scenarios, both private consumption and government spending will decline, with the latter decline being smaller than the former. This is because in the model government spending does not produce emission and therefore the impact on it is smaller. At the same time, foreign trade also declines, in which import declines due to a shrinking domestic economy and thus a falling demand for imports, especially investment, and export declines because of rising prices of export products caused by a stronger real exchange rate. Nevertheless, in general the fall in import exceeds that of export, and therefore trade surplus will be achieved. At the same time, as the country's real exchange rate appreciates, trade conditions also improve. The model shows that carbon tax will optimize China's domestic demand structure because the fall in investment exceeds that in consumption. Thus, carbon tax can, to a degree, help transform China's mode for development and restructuring (Tables 4.14 and 4.15).

3. **The impact on the energy sector**

In general, emission reduction will have a negative impact on all industries in China, and the sooner the emission peaks, the greater the impact. On average, at the peaks in 2025, 2030 and 2040, output in 17 industries will fall on average by −31.9, −24.5 and −15.8% respectively. The scale of the impact is basically the same, with the greater impact being on the industries in oil, natural gas, coal, construction, electricity and finished petroleum products. There will be less impact on agricultural produces, food, trade and services (Table 4.16).

**Table 4.14** Macroeconomic effect from emission peaks in China by year (aggregate effect in 2050, %)

| 2050 | GDP | Investment | Private consumption | Governmental spending | Export | Import | Commodity prices |
|---|---|---|---|---|---|---|---|
| 2025 | −20.86 | −40.56 | −15.77 | −5.55 | −10.10 | −14.04 | 13.47 |
| 2030 | −14.79 | −31.55 | −10.95 | −3.98 | −5.62 | −10.48 | 8.24 |
| 2040 | −8.68 | −19.33 | −6.22 | −2.33 | −3.00 | −6.20 | 4.33 |

*Data source* Dynamic GTAP-E simulation result

**Table 4.15** Macroeconomic effect from emission peaks in China by year in aggregate (GDP %)

| Peak year | 2015 | 2020 | 2025 | 2030 | 2035 | 2040 | 2045 | 2050 |
|---|---|---|---|---|---|---|---|---|
| 2025 | −0.4 | −1.3 | **−2.7** | −5.6 | −9.2 | −13.1 | −16.8 | **−20.9** |
| 2030 | −0.2 | −0.8 | −1.9 | **−3.5** | −5.9 | −8.5 | −11.5 | **−14.8** |
| 2040 | −0.04 | −0.3 | −0.8 | −1.7 | −3.0 | **−4.7** | −6.7 | **−8.7** |

**Table 4.16** Economic effect from emission peaks in China by industry (aggregate effect in 2050, %)

| Industry type | 2025 | 2030 | 2040 |
|---|---|---|---|
| Agricultural produces | −10.2 | −6.7 | −3.6 |
| Food | −12.4 | −8.3 | −4.6 |
| Coal production | −49.5 | −37.5 | −23.4 |
| Oil production | −91.2 | −79.5 | −56.6 |
| Natural gas production | −59.4 | −51.1 | −38.9 |
| Finished petroleum products | −31.4 | −22.9 | −13.7 |
| Electricity | −39.7 | −29.9 | −18.7 |
| Construction industry | −39.4 | −30.6 | −18.7 |
| Trade | −18.4 | −13.0 | −7.6 |
| Steel | −31.5 | −23.1 | −14.1 |
| Manufacturing industry | −22.6 | −16.0 | −9.5 |
| Other types of transport | −20.0 | −14.4 | −8.6 |
| Maritime transport | −22.4 | −16.2 | −9.7 |
| Air transport | −20.4 | −14.4 | −8.5 |
| Chemical industry | −27.1 | −19.3 | −11.6 |
| Mineral products | −30.3 | −22.7 | −13.8 |
| Services industry | −16.0 | −11.4 | −6.6 |

*Data source* Dynamic GTAP-E simulation result

Industrial changes can be divided into two types by influence factors. The first type is changes to the energy industry (coal, oil, natural gas, finished petroleum products and electricity); the second type is changes to the non-energy industry (the other 12 products). In general, the impact on the energy industry is greater, whereas that on the non-energy industry is relatively smaller.

(1) **Effects on the output of the energy industry**

First, with regards to energy industry, the impact of demand decrease and cost increase leads to falling output and rising prices. First, carbon tax makes energy-related products more expensive, and leads directly to decrease in demands for these products, reducing output together with prices in energy industry. However, we find that instead of a drop, prices in energy industry rise sharply. The reason is that the energy-related product itself forms a large part in the input mix in the energy sector. A direct tax on carbon emission leads to a substantial rise in cost, which in turn leads to price increase and falling output. Changes to coal, oil, natural gas and finished petroleum products fall into this type.

An explanation is needed as to the reason why the fall in the output of crude oil far exceeds that of other energy-related products. Nearly 90% of crude oil usage is for finished petroleum products. Therefore, changes to the output of finished petroleum products directly affect the output of crude oil. However, the output of finished petroleum products declines by 31.4%, only 1/3 of that of crude oil. There are two reasons: firstly, compared with imported crude oil, domestically produced crude oil becomes more expensive. A carbon tax leads to a sharp rise in the domestic prices of finished petroleum products, but there is little change in the price of imported crude oil. As a result, the industry makes extensive use of imported crude oil instead of domestically produced crude oil. Secondly, in domestic oil usage, the proportion of imported crude oil is much higher than domestically produced one. The model's databank shows that in China over 80% of crude oil used for finished petroleum products is imported, and only 20% is domestically produced. This results in an even greater price substitution effect, which further reduces the output of domestically produced crude oil.

There is another question. It is usually thought that carbon dioxide emission by the electricity industry is high, so why is there not a big drop in the energy industry? The reason is that in the emission databank, the direct demand for electricity of industries does not emit carbon dioxide. In other words, for the electricity industry, we use the data of output side rather than the end-use or the consumption side in the emission calculation. Carbon dioxide is emitted only when electricity is produced. Therefore, the electricity industry is different from other energy industries in that the impact is from the supply side, not the demand side. Thus, the impact on the electricity industry is relatively small. Moreover, it is possible for the electricity industry to use alternatives for energy-related products, but this cannot happen with other energy industries. This is because the energy-related products are mostly converted by other industries rather than consumed by burning, and therefore there can be no alternatives. Thus, the impact on electricity is smaller.

Among all the energy-related products, finished petroleum products witnesses the smallest decline in output. The main reason for this is that the impact on cost is relatively small for finished petroleum products industry. According to the GTAP-E V7 data, carbon dioxide emission by finished petroleum products industry only comes from burning natural gas,[4] whereas coal and crude oil are converted and do not produce emission. Natural gas as a sare of cost accounts for less than 0.0001 in the finished petroleum products industry. As such, compared with other energy industries, a direct carbon tax has little cost impact for the finished petroleum products industry.

(2) **Effects on the output of the non-energy industry**

Changes in the output and price for the second type, namely non-energy-related products are mainly due to emission cost. The carbon tax directly pushes up prices of the energy-related products used by the non-energy-related industries. As there is no impact from direct demand, there is little overall effect on the non-energy industries. However, sharp falls in output also happen to some non-energy

[4]In the 2004 carbon baseline database, the emissions from the coal industry was 1.8 million tons, 7.7 million tons from the oil industry, 2.8 million tons from the natural gas industry, only 0.001 million tons of carbon dioxide equivalent was from finished petroleum products, which is less than 1 percent of the three energy-related products.

industries, as in the construction industry, and steel and mineral products, because of the influences from upstream and downstream industries. In the construction industry where 90% of energy product consumption is for investment, an overall drop in investment causes a fall in output in the industry. Steel and mineral products are the upstream of construction and manufacturing industries, and a declining output in downstream causes the upstream industry to contract.

# Part II
# Strategic Choices for China's Industrial Upgrading

# Chapter 5
# Evolving Comparative Advantage and Choosing a Pathway for China's Industrial Upgrading

**Qizi Zhang**

In a globalized world, transforming China's economic growth model in effect is to change the comparative advantage, so that the country can improve its position in the international division of labour to achieve industrial upgrade. Although the objective for China's industrial upgrade is now clear, which path to choose remains an issue for further study. There were many factors for China's economic slowdown in the first half of 2008, one of which was the fact that we have not resolved the stated problem.

## 5.1 A Model for the Way Forward to Industrial Upgrade

Three issues are to be addressed in deciding the way forward for a country's industrial upgrade. These are: the direction of the industrial upgrade, the extent of the industrial upgrade, and avoiding risks that disrupt industrial upgrade. The traditional theory on comparative advantage cannot provide convincing solutions to these issues, and is of limited relevance in practice. In recent years the theory on comparative advantage evolution compensates to a large degree the shortcomings of the traditional theory, and is useful for addressing these three issues.

1. **Model of comparative advantage evolution**

According to the standard theory on comparative advantage, to change a country's position in the international division of labour is to change the factor

Q. Zhang (✉)
Chinese Academy of Social Sciences, Beijing, China
e-mail: zhangqizi65@126.com

 
Q. Zhang (ed.), *Transforming Economic Growth and China's Industrial Upgrading*, Research Series on the Chinese Dream and China's Development Path,
https://doi.org/10.1007/978-981-13-0962-5_5

endowments of that country. For instance, in the international division of labour, if a country mainly produces labour intensive products and wants to become a country that produces capital intensive products, then it must change the factor endowments in the mix of its labour relative to the abundance of capital. This theory has produced an answer as to what a country should produce, but it has not given a workable suggestion as to how a country can make the formidable leap from a producer mainly of labour-intensive products to that of capital-intensive products. Ricardo Hausmann and Bailey Klinger have put forward the theory of comparative advantage evolution in recent years. This theory criticises the existing comparative advantage theory for its disregard of the effect from the initial division of labour on a country. Their research shows that changes to a country's product mix is connected with that country's product space. The initial mix in a country's product space has a significant impact on that country's product output and has implications for the country's development (Hidalgo et al. 2007). Following the convention in international economics, we call this theory the HK model.

The HK model is very simple. Assuming that the production of any product needs a specific series of factors, we found that factors for one product are not entirely suited for another, i.e. they are imperfect substitutes. Let us suppose that in moving from the current product to another product, the return is $\Delta P_{i,j}$

$$\Delta P_{i,j} = f\delta_{i,j}$$

Of which $\delta_{ij}$ represents the difference in technology between product i and product j. If i = j, $\delta_{ij}$ is 0; otherwise it is larger than 0. The cost of moving from product i to product j increases with the difference in technology, such as

$$C(\delta_{ij}) = \frac{c\delta_{ij}^2}{2}$$

The price of the product also increases as the difference in technology increases. The problem that needs resolving by the corporation is how to maximise profits in upgrading from product i to product j, i.e.:

$$\max_{\delta_{i,j}} \Pi = f\delta_{i,j} - \frac{c\delta_{i,j}^2}{2}$$

Therefore, for a corporation, the optimal difference for a rapid upgrade is:

$$\delta_{i,j}^* = f/c$$

If interaction between enterprises is not taken into account, then clearly, the capability for industrial upgrade is limited as enterprises are conditioned by their past (Hausmann and Klinger 2007). If government disregards historical conditions and imposes over-demanding industrial upgrade targets, the result is that enterprises will perish in making this formidable leap. According to this theory, the direction for industrial upgrade is moving from the present position towards an upgrade with the optimal difference.

## 2. **Extending the HK model**

The HK model is rather simple. It assumes a linear industrial upgrade with no consideration given to interactions between corporations. However, industrial upgrade may not be linear, and during the process there is interaction between corporations. If an enterprise's current industry has identical technology distance with more than one industries, how should the enterprise choose? Let dots represent industries, and lines represent the technology difference between the industries. Then the industrial upgrade for the enterprise can be shown as in Fig. 5.1. Figure 5.1a shows the research as carried out for the HK model. The situation in Fig. 5.1b is different: the enterprise faces many choices.

In order to forecast the behaviour of the enterprise with so many choices, we need expand the HK model as required. From Fig. 5.1b, it can be seen that after choosing industries B and C, the subsequent industrial upgrade will be completely different. In the figure, the industrial upgrade for B or C can be measured by the degree of vertex B or C. A degree is a concept in graph theory, measured by the number of edges that connect to the vertex. A large degree indicates a high possibility in the industrial upgrade. For convenience, we will call the possible upgrade of the industry as the industry degree. After introducing this factor, when implementing the industrial upgrade, we should consider not only the difference in technology between the industries, but also the opportunity for subsequent upgrades. The industry degree is represented by d. Its influence in the upgrade decision is on the cost of upgrade. When an enterprise upgrades to a new industry, the more sequent opportunities the new industry provides, the less possible that the enterprise gets "trapped" This is analogous to an enterprise having invested in fixed assets, and if the assets are versatile enough, the risk of being locked in is also quite small.

**Fig. 5.1** .

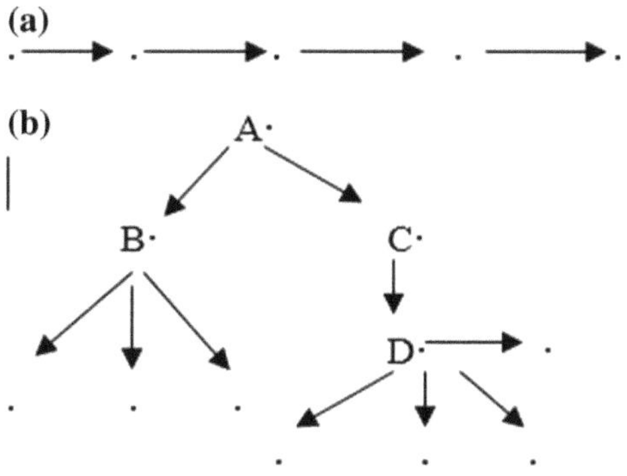

Let us suppose that in moving from the current industry to another industry, the return is still $\Delta P_{i,j}$

$$\Delta P_{i,j} = f\delta_{i,j}$$

After introducing the industry degree, the cost for industrial upgrade becomes:

$$C(\delta_{ij}) = c\delta_{ij}^2/2d$$

The optimal difference for the enterprise to implement industrial upgrade is:

$$\delta_{ij} = df/c$$

## 3. The implications of introducing the industry degree

Introducing the industry degree into the HK model helps us understand the leapfrogs in industrial upgrade and the "wave phenomenon" in the industrial investment of developing countries.

The HK model does not accommodate upgrade leapfrogs but the expanded HK model does. According to the HK model, it is impossible for an enterprise to jump from A directly to D, but in an expanded HK model, it is entirely possible. So long as the industry degree of D is very large, the enterprise will have the momentum to jump from A to D.

The HK model cannot explain the "wave phenomenon" in the industry investment of developing countries, whereas the expanded HK model can provide an answer from a new perspective. According to Professor Lin Yifu, wave phenomenon in the industry investment exists in developing countries, instead of developed countries. In developed countries, the way industries innovate and their direction can be determined. As all the industries are already at the forefront of global industry value chain, each enterprise has a different outlook in most cases on which is the next promising industry. There is no consensus in society, and even governments do not possess more accurate information than the enterprises. In contrast, in countries undergoing rapid development, in order to achieve industrial upgrade, enterprises need to invest in industries with mature technology, existing product markets and position in the global industry value chain. It is easy to reach a consensus on which is the new and promising industry in this developing country, and then investments by enterprises will roll towards the same certain industry, like waves upon waves. At each wave, enterprises will expect high return on investment, and financial organisations, swayed by the herd behaviour, will also be willing to back these investments. But the large total investment of all enterprises inevitably led to these consequences: heavy losses, overcapacity, and a sharp rise in bank loans on bad debts. Even though there is already overcapacity in existing industries, the rush to invest in the new sector may continue (Yifu 2007).

The "wave phenomenon" describes a state of large scale investment rushing towards a certain sector. In fact, it describes how an industry emerges, dies and is replaced. However, the rise and fall of industries is not confined to developing countries—it also applies to developed countries. Enterprises in developed countries can also be divided into the pacesetter and the follower. The pacesetter develops new products and achieves efficiency, and afterwards the followers easily reach a consensus on the prospect of the new industry, with many enterprises investing in droves in this industry. Then why is the "wave phenomenon" in developed countries much weaker than in developing countries? The answer can be found in the difference in the industry degree between the developing and developed countries. The industry degree at point C in Fig. 5.1b is 1. Assuming that there are N enterprises in industry C, then there are N enterprises making industrial upgrade towards D. The industry degree at A in the figure is 2. If there are N enterprises in industry A, then for these enterprises, whether they upgrade toward industry B or C makes not much difference, so the number of enterprises that upgrade to B or C should be N/2. The industry degree for B and D are 3 and 4 respectively. Likewise, the number of enterprises from B and D that upgrade to any industry should be N/3 or N/4. Therefore, as the industry degree gets bigger, the rolling wave effect of the industrial upgrade becomes weaker. The reason that the rolling waves effect in developed countries is much weaker than in developing countries lies in the fact that the industry degree is higher in developed countries; there are more varied ways for enterprises in the same industry to upgrade.

## 5.2 Bifurcation in the Evolution of Comparative Advantage and Direction for Industrial Upgrade

As mutations happen during the evolution of species, bifurcation happens during the evolution of comparative advantage. Then, industrial upgrade is not necessarily linear—it can also bifurcate, with cross-overs happening for upgrades both intra– and inter-industry. Therefore, as a country upgrades it industries, it needs to manage both linear and non-linear upgrades, as well as both intra–and inter-industry upgrades. Since the reform and opening-up, a vital characteristic in the process of China's industrial upgrade is the emergence of bifurcation. And it is because of this that China has maintained a rather high rate of economic growth and exports, and from which we have the Chinese exports conundrum.

1. **The path for comparative advantage evolution and the types of industrial upgrade**

When discussing the new international division of labour, different scholars hold different perspectives and have different concepts (Frobel et al. 1978; Sturgeon 1997; Gereffi 1999; Boy 2002; Deacon 2007; Su 2007). However, the one thing in

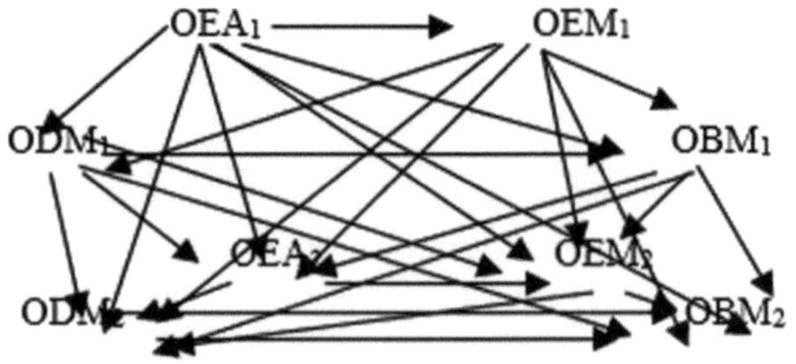


**Fig. 5.2** A complex network of an evolving comparative advantage

common is the emphasis on the role of intra-industry division of labour in the new international division of labour. An essential feature of the new international division of labour is a global network of the intra-industry division of labour. And it is because of this intra-industry global network that makes such a division of labour so important. With the emergence of an intra-industry division of labour, the path of comparative advantage evolution becomes even more complicated. Figure 5.2 lists the possible paths that comparative advantage can evolve in two industries—combining the possibilities for both intra–and inter-industry. It is not difficult to see that bringing in intra-industry division of labour turns the comparative advantage evolution into a complicated network.

In Fig. 5.2, $OEA_1$, $OEM_1$, $ODM_1$, $OBM_1$ and $OEA_2$, $OEM_2$, $ODM_2$, $OBM_2$ represent the production links, such as assembly line and processing, consigned processing, independent design and processing, and own brand production in industry 1 and industry 2 respectively. From $OEA_1$ to $OEM_1$, $ODM_1$, and $OBM_1$, shown as intra-industry division of labour, from $OEA_1$ to $OEA_2$, shown as inter-industry upgrade, where the bifurcation happens during industrial upgrade.

Based on whether bifurcation occurs, comparative advantage evolution can be divided into types: linear and non-linear. Accordingly, industrial upgrade can be called linear and non-linear upgrades.

Linear upgrade includes intra-industry or inter-industry upgrade. From the global value chain point of view, Humphrey and Schmitz put forward four types of upgrade: process upgrading, product upgrading, functional upgrading, and inter-sector upgrading (Humphrey and Schmitz 2000). Of these, the first three types are intra-industry upgrades. Ernst divide industrial upgrade into five types—inter-industry upgrade: moving along the industrial hierarchy from low added-value (such as light industry) towards a higher tier (such as heavy industry and high-tech industry); factor upgrade: moving along the factors hierarchy from endowed assets or natural capital (natural resources or unskilled labour force) towards created assets, i.e. physical capital, human capital and social capital; demand upgrade: moving along the consumption hierarchy from the essential products towards convenience products, and then to luxury products; functional upgrade: moving in the value chain hierarchy from sales and distribution to final assembly, testing, components manufacturing, product development and systems integration; linkage upgrade: in the forward and backward linkages moving from tangible products to intangible, knowledge-intensive support services (Ernst 2001). Of Ernst's five types of industrial upgrade, the latter four are intra-industry upgrades.

The upgrades proposed by Humphrey and Smitz, as well as Ernst are all linear upgrades. However, industrial upgrade may be non-linear. During the upgrade, the industry may bifurcate, i.e. intra-industry and inter-industry upgrade happens alternatively. Non-linear industrial upgrade can also be divided into upgrade prioritised for intra-industry bifurcation and prioritised for inter-industry bifurcation. Upgrade prioritised for intra-industry bifurcation is to first implement intra-industry upgrade and then jump to another industry when intra-industry upgrade reached a high standard. When a country's industrial upgrade has reached a high level, it can jump to a higher position on the inter-industry upgrade. Upgrade prioritised for inter-industry bifurcation is to first achieve inter-industry upgrade, followed by intra-industry upgrade. Generally speaking, when a country upgrades to a new and higher industrial level, this can in turn facilitate intra-industry upgrade for industries at a relatively lower level. Whether a country facilitates inter-industry upgrade via intra-industry upgrade or vice versa is not determined by how smart we are, but by comparing the technology difference. If the technology difference for inter-industry upgrade is smaller than that for intra-industry, then we should prioritise the strategy for inter-industry upgrade. From China's reality, prioritising inter-industry upgrade is more conducive to maintaining high growth for the economy and exports.

2. **Bifurcation of industrial upgrade paths and Chinese exports conundrum**

To analyse the technology content of exports, Hammel et al. developed an export sophistication index, which converts the technology content of exports into per capita income. Using the PRODY methodology, Professor Freound at Harvard University, USA, estimate China's export sophistication and found that during 2000–2004 the average income on Chinese exports was approximately USD8308, whereas the actual per capita income in China in 2006 was only USD2010. A study by Peter K. Schott found also that the similarity between Chinese products and those from OECD countries is much higher than other countries with the same endowments. Other estimates show that the sophistication index of China's exports in 1995 was equivalent to USD10,478 per capita income, and in 2005 this reached USD15,867 (Yuzhen 2007). A study by Rodrik also found that the average income level on Chinese exports is three times higher than other developing countries with the same income level (2006). Rudai and Yang conducted a study on Chinese exports from the perspective of limited catch-up. They found that to an extent Chinese exports have advanced features (2007). This phenomenon is the so-called conundrum of Chinese exports.

Why has this conundrum of Chinese exports emerged? An explanation attributes this to China's implementation of the catch-up strategy, and to the intervention by the Chinese government which distorted comparative advantage. However, this explanation is not very convincing. Since China adopted reform and opening-up policy, the role of the market economy becomes greater, then why has not the

Chinese exports conundrum disappeared? From the perspective of comparative advantage evolution, the conundrum can be attributed to a bifurcated process of industrial upgrade. Unlike the former one, this explanation holds that the Chinese exports conundrum is manifested as a better way to use comparative advantage rather than a distortion of it.

As evidence for a bifurcated process in China's industrial upgrade, the growth in Chinese exports is dependent to an extent on continuously introducing new export industries. During 1980–2006, the overall Chinese trade competitiveness index gradually rose from the negative figure in the 1980s to a positive figure by later the 1990s. Looking at it by industry, the trade competitiveness index of primary products declined continuously, but that of manufactured goods rose steadily. Looking at the structure in primary products, the more competitive sectors are food and live animals mainly for consumption; the beverage and tobacco sectors had a degree of international competitiveness, but in recent years have declined sharply. There has been a continuous decline in the competitiveness of primary products for non-food raw materials, mineral fuels, lubricants and related materials, animal and plant oils and wax. Looking at the structure in manufacturing products, the international competitiveness for miscellaneous manufactured goods remain high, chemical and related products remain low, whereas the weakness of textile, rubber products, mining products, machinery and transport equipment is gradually rising to a level that can compete internationally (see Figs. 5.3 and 5.4). Of course these structural changes in industrial competitiveness can be regarded as achievements in China's industrial upgrade. However, it is clear that China's industrial upgrade has been achieved via bifurcation, that is, continuous introducing new industries has helped maintain comparative advantage.

Another evidence for bifurcation in China's industrial upgrade is that while China has maintained a fast growth in exports, for the same product there has been

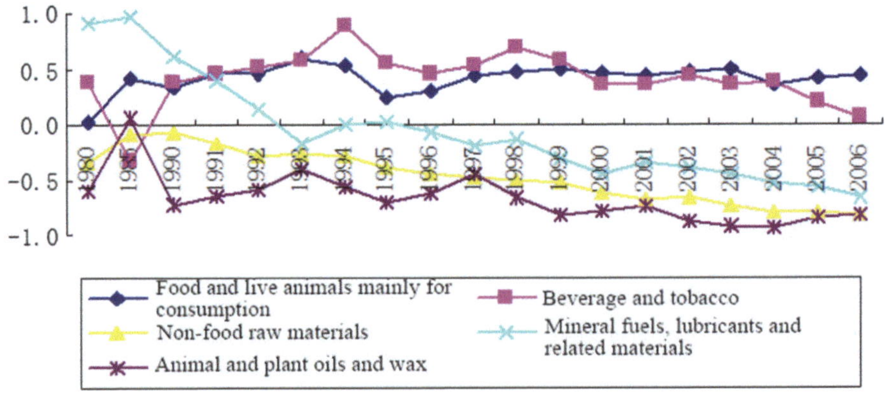


**Fig. 5.3** Changing trends in the trade competitiveness index of China's primary products by industry *Data source* Zhang Qizi, Guo Chaoxian: A research report on the quality and efficiency in China's economic growth, unpublished, 2008. Same as in Fig. 5.5

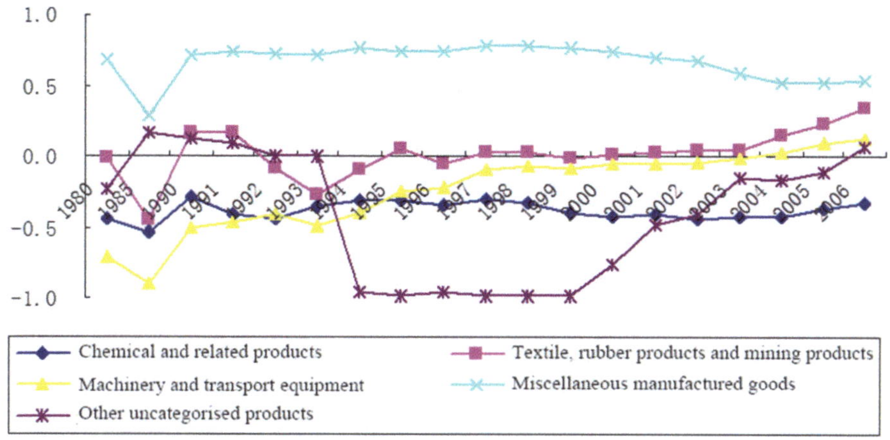


**Fig. 5.4** Changing trends in the trade competitiveness index of China's manufacturing products by industry

limited progress in product quality. Professor Rodrik's study has been criticised by Xu Bin. Xu (2007) believes that Rodrik did not give consideration to factors such as the low quality of Chinese products; And that although Schott analysed the difference in quality between Chinese products and those of other countries, in calculating China's export sophistication index this factor has been omitted. After considering the difference in product quality, he reappraised China's export sophistication for 1990–2001, and found that during the first half of the 1990s the technology content of China's exports exceeded its growth, whereas technology content and growth tallied up during the second half of the 1990s. As this criticism uses the framework of intra-industry upgrade, it does not entirely refute the Chinese export conundrum, because the Chinese export conundrum is not only concerned with intra-industry upgrade but also inter-industry. When calculating a product's technology content, if the quality factor is taken into account, then conversion must be carried out on the quality of different products. If not, this kind of criticism only serves to confirm the limitation in China's intra-industry upgrade.

3. **Should priority be given to inter–or intra-industry upgrade?**

Since the reform and opening-up, China has bolstered export and economic growth via bifurcated industrial upgrade. Is the strategy that has taken us so far no longer effective? With the emergence of intra-industry division of labour and the growing popularity of the concept on industry value chain, intra-industry upgrade received more attention. A framework of linear upgrade—from process upgrade to product upgrade to functional upgrade and then inter-sector upgrade—has begun to steer a course in practice for China's industrial upgrade. It is understandable if this is just a strategy for enterprises, but as a national or regional strategy for the present stage, it is very questionable. From OEA, OEM to ODM, then to OBM, and then over to inter-industry upgrade can be non-linear. It is entirely possible for intra-industry upgrade to bifurcate after a certain stage, switching to inter-industry before totally completed. Inter-industry upgrade can in turn spur on intra-industry upgrade. This strategy of bifurcation with preference for inter-industry upgrade has long been an important force for bolstering fast economic and export growth for China. For the foreseeable future China still need to adopt the strategy of bifurcation prioritising inter-industry upgrade. This is not a subjective decision, but an objective requirement that at the current stage implementing inter-industry upgrade brings greater return for China than intra-industry upgrade. This can be further illustrated from the two perspectives of technology difference and industry degree.

Enterprises engaged in OEA, OEM, ODM and OBM activities can be regarded as providing the market with different products. There is much research to show that to achieve intra-industry upgrade from OEA to ODM, especially OBM upgrade is not much easier than achieving inter-industry upgrade. For example, it is much harder for the automotive industry to achieve intra-industry upgrade from OEA to ODM, and especially OBM upgrade than to achieve an upgrade from the automotive industry of OEA to the electronics industry OEA. Gereffi's research shows the East Asian garments industry starting from assembling imported inputs, to growing domestic output, to product design for other enterprises and their brands, and finally to selling their own product brands domestically or in overseas markets. Gereffi (1999) is optimistic that the upgrade prospect is good for manufacturers of developing countries and newly emerging industrialised countries operating in quasi-hierarchical global value chains. This is then followed by operating in design, sales and establishing their own brands. Martin Bell of Sussex University believes that what Gereffi describes is a benign escalator. From own design and processing to own brand design and manufacturing is not a matter taken for granted. Hobday carried out a comprehensive analysis of the switch from OEM to ODM and then to OBM, and found that there is more evidence on the switch from OEM to ODM than there is for ODM to OBM. A study of the global footwear industry value chain shows that manufacturers from China, India and Brazil face barriers in developing their design and sales capability (Knorringa 2000; Xiaoyan 2007).

Why are there different levels of impediment for functional upgrade in the global value chain? The reason is generally believed to be buyer power and capacity constraints (Humphrey and Schmitz 2002; Xiaoyan 2007). With further analysis on the barriers to functional upgrade in developing countries, we can list many factors. But no matter how many factors there are, all the studies on the failures of functional upgrade shows that it is more difficult for developing countries and regions to achieve functional upgrade; the upgrade difficulty for intra-industry is no less than that for inter-industry.

The level of difficulty for developing countries has impeded functional upgrade, but this is not the only reason for failure. Failure in functional upgrade in some developing countries and regions can be explained by their choice of the path prioritising inter-industry upgrade. Not only is inter-industry upgrade as a strategic priority more likely to succeed, it can also increase the industry degree. The process for inter-industry upgrade is also that for increasing the industry degree. Intra-industry upgrade is linear, with the industry degree at 1. Introducing a new industry brings more choices for the enterprise, and is conducive for intra-industry upgrade which brings more new growth potential. Ricardo Hausmann is in favour of prioritising inter-industry upgrade. His reason is that the nearer a product is from the forefront of quality, the slower its growth potential, and the farther it is from the forefront, the larger the growth potential. When new products are introduced into a country, the entry position is usually low, i.e. they enter where it is far from the forefront of quality, and its growth potential is much greater than the quality upgrade for existing products (Kugler et al. 2007).

Although inter-industry upgrade as a strategic priority can bring lots of benefits, this kind of strategy also has constraints—inadequate information. Kugler, Stein and Wagner are opposed to inter-industry upgrade as a strategic priority. They believe that industrial upgrade through the introduction of new products is more difficult than intra-industry upgrade. To introduce new products for industrial upgrade, the government or enterprises must know in advance what the product should be, but there is no such information before the new product is produced. There is a clear path for intra-industry upgrade—there is not the problem of not knowing where to upgrade due to a lack of information. Not only is intra-industry upgrade beneficial for inter-industry upgrade, it can also provide information for it (Kugler et al. 2007). For developed countries, the problem of insufficient information for inter-industry upgrade as identified by Kugler et al. is certainly there, but for developing countries this problem is not a serious barrier because developing countries can just adopt the 'follower' strategy, and achieve inter-industry upgrade by following the path taken by developed countries.

## 5.3 Risk of an Industrial Upgrade Stalling and How to Defuse It

In the framework of the traditional comparative advantage theory, industrial upgrade is continuous, and without the risk for sudden changes or stalling. However, this kind of risk exists in the model of comparative advantage evolution. In other words, during an industrial upgrade, the enterprise cannot know the optimal difference and this is when comparative advantage appears to stall, requiring a sudden change. This phenomenon has already occurred in some countries and has triggered recessions. China is at a critical juncture for industrial upgrade, and the threat from such risks are also growing. How to avoid the risk of stalling comparative advantage is a vital problem that must be resolved for China's industrial upgrade in the future.

1. **China faces the risk of stalling comparative advantage**

China is already ranked amongst middle-income countries. The task from now on is to forge ahead onto the ranks of the mid-to high-income countries, and be eventually ranked amongst high-income countries. However, having reached the ranks of the middle-income countries, and before China is ranked amongst the mid-to high-income countries, and to finally accomplish her historical mission of becoming a high-income country, there needs to be a 'mutation' of our comparative advantage. When the comparative advantage of a country is going through a sudden change, it often faces a higher risk of it stalling. Before some of the Latin American countries became middle-income countries, they had strong economic growth, but once they were amongst middle-income countries, growth stalled and the recession came. This is what we call Latin-American disease, and there is already a large volume of research on this. However, analysing this from the perspective of comparative advantage evolution, the fundamental reason is that comparative advantage has stalled. Some industries lost their comparative advantages due to the impact of other developing countries, and new industries have yet to develop their comparative advantages, and thus comparative advantage stalls.

As China's economic growth increases, wage and environmental costs will definitely rise bringing about severe challenges in labour intensive industries from low-income countries. To press on towards the high-income country target, China must make innovation on comparative advantage and its mutation, and develop technology–and capital-intensive industries. However, in the process of developing technology and capital intensive industries, China must challenge developed countries. If we cannot overcome the challenges from developed countries, the comparative advantage for China's development will stall, leading to a recession.

Some of the effects of China's stalling comparative advantage have already emerged. Since 2008, China's economic growth has slowed down. This slowdown is caused by many factors, with short-term and long-term factors intertwining, China's macroeconomic control since 2008 and stalling comparative advantage in parts of China. Up to May 2008, the six provinces and municipalities of Guangdong, Jiangsu, Shanghai, Shandong, Beijing and Zhejiang, where the revenue of enterprises above designated size exceeds RMB 100 billion, accounts for 73.6% of national income, whereas during January to May, the added value of industries over the designated size in the four regions in the West, North East, Central, and the East increased by 19.25, 18.77, 20.84 and 15.71% respectively. With regards the industrial growth rate of the East China, in the first half of the year, apart from Shandong with 18.5% growth and Tianjin with 21% growth, all other provincial cities had growth rates lower than the national industrial rate of growth. Clearly, under the current policy, China's eastern region is already under the pressure of stalling comparative advantage.

The meaning of stalling comparative advantage can be further explained in Fig. 5.5. In the figure, $\Delta C_{ij}$, $\Delta P_{ij}$, $\Pi_{ij}$, and $\delta_{ij}$ represent industry i's upgrade cost to industry j, price increase, and increased profits and the extent of industrial upgrade. If the enterprise cannot make further profits in industry i and is only capable of

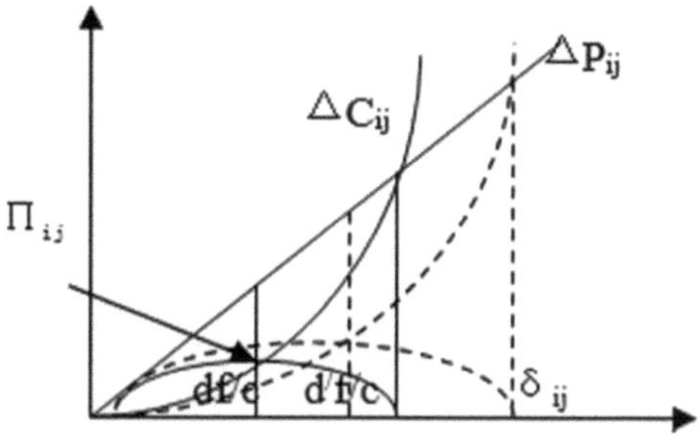


**Fig. 5.5** Stalling industrial upgrade

advancing to df/c, but policy and technology require that it advances to d′f/c, then we have stalling comparative advantage. Industrial growth in China's eastern region declines. The reason is that central government policies require the various enterprises to upgrade to d′f/c, but at the moment most of the enterprises are only capable of upgrading to df/c. While traditional industries are being suppressed, there is also a lack of new industries to take over. Some regions adopt the 'clear the cage and bring in new birds' strategy in order to solve the problem of environmental resources. There is nothing wrong with this kind of strategy, but in practice, the cage has been cleared, but new birds did not come. There are many reasons for this problem, such as an appreciation of the renminbi, signs of a recession in the USA, etc., but to a large extent, it has to do with the pace of China's industrial upgrade being too fast, and too impatient in getting there. This fast pace in industrial upgrade and the impatience add to the risk of the economy sliding back.

2. **Defusing risks—a strategy to prolong the life cycle of comparative advantage**

How to defuse the risk of stalling comparative advantage that has already emerged in some eastern regions, and prevent this partial stalling from turning into a full-scale stalling is the most arduous task facing China in the next phase. In short term, we can use spatial restructuring and a reasonable policy mix to prolong the life cycle of comparative advantage and reduce the extent of comparative advantage mutation.

**Firstly, a moderate push for reverse-outsourcing, promoting global distribution of industries.** The economic success of some Asian countries has prompted a large volume of theoretical research and outcome, producing all kinds of explanations. Of these theoretical models, the flying geese model is one of the more representative. Initially the flying geese model focuses on the rise and fall of a country's industry. Afterwards it extends to the changes in the industrial structure of specific countries and transnational transfer of industries. According to this theory, changes in a country's industrial structure will intensify, with capital–or technology-intensive being more pronounced in newly emerging industries compared to industries they replace. For example, the transition of Japan's core industries followed a sequence of textile, chemical industry, steel, automotive, and electronics.[1] This kind of change in Japan's domestic industrial structure went hand in hand with the flying geese transfer model in Asian industries. In other words, within Asia, the centre of textile industry has transferred following this sequence, namely from Japan to the four 'Asian tigers', to the ASEAN and then to China. With the emergence of intra-industry division of labour, this transition also manifests in the low-end process as going from Japan to the four Asian tiger economies, ASEAN, and China. Uneven development in the Asian region provided impetus for this kind of transition to take place, and it is this kind of transition that has created the Asian miracle. China should learn from this experience during industrial upgrade to transfer some of the processes that are gradually losing competitive advantage to other countries by reverse-outsourcing, thus taking full advantage of the resources and cost from other countries to facilitate industrial upgrade.

Product design and production modularisation can provide the technological basis, from which China can implement global distribution of industries. Product design and production modularisation brings a series of advantages including: reducing dependence on tacit knowledge and taking full advantage of distributed knowledge; reducing knowledge complexity and cost of learning; reducing risks in technological innovation; increasing options for innovation; increasing product diversification, etc. Taking advantage of modularisation will help maintain China's competitive advantage, but these are not the only implications. Product design and production modularisation can bolster technology and provide substantive power in driving China's strategy for economic globalisation.

The technology in modularisation makes vertical disintegration in industries possible and it also effectively reduces transaction cost following vertical disintegration. When asked why such a problem occurs for enterprises, the answer from Kos et al. is that there are transaction costs in the market and if these are reduced it will help market expansion. Modularisation of products and production processes makes it possible to break down the technology, but this does not necessarily lead to global distribution of the industry. When technology works, establishing global distribution of industry also relies on cost reduction in transport, communications and opportunistic transaction charges (Qizi et al. 2007).

Baldwin differentiates two types of transaction charges, one type is due to opportunism and moral hazard, the other is mundane transaction cost. Williamson's theoretical work gives much attention to transaction charges due to opportunism and moral hazard, whereas by comparison, mundane transaction cost is neglected. Baldwin's definition for mundane transaction cost includes charges for defining, quantifying, valuing and compensating. For integrated products, because there is a strong correlation of the 'factors' that make up the product, which also leads to a strong correlation between design and other production tasks, it is very difficult to

[1]Ozawa dubs textile and garment as the Hecksher-Olin model of labour-driven industry, steel as the resource–and scale–driven undifferentiated Smithian industries, automotive as the differentiated Smithian industry, electronics as Schumpeter's innovation industry, and in addition Ozawa also dubs information processing and transmission as McLuhan's network-driven industry.

break down the responsibilities and duties between the parties involved. This makes it easy for opportunism. Enterprise is one way of overcoming opportunism; shortening the distance with your trading partner is another. In other words, an enterprise's production should be configured as far as possible within specific geographical range. This helps reduce costs on both sides and increase interactions which can complement what is lacking in a contract. Modularisation reduces the correlation of the tasks between product design and production, making it easier to break down responsibilities and duties for both trading partners, which leads to reduced mundane transaction costs. This helps to curb opportunism costs, giving impetus not only to vertical disintegration, but also to distributed production (2007).

**Secondly, Geographical reconfiguration of domestic industries, a strategy of upgrade by steps.** To maintain sustained competitiveness and enduring economic growth and vitality, a country has to be bolstered by technological advancement. The capacity for technological innovation differs between enterprises, regions and industries. China's large enterprises and enterprises in the eastern areas have relatively greater technological capabilities. Therefore, China should first upgrade large enterprises and those enterprises that are technologically advanced in the eastern areas, thus laying the foundation for the next round of industrial upgrade. The government should encourage central and western regions to take on industries in their transition from the eastern region, and small and medium sized enterprises to take on industries in their transition from large enterprises. Through this kind of geographical reconfiguration and restructuring of industrial organisations, China, as a whole, can prevent comparative advantage from stalling and buy time for further industrial upgrade, accumulate resources, and avoid a full-scale 'industrial hollowing-out'.

**Thirdly, well-reasoned choice of policy mix and timing.** To encourage optimal industrial structuring and upgrading, China has adopted a series of measures which are necessary from a long term perspective. However, if most of these measures are implemented in the same and short period, they will create pressure for China's economic growth in the short term. To avoid new policies having too great an impact on enterprises, a well-reasoned choice on timing and policy mix has to be made. Pressure from policies on the operation of enterprises should be distributed over different periods of time to enable enterprises sufficient time to modify their production operations in order to comply with the new policy. In terms of policy mix, a carrot-and-stick approach should be taken to restrict development in some industries while offering supportive measures for those industries representing future development, thus offsetting the negative impact that the various restrictive measures have on economic growth.

3. **A strategy of open innovation to defuse risks**

To defuse the long term risk of stalling comparative advantage, China's industrial upgrade must fully utilise existing strengths while also embrace open innovation. Developed countries have already developed a range of cutting-edge technologies and China aims to catch up with these developed countries. Therefore, the open innovation in China is also a kind of post-open innovation.

The strategy of post-innovation is put forward by Enrst following a study on the experience in Asian countries of development in the electronics industry. For him, development in the electronics sector in Asian countries has gone beyond the general theory on innovation. As latecomers, Asian countries have adopted a post-innovation strategy in the international competition in the electronics sector. They have joined the ranks of international competition in innovation and have succeeded in post-innovation. As exports become industrialised, returns diminish; external impact, concerns that the economic power of the electronics sector is too concentrated in the USA, and the rise of China causing a decline in the traditional competitive advantage of other countries—all these contribute to the post-innovation strategy of the Asian electronics sector (Ernst 2004).

Henry Chesbrough from an affiliated school at Berkeley University, California, put forward the concept of open innovation. With 'open innovation' he calls for firms to pay attention to creativity and practice from outside of their own R&D so their firms can adopt and benefit from these. He calls for firms to be even more 'open' to external creativity (Committee for Economic Development Digital Connectivity Board 2006). Fundamentally different from closed innovation, open innovation states that the world's most talented people cannot be recruited into one firm, and that creativity emerges from networks. This idea is equally applicable to a country. No country can attract all the talented people. To be at the forefront of international creativity, a country must turn to resources in science and technology, build a global innovation network, and adopt an open innovation strategy. This is particularly important for developing countries.

From a functional point of view, systems of innovation can be divided into regional, sectoral, national, and global systems of innovation. Of these systems of innovation, China places greater importance to those at national, regional and sectoral levels, with particular emphasis for the regional system of innovation. By comparison, there is too little emphasis given to the global system of innovation. Proposals were made at the 17th Party Congress that in building a country for innovation, they must turn to resources in science and technology. This is an important signal that China will embrace a global system of innovation. Adopting post-innovation is building a global system of innovation.

Industrial modularisation offers the potential for China to build a global system of innovation and to adopt a post-innovation strategy. Processing and assembly becomes easier with modularisation, and with modularisation MNCs can also transfer out their processing and assembly, which serves to promote knowledge outsourcing. Sharing of knowledge is necessary for modularisation in order to make use of distributed knowledge; modularisation helps to prevent knowledge drain and protect intellectual property rights. As such more and more MNCs adopt open innovation, carry out knowledge outsourcing, or with the help of other firms exploit the knowledge they hold which is otherwise difficult to tap into. With modularisation, not only can MNCs transfer out their processing and assembly, they can further transfer other processes higher in the value chain, such as R&D,

procurement, marketing, services etc., placing more of the economic resources in the external environment. This provides new opportunities for China to turn to global resources in science and technology, and to play a part in the global knowledge and innovation network (Qizi et al. 2007).

## References

A report from the Committee for Economic Development Digital Connectivity Board: *Open standards, open source and open innovation*, 2006.

Baldwin, Carliss Y. 2007. *Modularity, transactions, and the boundaries of firms: A synthesis*. Working Paper for Harvard Business School, 08-013.

Dicken, Peter. 2007. *Global shift. Reshaping the global economic map of the 21st century*, Beijing: Commercial Press.

Ernst, Dieter. 2004. *Late innovation strategies in asian electronics industries—A conceptual framework and illustrative evidence*. Prepared for the Special issue of Oxford Development Studies in Honour of Linsu Kim.

Ernst, D. 2001. *Global production network and industrial upgrading-knowledge-centred approach*. East-Wester Centre Working Paper: Economic Series.

Frobel, F., J. Heinrichs, and O. Kreye. 1978. The new international division of labour. *Social Science Information* 17(1): 123–142.

Gereffi, G. 1999. International trade and industrial upgrading in the appareal commodity chains. *Journal of International Economics* 48(1): 37–70.

Gereffi, Gary. 1999. *A commodity chains framework for analysing global industries*. Duke University Working Paper.

Hausmann, Ricardo, and Bailey Klinger. 2007. *The structure of the product space and the evolution of comparative advantage*. CID Working Paper No. 146.

Hidalgo, C.A., B. Klinger, A.-L. Barabási, and R. Hausmann. 2007. The product conditions on the development of nations. *Science* 317(5837): 482–487.

Humphrey, J., and H. Schmitz. 2000. *Governance and upgrading: Linking industrial cluster and global value chains research*. IDS Working Paper No. 12, Institute of Development Studies, University of Sussex.

Humphrey, J., and H. Schmitz. 2002. How does insertion in global value chains affect upgrading in industrial cluster. *Regional Studies* 36(9): 1017–1027.

Kugler, Stein, and Wagner. 2007. *Product space, product quality and the emergence of new export sectors*. PPT for Economic Department Seminar of Wesleyan University Seminar.

Luthje, Boy. 2002. Electronics contract manufacturing: Global production and the international division of labour in the age of the internet. *Industry and Innovation* 9(3): 227–247.

Qizi, Zhang et al. 2007. *Modularisation and China's industrial upgrade strategy*. The Chinese Academy of Social Sciences Subject B Final Report on "A study on the modularisation of industrial structure".

Rodrik, Dani. 2006. *What's so special about china's exports?* NBER Working Paper 11947.

Rudai, Yang, and Yao Yang. 2007. *Limited catch-up and economic growth in China*. Peking University Centre for Economic Research Working Paper.

Schmitz, H., and P. Knorringa. 2000. Learning from global buyers. *Journal of Development Studies* 37(2): 177–205.

Sturgeon, T. 1997. *Turn-key production networks: A new American model of industrial organization?* Berkeley Roundtable on the International Economy, BRIEWP92A.

Su, Zhang. 2007. A critique on theory of a new international division of labour. *Teaching and Research* (1).

Xiaoyan, Zhou. 2007. *Modularisation and optimising industrial chain upgrade.* In *Modularisation and China's industrial upgrade strategy.* The Chinese Academy of Social Sciences Subject B Report. A study on the modularisation of industrial structure.

Xu, Bin. 2007. *Measuring the technology content of China's exports.* Working Paper, China's Europe International Business School.

Yifu, Lin. 2007. The rolling waves phenomenon and China's macroeconomic restructuring. *Economic Research* (1).

Yuzhen, Yin. 2007. *Competitiveness in the manufacturing sectors of China and Korea*—Complementarity and competition in the development of manufacturing between China and Korea. Seminar Paper (C), Beijing, 18 September 2007.

# Chapter 6
# Identify Opportunities for Industrial Upgrading

**Qizi Zhang and Hao Li**

When a country undergoes industrialisation or modernisation, it will manifest as structural change. For a government to have a role in structural change and for businesses to become a successful driver in economic growth—these are premised on the ability of the government and businesses to identify the direction for structural change as well as the industry with the best comparative advantage potential at different stages (Lin 2012, p. 204). However, to discover the latent comparative advantage of an industry is not an easy task. And for this purpose, there has been on-going efforts in Economics to come up with tools and methodologies,[1] but for a long time no detailed or operational instructions have been forthcoming. However, this situation has changed somewhat in recent years. There has been major research breakthrough in economics to identify industries with potential comparative advantage.

Whilst working at the World Bank. Lin Yifu and his colleagues put forward the Growth Identification and Facilitation Framework (GIFF). An important guideline from this framework for developing countries is to select industries from countries with roughly twice its own per capita income, similar resources endowment and similar industrial structure as the focus for catching up, and to incorporate successful private enterprises into the industry set with latent comparative advantage (Lin 2012, pp. 107, 203–238). The proponents of GIFF have undertaken case studies for this framework to demonstrate its application, but as the framework assesses the similarity in resource endowments between countries, the tricky question presented itself on how to assess resource endowments. Simply using the factors of capital or relative abundance in labour as the basis for assessment will

[1]These tools and methodologies include theories on comparative advantage, spearhead industries, import substitution, and imitation.

Q. Zhang (✉) · H. Li
Chinese Academy of Social Sciences, Beijing, China
e-mail: zhangqizi65@126.com



Q. Zhang (ed.), *Transforming Economic Growth and China's Industrial Upgrading*,
Research Series on the Chinese Dream and China's Development Path,
https://doi.org/10.1007/978-981-13-0962-5_6

lead to a point of contention which is "having similar resources and factor endowments, yet specialising in different products". This framework requires that a country keeps a check on the pacesetter, and because of the level of development, many developed countries are already at the top. As a result, even though the GIFF framework is good at resolving the difficult problem of assessing similar resource endowments, it cannot provide guidance for developing countries, and thus can only be a framework for guiding developing countries in their selection of industries.

Another theory that has emerged in recent years of discovering latent comparative advantage is that on product space put forward and developed by R. Hausmann, Bailey Klinger and C. A. Hidalgo at Harvard University (Hausmann and Klinger 2006; Hausmann et al. 2007). From the outset in 2006 when this theory emerged, numerous scholars and international organisations have applied it to studies on restructuring and industrial upgrade in specific countries or regions (Abdon and Felipe 2011; Bayudan-Dacuycuy 2012; Reinstaller et al. 2012). In 2008, China began to apply this theory in research to study how it guides China's industrial upgrade (Zhang 2008; Zeng and Zheng 2008). Since then a small number of papers and reports have reviewed this theory and attempted to apply it to explain China's industrial upgrade. However, the focus of most of the existing literature is on how to apply the theory of product space to measure economic complexity and furthermore to estimate its impact (Wu and Zhang 2011, 2012; Zhang et al. 2012; Wu et al. 2012). Although in China and abroad, a small number of literature has attempted to apply the theory of product space to uncover the potential for upgrade in China's industries, its application is limited due to data, such as using alternative algorithms for product proximity (Zeng and Zheng 2010); substituting the overall product space with partial product space (Wan and Qi 2012); lack of discussion on the proximity threshold that impacts on the selection of industries with latent comparative advantage; only one stage of industrial evolution was simulated (Zhang et al. 2013), etc. In an attempt to overcome the aforementioned constraints, this paper will identify the opportunities and potential for China's industrial upgrade based on the latest global trade data and the restructure of the global product space.

## 6.1 Global Product Space and Product Space Heterogeneity

According to the theory of product space the opportunity for a nation's industrial upgrade is defined by a capability function. To produce a new product or the transition to a new industry is determined by existing output capability. Thus, the key factor in finding a nation's latent comparative advantage is to take an analytical approach to identify its capabilities. To a large degree the success of the product space theory is determined its application to successfully solve this problem.

A long-standing theory used for guiding a nation's selection of industries and discovering its capabilities is the theory of comparative advantage. This theory requires a country to select its industries according to its comparative advantage. In the early versions of this theory, it had difficulties to convincingly explain how international trade can offset the phenomenon of the global division of labour as the economy was becoming more and more globalised. One of the responses of this theory to this defect is to take into account more and more factors. Expanding the theory in this way makes it possible to explain more of the issues in international trade, but also makes it less useful in practice as a guideline for countries to select industries. There are so many factors that determine what a country will or will not produce. As more and more factors matter in the decision, decision-makers face greater difficulties. Although theoretical research can uncover a series of determining factors, it cannot exhaust them all, and it is easy to become bogged down in endless debate on what is decisive in a country's comparative advantage.

The theory of product space differs from the traditional theory of comparative advantage in how it uncovers a nation's capability. The theory of comparative advantage discovers a country's comparative advantage and capability via input factors, whereas the theory of product space puts emphasis on output. The capability of different countries can be measured by their product space. The products currently produced by a country reflect that country's production capability,[2] therefore, from the perspective of the product space theory, a country's position in the product space structure determines its direction and path for industrial upgrade and performance in future economic growth. The opportunities for a country's industrial upgrade can be discovered in the product space structure. This kind of operational approach can effectively prevent the complex argument on what comparative advantage a country possesses arising from input analysis.

If a country's capability can be measured by its product space, then in order to identify a country's opportunities for industrial upgrade using the theory of product space, it is necessary to first construct the product space. Product space is formed by all products that can be produced and the relationship between them. Product relatedness means the similarity in the capability required for producing the different products. At the operational level, this similarity can be measured by product proximity. When products A and B are compared with products A and C, with the production of these products being carried out in many countries, then the relationship between products A and B, compared to the relationship between products A and C, can be defined as having greater proximity. The latent comparative advantage of an industry or a product must bear certain characteristics of proximity.

The purpose of constructing the product space is to find the complete set of products that can be produced. To identify a product's latent comparative advantage is to find a subset that satisfies specific conditions from this total set of products. Clearly, the more product categories there are in the complete product set, the more

[2]This practice of using output to reflect on a country's comparative advantage can be traced back to a time when B. Balassa first proposed revealed comparative advantage in 1963.

accurate will be the set of products with latent comparative advantage. Theoretically, the complete product set should include existing products, as well as future products. However, future products are not yet out, and so, in the process, what is called a complete product set only includes products that have been produced. Since the types of products produced around the world are changing all the time, this product set must also be continuously revised. In order to identify the latent comparative advantage in China's industries, with available data, we have constructed the global product space based on trade data during 2009–2011, including 3118 categories of tradeable products.

The capabilities theory put forward by Hausmann and Hidalgo, is called theory of the evolution of comparative advantage—its name also includes the word "comparative advantage"—but this theory differs from other theories of comparative advantage. Other theories are based on the basic assumption of the homogeneous nature of the product space, which means that there is an equal 'distance' between products. In the models of the various economic growth theories, there is a model called a product line extension, which specifically looks at the impact on economic growth by expanding product types. This kind of model assumes that the product space is homogeneous (Barro and Xavier 2000, pp. 198–216). However, we can imagine that if the product space is not heterogeneous, then there is no difference in the capability for producing different products. For a country it makes no difference whether to produce this or that product in the next stage, and thus it can choose randomly. In research, it is then impossible to differentiate the capability between countries based on product space. The successful application of the theory of product space is predicated on the heterogeneous nature of the product space.

The theory on product space as put forward by Hausmann et al. is based on their actual research on product space. They used the 1962–2000 international trade database built by Feenstra and Lipsey to construct a picture of global product space that included 775 categories of products. This image of the global product space, as they found, manifested a core-periphery model: the periphery of some products appears dense when compared with other products, and the periphery of some products appears sparse when compared with other products—there is no uniformity in the global product space. This conclusion raises two questions from the point of view for research. Firstly, is their conclusion only applicable to special periods? Secondly, if real production data is used, will the heterogeneity in product space disappear? To identify a country's output capability based on product space, the best method is to use production data, but detailed production data from various countries is not available. Instead, export data on products is used as the next best option. The question raised from this is that if the product space diagram is constructed from production data, will there still be heterogeneity in the product space?

To solve the first question, we used the same methodology as Hausmann et al. when they analysed the global product space diagram, but with different data to reconstruct the global product space diagram. Figure 6.1 used the UN Comtrade Database to map the global product space for the periods 1992–1994, 1999–2001, 2004–2006, and 2009–2011. To reduce unexpected fluctuations in the different periods, we constructed the diagrams by calculating the average proximity of

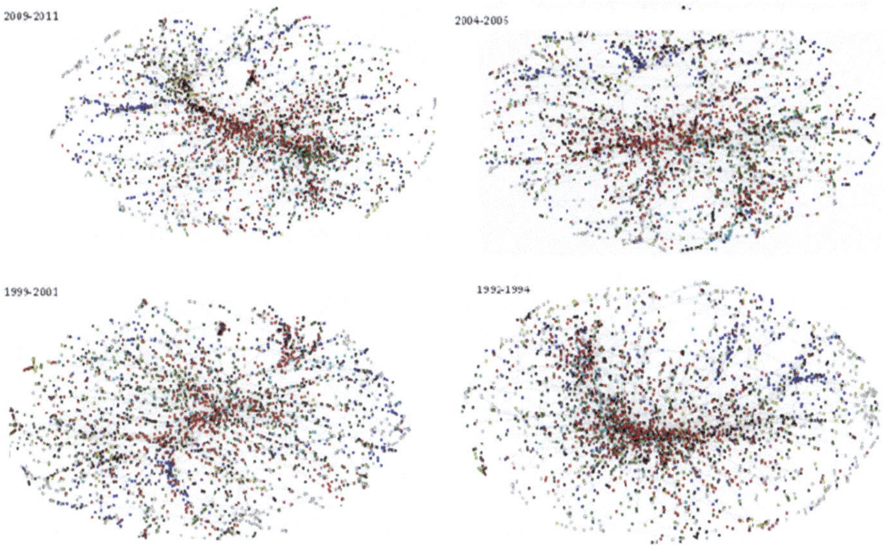


**Fig. 6.1** Comparing different periods of the global product space structure

products in these periods. The network of product space in Diagram 1 clearly shows the core-periphery characteristic. If specific industries are marked on the nodes in the diagram, then we find that the high-end manufacturing industries of electromechanical, chemical and instrumentation are positioned in the core, and primary products from agriculture, animal husbandry and fishery, as well as the minerals and mining industries are positioned in the periphery.[3] Comparing the product space diagrams of the different periods, we can easily see that although the connectedness in the product space is somewhat different for the different periods, the product space heterogeneity is there throughout.

To solve the second question, the most scientific method is to collect production data from around the world. Using this as the basis, the proximity between products is recalculated and the global product space diagram is constructed. However, this is not realistic at the moment. Our next best option, therefore, is to try and use China's production data to calculate the proximity of the various products and map out China's product space. Figure 6.2 is drawn with data from the 2006 China

[3]In the product space diagram, the connection (edge) between the nodes is constructed using the standard international trade classification (revision 3) (SITC rev 3) 5-digit product code as nodes and based on the adjacent product matrix elements, i.e. the degree of proximity of each pair of products. To reflect that all the products are effectively connected, we first mapped the maximum spanning tree that connects all the product nodes. From this, we took the edges with a proximity value greater than a certain threshold (0.55) and add them to the maximum spanning tree to finally form the product space diagram. Proximity values that are non-essential for forming the edges of the maximum spanning tree, of less than the specified threshold, are not taken into consideration for now.

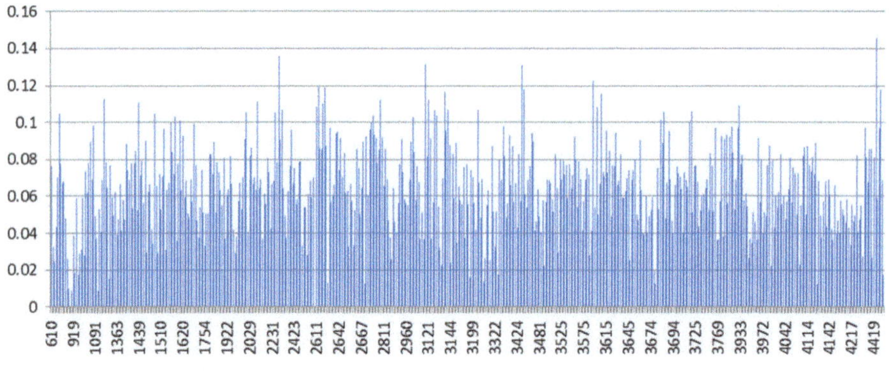

**Fig. 6.2** A comparison of the product proximity for different Chinese products (drawn from provincial production data). *Note* Horizontal axis shows the product category number

industrial enterprise database, and calculations are based on the average proximity for each product by province. The horizontal axis gives each of the product number, and the vertical axis is the product's average proximity, which equals the sum of the proximity of a product and all other products divided by the number of product categories. If the product space is homogeneous, then the height of the various columns will be consistent in Fig. 6.2, but instead these are of different heights. It shows that different products have different average proximity. The product with the highest proximity is nearly 20 times that of the product with the lowest proximity, and therefore, to correspond with this, the product space in the diagram must be heterogeneous. If a product space diagram is drawn according to product proximity, with the name of the product indicated on the node, and also indicated on the nodes in Fig. 6.1, we will find the relatedness of these two figures, with slightly different space for the same product but still exhibiting the heterogeneous core-periphery pattern. This example shows that using production data to reconstruct the product space will not alter the heterogeneous nature of the product space. This guarantees the feasibility of using product space to identify latent comparative advantage and products.

## 6.2 Selecting Industries with Latent Comparative Advantage

### 1. Three principles for selecting industries with latent comparative advantage

According to the theory of product space, among China's current products with comparative advantage, those have the greatest potential for comparative advantage should be the two products with the highest proximity in the product space, because the capability differential is the lowest between two such products, and the upgrade cost is the lowest going from one product to the other. Given the set prices of the two products, firms can reap the greatest profit (Zhang 2008). This is the overarching principle. However, getting down to determine product proximity and which products with the same proximity should be included in the set of products with latent comparative advantage requires examination based on the three principles as follows.

Firstly, currently there is no comparative advantage, i.e. the revealed comparative advantage index is smaller than 1. To categorise products according to their revealed comparative advantage—products either have or do not have revealed comparative advantage—an industry has to satisfy the potential for comparative advantage by its degree of proximity. However, if the industry already has revealed comparative advantage, it cannot be included in the industry set with latent comparative advantage.

Secondly, the technology content of the target industry is greater than that of the industry at its embryonic stage of industry evolution. Target industry is the industry we want to find with latent comparative advantage; embryonic industry is the industry with comparative advantage at the time and satisfies the proximity requirement of an industry with latent comparative advantage. The evolutionary trend in comparative advantage suggests that to have continuous development, a country's industry evolves from relatively low technology content to high technology content. Therefore, selecting a product set on the basis of proximity, with the latent ability to evolve, is more appropriate than removing existing low-tech products. Theoretically the evolution of an industry can also experience technological regress from high-tech content to low-tech content, but this change does not require new capability facilities and may result in idle capability. Thus, from a business perspective, such a decision is unlikely unless there is a major economic recession.

Thirdly, the proximity threshold. In selecting industries with latent comparative advantage, a business needs to set a critical distance for the jump, which is setting the proximity threshold. We can calculate the proximity for any two products, the difference being the degree of proximity. There may be high proximity, or low proximity, or significantly low proximity. If a proximity threshold is not set, then an industry with comparative advantage but which may not be in proximity to any industry at that time can still be included within the ranks of industries with latent comparative advantage. This action assumes that firms have limitless capacity so as to make a formidable jump that spans any distance. If we accept this assumption it makes the selection of industries with latent comparative advantage meaningless because it assumes that any industry is viable for business, the only constraint being that of demand. Clearly, this is unreasonable. Therefore, having satisfied the above two conditions, an industry will still need to satisfy the proximity test. Before identifying an industry with latent advantage, we need to determine the proximity threshold.

The proximity between products can also be defined by capability distance. If the capability distance is defined as 1 for a pair of goods requiring two completely different production capabilities specially in making them, then for two products that require certain similar production capabilities, the capability distance can be defined as the difference of 1 and the proximity value. Therefore, determining a proximity threshold can be interpreted as the capability distance to be traversed by a country and businesses for industrial upgrade, which can also be defined as the extent of industrial upgrade.

2. **Comparing industrial upgrade opportunities under different threshold values**

In order to use the three criteria to determine the industry set with latent comparative advantage, we use the 2000–2011 database for global trade in products to calculate the revealed comparative advantage of China's different products. Averages are then calculated and if the value is smaller than 1, it can be included in the latent comparative advantage short list. Since the industry set selected is undirected, it must therefore include some products with lower technology content than those at the embryonic stage. It is then necessary to further narrow down the categories of industries with latent comparative advantage according to the technology content indicated by the products.

To identify the technology level of a product, Hausmann et al. (2007) put forward the PRODY index. This paper also adopts this method for measuring the technology content of a product. In calculating PRODY the data for export products is taken from the UN Comtrade Database, the per capita GDP for the various countries is taken from the World Bank World Development Indicators, and calculations are based on the 2000 US dollar at constant prices. The 1999–2011 annual PRODY is the selection benchmark for an industry's potential advantage. Any product with a PRODY that is smaller than that at the embryonic stage is eliminated.

Following the revealed comparative advantage index and the level of technology content, industries with latent comparative advantage are selected and which should be further screened with proximity. The difficulty in using such criteria for selection is how to determine the critical distance. Studies so far all make an assumption based on a certain distance for the jump (Bayudan-Dacuycuy 2012, pp. 59–66), but is this a reasonable assumption? What criteria can we use to evaluate its appropriateness? We can use two criteria: the first is to see whether such a jump will have a significant impact on economic growth, and the second is to see whether such a jump is too far or not enough by comparing it with other countries around the world.

Setting the threshold will directly affect the forecast on China's industries with latent advantage. Figure 6.3a, b use different methods to display the changes in the type of industries with latent advantage in China under different threshold values. The horizontal axis in Fig. 6.3a represents different threshold values, and the vertical axis represents the categories of industries with latent advantage. Thus the curve in the figure represents the categories of products with latent advantage during the same evolutionary period. The horizontal axis in Fig. 6.3b represents the stages in an industry's evolution, the vertical axis represents the categories of industries with latent advantage. The curve in the figure represents the changes in the categories of industries with latent advantage at different evolutionary stages

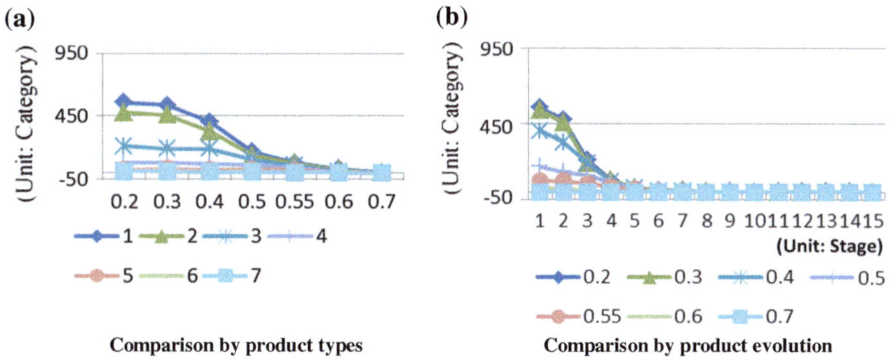


**Fig. 6.3** **a** Products with latent comparative advantage at various stages under different threshold values. **b** Latent advantage under different threshold values

with the same threshold value. From Fig. 6.3a, b, we discover a rather interesting characteristic in industry evolution: the changing trend suggests that 0.5 appears to be a tipping point. Once pass this point, the categories of industries with latent advantage decreases exponentially as the threshold value goes up.

In terms of quantities, if the extent of industrial upgrade is set at 0.2, then there are over 1400 categories of industries with latent advantage; setting the threshold at 0.55 yields 270 types of industries with latent advantage. If it is set at 0.5, the yield will increase to 522 types, but beyond 0.6 products with latent comparative advantage will basically disappear in China, and if it exceeds 0.7, then there will be no industries with latent comparative advantage in China. Assuming a linear relationship between economic growth and product types means that to maintain the same level of growth, for businesses to cross over this threshold of 0.5 to arrive at an industry with latent advantage, the average extra output by each industry is equivalent to a threshold at 0.2, an increase by 1.6 times; setting the threshold at 0.55 will increase it by 4.2 times. Proximity is a measurement of similarity between products. Evidently, as proximity increases industries are required to raise average output. Given the same extent of upgrade, the more diversified the products, the better will be the economy in maintaining a faster pace of growth. If industrial upgrade requires higher proximity, there is less product diversification, which then weakens the case for increased product types as a basis to bolster economic growth. Setting the extent for industrial upgrade to 0.5 can effectively maintain China's product diversification.

In comparing opportunities for industries under different proximity threshold values, we need to compare the categories of industries with latent comparative advantage as well as the mix of industries. Setting the proximity threshold at 0.5 for identifying industries with latent advantage will maintain China's advantage in industrial diversification, but more importantly this will include many traditional industries belonging to the periphery in the product space. Examining this by industry, we can find that those can make a small jump to achieve industrial upgrade are mainly sectors in the chemical, electromechanical and instrumentation industries. At a proximity threshold of 0.55 the list of products belonging to the chemical, electromechanical and instrumentation industries amount to around 55%. A large number of labour intensive industries, agriculture and raw material industries are excluded. However, at a proximity threshold of 0.5, a large number of these industries will be subsumed under industries with latent comparative advantage. Looking at the evolution of China's product space in the future, as the proximity threshold is raised, the periphery of the product space will become sparser, with the core becoming denser. At a proximity threshold of 0.65, the density towards the centre of the product space begins to thin out compared with that at a threshold of 0.5 (see Fig. 6.4).

In order to study what constitutes a reasonable proximity threshold value in the selection of China's industries with latent comparative advantage, we conducted a simulation of the industrial upgrade by 158 countries at different threshold values. Figure 6.5 shows the outcome. In Fig. 6.5 the horizontal axis represents the categories of industries with comparative advantage plus those with latent advantage; the vertical axis represents the number of countries. As can be seen in Fig. 6.5, when the threshold value is 0.2, the number of products for most of the countries

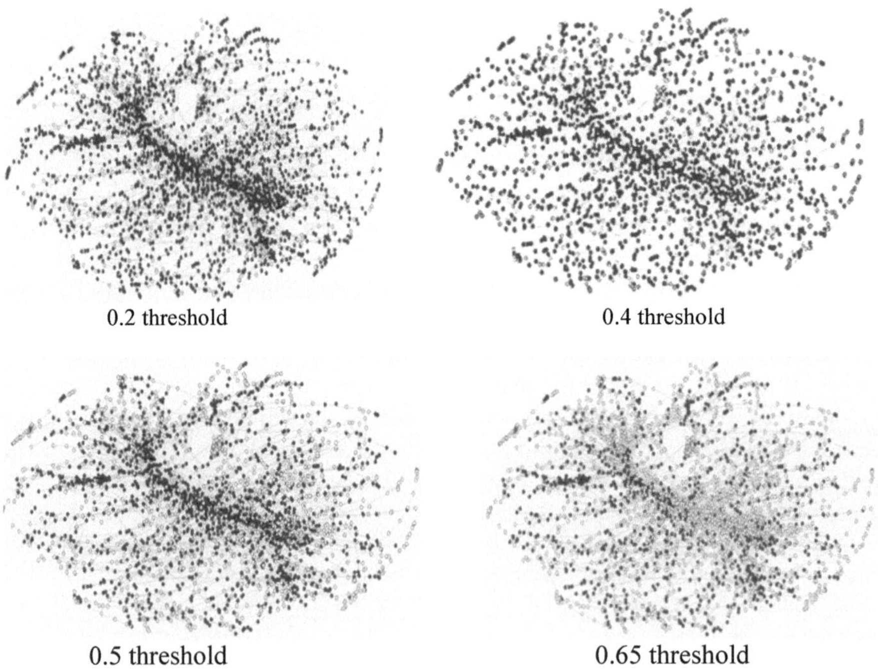


**Fig. 6.4** Structure of China's product space under different threshold values. *Note* This diagram is obtained by inserting China's product space into that of the global, and the darker dots represent China's products with comparative advantage

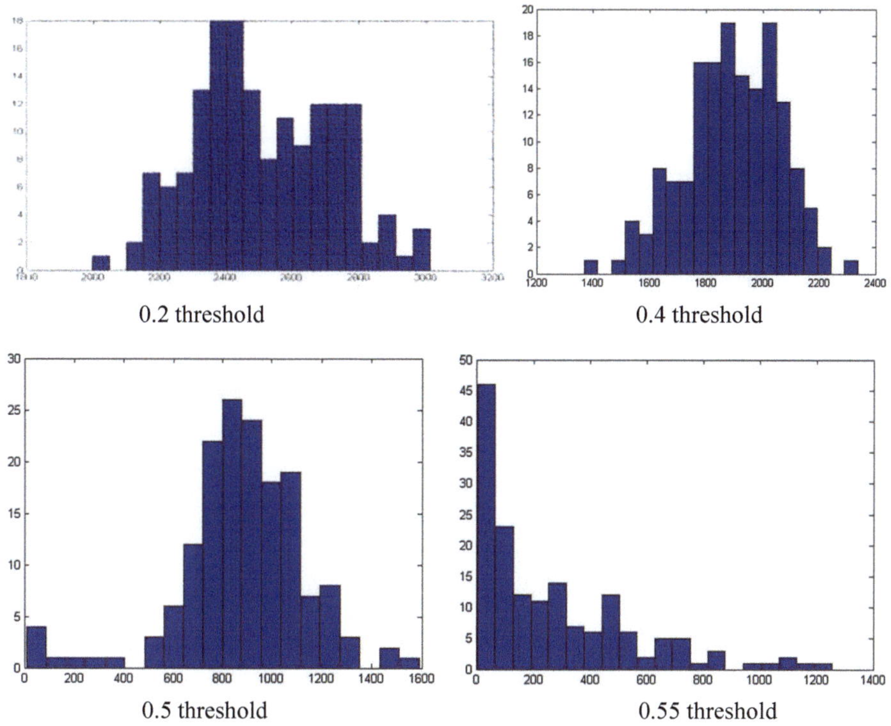


**Fig. 6.5** Relationship between categories of products with latent advantage and the number of countries by threshold values

with latent and existing advantages exceeds 2000; at a threshold value of 0.5, this figure for most countries is between 500 and 1,200. If the threshold value is 0.55, then this number will be less than 500 for most countries, with less than 100 types for many countries. At a threshold value of 0.5, the graph displays the familiar bell shape. However, what is most surprising is that the threshold value of 0.5 is also the tipping point for developed countries such as the USA (see Fig. 6.6). Thus, globally, to maintain steady growth, a proximity value of 0.5 is needed on the whole for industrial upgrade, which means having the capability distance to cross the threshold value at 0.5. For China to maintain steady growth, at a minimum average and for the short term, it must overcome the capability distance at 0.5.

3. **Assessing China's potential capability for industrial upgrade**

The difference in the capability between countries for industrial upgrade manifests firstly as industry categories with latent advantage. A country having more types of industries with latent advantage will have stronger capability for industrial upgrade. Figure 6.7 compares China's potential for industrial upgrade with the global average. It clearly shows that currently there are far more categories of products with advantage in China compared with the global average, but China

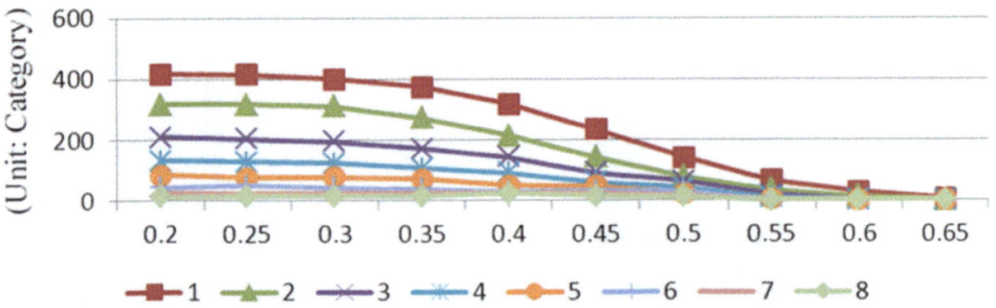


**Fig. 6.6** Evolutionary path of American industries with latent advantage by threshold values

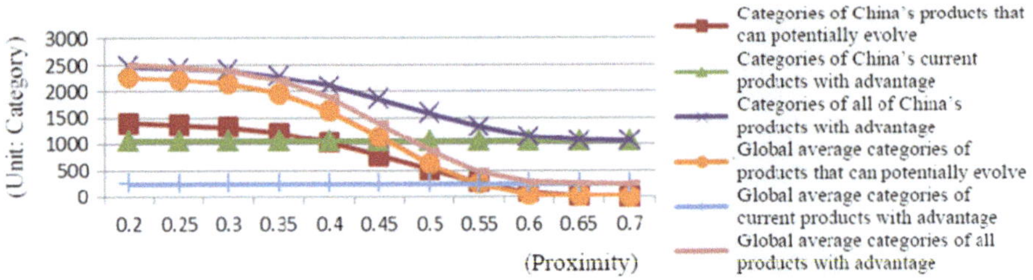


**Fig. 6.7** Comparing the evolution of China and the world's industries with latent comparative advantage

lacks obvious advantage in the potential for industry evolution. The number of China's product lines with potential is lower than the global average when the proximity threshold value is smaller than 0.5, and begins to approach the global average only when the proximity threshold value is greater than 0.5.

The difference in the capability between countries for industrial upgrade not only manifests itself in the number of industries with latent advantage, but also in the sustainability of industrial upgrade. Given different types of industries and the difference in technological capabilities, countries can make jumps of different distances. There are two meanings in the distance of the jumps. One meaning refers to the difference between products, measured by their proximity. The greater the difference in the product space, the greater will be the distance of the jump between the products. The second meaning refers to the number of steps for the jump. From the point of view of graph theory, each product corresponds to a node in the graph. The so-called steps in the jump refer to the number of nodes a product will jump to when upgrading to another product, which we call evolutionary stages in this paper. The number of products that can potentially evolve can be used as a measure for product lines with latent advantage; the stages of an industry's evolution can be a measure for the sustainability of industrial upgrade.

Compared to global standards, when the evolutionary stages of China's industries will be on a par with the world only when the proximity threshold reaches 0.6. Compared with developed countries, China's evolving product lines are not at a

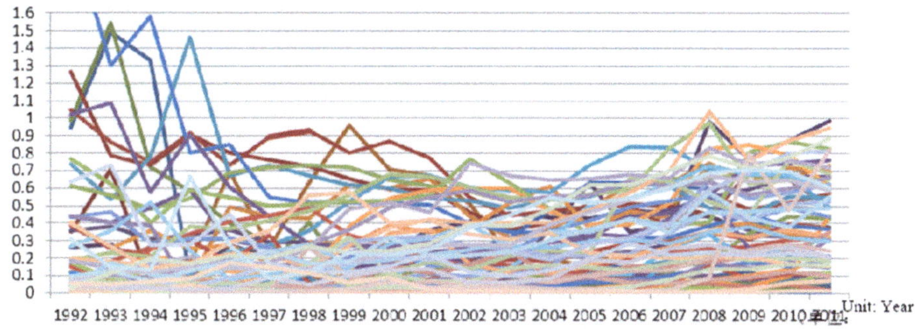


**Fig. 6.8** Evolving revealed comparative advantage of some industries with latent advantage. *Note* Each curve in the diagram represents a product which is not indicated in the diagram because there are too many of them

disadvantage, but the evolution of China's industries does not have sustainable advantage. For sustainable evolution, China is equal to developed countries only when the driving force for industrial upgrade in developed countries is very low. This is shown as a very high proximity threshold value in Fig. 6.8.

Compared with developed countries, there are fewer evolutionary stages for industries with latent advantage. In addition, after a certain period of time, the position of product lines with latent advantage is weakened, as shown by the contrast between China and the USA. Table 6.1 lists China's industry types with latent comparative advantage at different periods with different threshold values. If the distance for industry jumps are divided into big, medium and small—threshold values greater than 0.55 is a small distance, 0.35–0.5 is a medium distance, below 0.3 is a big distance—then in upgrading China's industries there are 77 types that need to achieve small jumps in the near future, and 270 types in the long term; for medium jumps 410 types in the near future and 947 types for the long term; for big jumps 72 types in the near future, making a total of 190 types for the various periods. In terms of numbers, the majority of industries in China can achieve medium jumps. Table 6.2 lists the evolving industry types in the USA with latent comparative advantage at different periods with different threshold values. As the table shows, 43 types of industries in the USA can achieve upgrade via big distance jumps in the near future, with only 187 types in the long term; 312 types of industries achieving upgrade via medium distance jumps in the near future and 952 types in the long term; 63 types of industries achieving upgrade via small distance jumps in the near future and 131 types in the long term. Clearly, compared with the USA, China's position is not poorer in evolving product lines, but neither is it stronger in sustainable industry evolution. China's industry evolution will be overtaken by the USA after the fourth life cycle stage in terms of the number of industries with latent advantage (for details see Tables 6.1 and 6.2).

**Table 6.1** China's industry evolution by different threshold values

| Stages of evolution | 0.2 | 0.25 | 0.3 | 0.35 | 0.4 | 0.45 | 0.5 | 0.55 | 0.6 | 0.65 | 0.7 |
|---|---|---|---|---|---|---|---|---|---|---|---|
| 1 | 559 | 556 | 539 | 487 | 404 | 282 | 167 | 77 | 33 | 4 | 1 |
| 2 | 481 | 476 | 461 | 410 | 329 | 232 | 136 | 74 | 25 | 3 | 0 |
| 3 | 213 | 209 | 190 | 199 | 192 | 160 | 109 | 57 | 11 | 0 | 0 |
| 4 | 77 | 74 | 78 | 84 | 71 | 70 | 62 | 36 | 3 | 0 | 0 |
| 5 | 23 | 24 | 32 | 26 | 24 | 23 | 26 | 19 | 1 | 0 | 0 |
| 6 | 15 | 15 | 15 | 8 | 8 | 11 | 12 | 5 | 1 | 0 | 0 |
| 7 | 12 | 8 | 11 | 3 | 5 | 6 | 8 | 2 | 2 | 0 | 0 |
| 8 | 2 | 5 | 5 | 0 | 1 | 1 | 2 | 0 | 0 | 0 | 0 |
| Total types | 1407 | 1376 | 1333 | 1217 | 1035 | 785 | 522 | 270 | 76 | 7 | 1 |

**Table 6.2** Evolution of latent comparative advantage in the USA by different threshold values

| Stages of evolution | 0.2 | 0.25 | 0.3 | 0.35 | 0.4 | 0.45 | 0.5 | 0.55 | 0.6 | 0.65 | 0.7 |
|---|---|---|---|---|---|---|---|---|---|---|---|
| 1 | 418 | 416 | 400 | 375 | 317 | 232 | 140 | 63 | 27 | 5 | 1 |
| 2 | 317 | 318 | 311 | 272 | 214 | 143 | 76 | 33 | 11 | 2 | 0 |
| 3 | 209 | 203 | 193 | 171 | 141 | 90 | 61 | 19 | 1 | 1 | 0 |
| 4 | 132 | 127 | 122 | 105 | 90 | 60 | 40 | 8 | 1 | 0 | 0 |
| 5 | 84 | 75 | 78 | 71 | 49 | 46 | 23 | 4 | 0 | 0 | 0 |
| 6 | 43 | 49 | 42 | 38 | 30 | 32 | 28 | 4 | 0 | 0 | 0 |
| 7 | 23 | 22 | 22 | 23 | 24 | 22 | 17 | 0 | 0 | 0 | 0 |
| 8 | 11 | 15 | 14 | 15 | 23 | 13 | 12 | 0 | 0 | 0 | 0 |
| Total types | 1270 | 1233 | 1201 | 1083 | 900 | 652 | 408 | 131 | 40 | 8 | 1 |

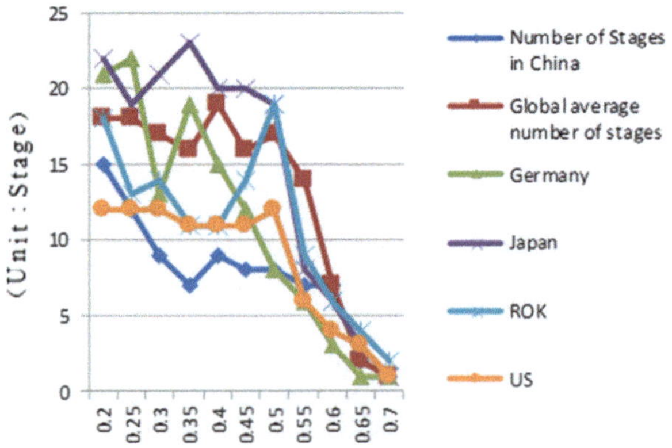


Firms and governments can choose the number of steps for industrial upgrading to achieve leap-forward upgrade. Clearly, the tendency is that, the greater the upgrade extent is, the fewer the number of industries with latent comparative

advantage. And there will be a rapid reduction in the opportunities for industrial upgrade. So, at a threshold value of 0.2, if the extent for industrial upgrade is defined as 1, which corresponds to the evolutionary stage in Table 6.1, then there are 559 types of industries with latent comparative advantage that can be developed; if it is defined as 2, the number falls to 481 types; when it is defined as 4, the types of industries with latent comparative advantage that can be developed fall to 77 (see Table 6.1). Without exploring new capabilities, we will quickly exhaust the opportunities for industrial upgrade. If the USA adopts a strategy for leap-forward upgrading, with industries taking jumps in 2, 3 or 4 steps, its opportunities for industrial upgrading will also begin to taper off but this effect will be less severe on the whole than it is for China (see Table 6.2).

A country's choice of strategy for upgrade will impact on its capability for industrial upgrading. However, whatever the scenario in simulation, the capability of China's industries for sustainable jumps is not promising. In simulating the future of China's industry evolution, a phenomenon that requires much attention is: whatever strategy China chooses at the initial stage, by the fourth stage of product evolution, for strategies with a threshold value below 0.5, the number of their products with latent comparative advantage begin to converge. By then, to maintain a fast pace of growth will depend on bringing out new products and China's comparative advantage in producing these new products. If at that time the set of global products has extended and China cannot keep pace with global innovation, even China's economic growth will be at stake. Under an optimistic view on global capability for innovation, the determining factor is how can China win comparative advantage in the future for innovation in new products and their production. This requires capability accumulation. For maintaining economic growth, China's choice of achieving industrial upgrade for industries with proximity at 0.5 is a good target. However, from a long term perspective, it is necessary that China's industrial upgrading keeps pace with the rest of the world. Sustainable economic growth requires that China's capability accumulation cannot be slower than the global average. According to China's position in international competition, a greater extent of industrial upgrading that is above the global average is a better choice for China. What we mean by a greater extent of industrial upgrading refers not only to new hi-tech industries, but also traditional industries, labour-intensive industries and resource-intensive industries.

## 4. A further discussion on the identified outcome

Having identified industries with latent advantage, we have to ask whether the results based on existing product space is valuable. Although it will not be easy to answer this question, we will still make attempts to give a preliminary answer via two methods. The first is to compare the evolution direction we predicted to ascertain that it is appropriate for the overall direction for economic development. Another method is to analyse how the revealed comparative advantage of the products under prediction goes in recent years, in order to examine the value and suitability of this method.

To catch up with the GDP per capita of developed countries, China needs a broadly similar industrial structure. To examine whether the direction of the product space is evolving in line with the overall trend for economic development is to examine whether China's product space in the future will become more similar to that in developed countries or regions. We have constructed images of the evolution in product space for the USA, Japan, Germany and the four 'Asian tigers'. The product space evolutionary path of these countries or regions shows that developed countries or regions that are industrialised also have comparative advantage in more products, with greater density in areas around the core. The product space of the four 'Asian tigers' is also evolving more and more around the core (Zhang et al. 2013). The majority of the industries we have identified with latent comparative advantage are located in the core of the global product space. Thus, there is consistency between the forecast industries with advantage and the overall direction that comparative advantage is evolving.

As an industry with latent advantage for the immediate future, its overall trend should be one of growth when measured by its revealed comparative advantage. However, the value of the product space theory will be much reduced if, according to this theory, sectors with latent comparative advantage can be identified by data from the revealed comparative advantage index. There are two categories of industries identified with latent comparative advantage according to the revealed comparative advantage index. The first is an increase in comparative advantage in the recent yeas, and the second is a decline. The former category can be further divided into two types: industries with very low revealed comparative advantage index and those with relatively high index. Industries with declining comparative advantage can also be divided into two types: those used to have explicit

**Table 6.3** Revealed comparative advantage index for some industries

| | 51574 | 51614 | 87443 | 65311 | 71323 | 73123 | 73735 | 77883 | 78434 |
|---|---|---|---|---|---|---|---|---|---|
| 1992 | 0.0848 | 0.0036 | 0.0724 | 0.1705 | 0.1753 | 0.0393 | 0.4387 | 0.0198 | 0.0110 |
| 2000 | 0.1328 | 0.0189 | 0.1330 | 0.1112 | 0.0144 | 0.0321 | 0.0388 | 0.0402 | 0.0408 |
| 2005 | 0.1363 | 0.1677 | 0.1926 | 0.1126 | 0.0050 | 0.0187 | 0.0841 | 0.1061 | 0.0220 |
| 2006 | 0.3089 | 0.1473 | 0.1783 | 0.0832 | 0.0090 | 0.0334 | 0.0738 | 0.1243 | 0.0352 |
| 2007 | 0.4779 | 0.0421 | 0.2554 | 0.0543 | 0.0252 | 0.0608 | 0.0752 | 0.1300 | 0.0809 |
| 2008 | 0.7352 | 0.0046 | 0.2788 | 0.1628 | 0.0341 | 0.0543 | 0.1781 | 0.2031 | 0.1404 |
| 2009 | 0.6804 | 0.0013 | 0.2308 | 0.0828 | 0.0273 | 0.0360 | 0.1425 | 0.2520 | 0.1359 |
| 2010 | 0.6616 | 0.0009 | 0.2680 | 0.1161 | 0.0570 | 0.0497 | 0.1742 | 0.2852 | 0.1693 |
| 2011 | 0.7311 | 0.0007 | 0.208535 | 0.1100 | 0.1217 | 0.020153 | 0.3120 | 0.2452 | 0.1636 |

*Note* 51574, heterocyclic compounds containing nitrogen heteroatoms, with a non-fused pyrazole ring, regardless of whether they have been structurally hydrogenated; 51614, propylene oxide (epoxy propane); 87443, spectroscopy, spectral photometer and spectrometer using optical radiation (ultraviolet, visible, infrared); 65311, high strength fabric made of nylon or other polyamides or polyester yarn; 71323, compression-ignition internal combustion engines (diesel or semi-diesel engines) for propulsion of vehicles listed under Class 78; 73735, fully or partly automated metal arc welding (including plasma metal arc welding) machines and equipment; 77883, electrical signalling, safety or traffic control equipment parts for railways, tramways, roads, inland waterways, parking facilities, port facilities or airports; 78434, gear boxes and parts comparative advantage which has declined, and those without comparative advantage but are now declining further. The curve in Fig. 6.8 shows how the revealed comparative advantage index has been changing during the past 10 years of some industries with latent advantage. What we see in the figure is that the revealed comparative advantage index for the majority of industries with latent advantage was on the rise, but for some industries latent advantage is still very low on the index (see Table 6.3). To an extent what this tells us is that the product space theory can help discover some potentially hard to find industries with latent advantage which cannot otherwise be found just by means of the changes in the revealed comparative advantage index.

## 6.3 Conclusion and Policy Discussion

As a developing country, during the course of economic development China took lessons from countries including the former Soviet Union and Japan in industrial restructuring. In the choice of productions, firms have not stopped to keep pace with developed countries in the West through imitation but they have not always been successful. The reason might be that such industrial choice is not entirely appropriate as their capability is constrained. We need to discover our own capability; and with this as the bedrock, we find new products or industries that will lead to success. Otherwise, the risk of failure is high. Factors that have a bearing on finding new industries or products with latent advantage are the ones in the future. Price signals in the market cannot always play their role, so we need a method that can discover capabilities. The theory of product space argues that the bedrock of a country's capability can be discovered by its product space, and it is based on this capability that a workable methodology for identifying industries with latent advantage is forthcoming. In this paper we have tried to adopt this methodology to forecast China's industries with latent advantage, and, under different proximity values, we have found industries with latent comparative advantage. In identifying industries with latent advantage, it was not possible to rely entirely on the changing revealed comparative advantage index or the traditional theory of comparative advantage, thus leaving room to apply the theory of product space in the identification of industries with latent advantage.

In this paper, the basis for identifying opportunities for China's industrial upgrade is the global product space diagram reconstructed from the latest data in global trade. However, there were still limitations in identifying opportunities for industrial upgrade: non-tradeable goods, the service industry, and entirely new types of industries have not been included. The best way to construct a country's product space structure is to use production output data, but we cannot go this far at the moment because of the availability of data. Unlike global output data, export data is relatively comprehensive. Thus, the industries with latent advantage discovered here are based on the product space constructed using export data. It is difficult to discover China's capability in non-tradeable goods using the product space constructed from export data. The service industry is not included in the existing product space either. All the industries currently existing form the basis in the use of the theory of product space to identify opportunities for industrial upgrade, but it is entirely possible that brand new sectors emerge in future developments. However, the theory of product space cannot predict such developments. Due to the aforementioned limitations, industries with latent advantage so far identified do not represent the entirety of China's industries with latent advantage. However, those identified so far can still be the focus for the nation and business. Moreover, during the course of analysing industries with latent advantage, we come across policy implications which can be instructive: currently, in examining comparative advantage, the revealed comparative advantage in some industries identified is very low, and for others it is even on the decline. In particular, some key sectors already have advantage but are currently very low on the revealed comparative advantage index. This requires that the government make some relevant policy adjustment to remove obstacles that impinge on these sectors in becoming industries with latent comparative advantage. Where key sectors cannot be identified as having latent comparative advantage, it is crucial that their capabilities are strengthened.

Currently there is no lack of critics on China's industrial transformation and upgrading. Governments at all levels are yearning for faster industrial transformation and upgrading, and to quickly transform the mode for development via restructuring. However, 'stalling' can occur if the pace is too fast during industrial upgrading. To be able to predict such a phenomenon is what makes the theory on capability by Hausmann and Hidalgo so unique. In the theory on comparative advantage, a nation and her industrial upgrading cannot stall. In fact, this is not the case as demonstrated by our study through a simulation on industry evolution in China and other countries. During economic growth, China must beware of risks of stalling in the upgrade and transformation of her industries.

A most interesting finding in our study is that where the extent of industrial upgrading exceeds the 0.5 threshold, the number of industries with latent advantage drops sharply. This finding is not only applicable to China but also to developed countries like the USA. No matter what initial strategy China adopts for industrial upgrade, the room for upgrading will be exhausted after 4 stages of upgrade. The policy implication of this finding is that if the pace of China's industrial upgrading is too fast the outcome will not be as one would like, but if the pace is too slow then equally it cannot ensure that China's economic growth can be sustained.

To ensure that China's economic growth can be sustained, the pace of industrial upgrade cannot be slower than the global average. The problem, however, is that China's capability for industrial upgrading is not better than the global average. To address this problem, in industrial upgrading we can choose an inclusive strategy. This means that industries with fewer upgrade opportunities can, by taking small, brisk steps and by intra-sector upgrade, accumulate new capabilities. When industries have more opportunities for upgrading, they are encouraged to take big steps at a brisk pace to catch up with world-leading industries; industries with middling upgrade capabilities are encouraged to proceed at a medium-fast pace.

When different industries upgrade they will have different demands for labour in terms of quality and types. In view of sectoral characteristics, different upgrade policies should be adopted to allow different types and qualities in the labour force to be included in the industrial upgrade process and to share in its outcome, so as to full use of China's rich human resources and the advantage of their diversity. With such a strategy more labourers can be engaged in the process for industrial upgrade, and this is why this strategy is also called an inclusive strategy for industrial upgrading. This strategy can work in tandem together with inclusive growth, and provides underpinning to achieving inclusive economic growth. It can help avoid 'biting off more than we can chew' during the process of industrial upgrading.

As is clearly shown by the global product space, different industries have different upgrade opportunities. Therefore, businesses occupy different positions in the product space, with some businesses located in the core while others in the periphery. Industries located in the core, such as the electromechanical and chemical industries, are at a more advantageous position, and thus regions where these industries are located and businesses in these sectors can easily find favour with the government and make a leapfrog in their upgrade. After a business in the core has a jump-start upgrade, its original position is left vacant, but whether this vacant space can be transferred to other regions or businesses in the country depends entirely on the ability of the new-comer to take it on. The process for economic development in a country is that the product lines that have an advantage in the core of the product space will increase by volume and scale, which means that, by accumulating capabilities, businesses in the periphery will continuously move towards the core. Only when businesses in the periphery have the opportunities to accumulate and take on industries passed down from businesses in the core can we avoid a passing fancy. Having resources so highly concentrated in businesses in the core makes those in the periphery or regional businesses lack incentives or resources to foster essential capabilities. When new industries develop and vacate some product space, those in the periphery have no capability to take over the new vacant product space. Subsequently, there must be some industries fading or transferred to other countries. This is the 'bit off more than we can chew' phenomenon, with the result that we will quickly exhaust the potential and the room for industrial upgrading. This will have a massively negative impact on the economy.

China's greatest advantage is in her diverse and multifaceted industries. Currently the number of China's industries with advantage is well above the global average. A strategy for inclusive industrial upgrading can bring a mix that can both avoid industrial upgrading going too fast and having a major impact at the time and prevent insufficient capacity in future industries if the industrial upgrading is too slow. Adopting a strategy for inclusive industrial upgrading is to accept that the potential for upgrade varies from industry to industry. With this strategy, the government can play a key role are in providing essential information for businesses to discover sectors with latent comparative advantage, and in creating a level playing field where businesses can perform according to their strengths. In order to promote industrial upgrade, the easiest measure for countries to adopt is to give subsidies. However, China should be cautious in using subsidies to support industrial upgrade. In fact, this kind of measure will not allow businesses to fully function to achieve a jump-start that is in keeping with their own capabilities, which can in turn slow down industrial upgrading across the board.

Globally, the government intervention in industrial development is on the rise. *The Economist* published an article on 5th August 2010, which claimed that following the international financial crisis there is renewed interest around the world in industrial policy. The *2013 Human Development Report* identified the government support in developing some industries as an important factor for success, and incorporated it into the recommendations framework for developing countries. Although the theory of product space structure in discovering industries with advantage is instructive for governments to implement industrial policies, it does not necessarily follow that it should be the latest fad. A more important purpose for using the theory of product space to discover industries with latent advantage lies in revealing the many institutional and policy barriers that prevent such industries from fulfilling their comparative advantage and in revealing capability shortfalls during industrial upgrade, so that the market can better play its role in providing insights.

## Bibliography


Abdon, Arnelyn, and Jesus Felipe. 2011. The product space: What does it say about the opportunities for growth and structural transformation of Sub-Saharan Africa? [EB/OL]. The Levy Economics Institute Working Paper No. 670.

Barro, Robert J., and Sala-i-Martin Xavier. 2000. *Economic growth*. Beijing: China Social Sciences Press (translated by He Hui, Liu Mingxing).

Bayudan-Dacuycuy, Connie. 2012. The Phlippine export portfolio in the product space: potentials, possibilities and policy challenges. *Economic Bulletin* 32.

Hausmann, Ricardo, and Bailey Klinger. 2006. The structure of product space and evolution of comparative advantage [EB/OL]. Harvard University Centre for International Development Working Paper number 128.

Hausmann, R., J. Hwang, and D. Rodrik. 2007. What you export matters. *Journal of Economic Growth* 12: 1–25.

Lin, Yifu. 2012. *New structural economics*. Beijing: Peking University Press. (translated by Su Jian).

Reinstaller, Andreas, Werner Hölzl, Johannes Kutsam, and Christian Schmid. 2012. The development of productive structures of EU Member States and their international competitiveness. This report has been prepared in 2012 for the European Commission, DG Enterprise and Industry under Specific Contract No SI2-614099 implementing the Framework Contract ENTR/2009/033, 2012.

Wan, Jin, and Chunjie Qi. 2012. Product space structure and dynamic comparative advantage in agricultural products—an analysis and forecast based on high-dimensional panel data. *Journal of International Trade* 9.

Wu, Yejun, Qizi Zhang. 2011. On the theory of the 'middle income trap'. *Review of Industrial Economics* 10.

Wu, Yejun, and Qizi Zhang. 2012. An evolution of comparative advantage and economic growth. *China Industrial Economics* 2.

Wu, Yejun, Qizi Zhang, and Juan Xu. 2012. A discussion of product space and the evolution of comparative advantage. *Economic Review* 4.

Zhang, Qizi. 2008. An evolution of comparative advantage and China's choice for a route to industrial upgrade. *Industrial Economy of China* 9.

Zhang, Qizi, Yejun Wu, and Lei Wang. 2012. Economic complexity, regional specialisation and economic growth. *Economic Management Journal* 6.

Zhang, Qizi, et al. 2013. *A report on China's industrial competitiveness*. Beijing: Social Sciences Academic Press.

Zeng Shihong, and Jianghuai Zheng. 2008. How the theory of product space structure inspires the transformation of China's mode for economic development. *Economic Review* 11.

Zeng, Shihong, and Jianghuai Zheng. 2010. 'Cost finding' by entrepreneurs, evolving comparative advantage, and restructuring the product space—a case study on Jiangsu's economic development. *Review of Industrial Economics* 1.

# Chapter 7
# The Flying Geese Formation Strategy of Industrial Upgrading and Coordinative Regional Development

**Qizi Zhang**

After World War II, economic development in Asia appeared to quicken, which once dubbed the Asian miracle by the World Bank. This miracle forms a sharp contrast to the economic stagnation at the same period in Latin America, and as such has prompted much research into the reasons for its success. As early as the 1930s Japanese scholars put forward the flying geese formation development model, which became one of the theoretical frameworks for explaining the Asian miracle. The flying geese model was first devised by Japanese scholars to analyse international industrial transition and the question of the industrial division of labour, and there is still debate as to whether the flying geese formation is an appropriate model for the development in Japan or the East Asian region (Ono 2008; Akamatsu 1962; Kasahara 2004a, b). However, developing countries have achieved sustained economic development by taking on industries passed down from developed countries, and the model is even used to coordinate regional development within a country, rendering this strategy still worthy of in-depth research. In 2009, Cai Fang applied the flying geese model to analyse the inter-regional industrial transition and upgrading in China (Cai et al. 2009). In 2010, Ruan Jianqing and Zhang Xiaobo applied the flying geese model in a study on the changes in the spatial configuration of China's textile industry (Ruan and Zhang 2010). In 2013, using provincial sample data, Qu Yue et al. investigated whether China had already had a flying geese style industrial upgrade, and concluded that this has already occurred (Qu et al. 2013).

Although attention to the flying geese style industrial upgrade within a country only started in recent years, the theoretical and practical implications of research on this question is significant. During the course of development, some countries are easily stuck in stages of the Malthusian Trap or the middle income trap. Some countries have successfully escaped these traps whereas others are stuck. China is

Q. Zhang (✉)
Chinese Academy of Social Sciences, Beijing, China
e-mail: zhangqizi65@126.com



Q. Zhang (ed.), *Transforming Economic Growth and China's Industrial Upgrading*, Research Series on the Chinese Dream and China's Development Path,
https://doi.org/10.1007/978-981-13-0962-5_7

now within the ranks of middle income countries, but will it get stuck in the 'middle income trap' like its counterparts? As a large country, coordinative regional economic development and success in transferring industries that have lost their comparative advantage in developed regions into relatively poorly developed regions can help China effectively avoid stalling industrial upgrade and cross over the 'middle income trap'. If this theory stands, then it suggests that the notion of the middle income trap is not applicable to large countries. This paper aims to find out whether China can cross over the middle income trap by adopting the flying geese model strategy for industrial upgrading to overcome the problem of stalling comparative advantage. If this is not possible, then what problems do we encounter and what is required to solve them.

## 7.1 Flying Geese Style Industrial Upgrading and Comparative Advantage

1. **The flying geese model and the capability-based theory of comparative advantage**

The early version of the flying geese model derived from the experience of the Japanese economic development by Kaname Akamatsu. The real value of this theory is that apart from analysing factor endowments, it opened up a new approach to assessing a country's industrial development trend, but in the early stage this theory was entirely historical and experiential. In order to explain the facts from history and experience, Akamatsu's student Kiyoshi Kojima incorporated it within the framework of comparative advantage, and explained the rationality of the flying geese model by changing factor endowments (Kojima 1960). The unique value of the flying geese formation as a development theory is actually lost using this line of theorising, limiting its instructive purpose in the selection of industries. For example, in theorising the flying geese formation model, Kiyoshi Kojima only discussed three main industries: agriculture, light and heavy industries. However, the reality is much more complex than this, so the argument needs to be bolstered by a new theory of comparative advantage. Let us call this new theory the capability-based comparative advantage theory.

The theory of capability-based comparative advantage is extended from the traditional theory of comparative advantage. We can say that the traditional theory of comparative advantage is based on factor endowments, meaning that the comparative advantage of a country or a region is categorised from the perspective of its factor endowments. By the relative abundance between the factors, comparative advantage is divided into advantages in labour, resources or technology. When Cai Fang et al. discussed at what stage did the flying geese model of industrial production emerge in China, they focused mainly on changes in the cost of the factor: as the cost of factor rises, some industries in coastal regions lose comparative advantage and have to transfer towards central and western regions where cost is relatively low (2013). This is the same methodology in comparative advantage and that is why the traditional theory serves well as the basis from which to undertake analysis. However, the limitation of this methodology is that it cannot fully explain the difference in the international division of labour. In investigating elements that affect the international division of labour, most studies have found that the difference in this term is far more complex than that in factor endowments. The difference in the industrial division of labour is determined not only by factor endowments but also by factors much more complex. Analysing the risks involved in transforming comparative advantage is still difficult with this method. Within this framework, as long as there is a differential in the cost of the factor between regions, industries from high-cost regions will move towards low-cost regions. Since economic development manifests itself as a continuous process of industrial upgrade, less developed regions will not have long periods of stagnation. Factors affecting a country or a region's comparative advantage are far more complex than those involved in traditional comparative advantage. The theory of capability-based comparative advantage attempts to incorporate these factors and therefore it does not dismiss the traditional theory of comparative advantage. Instead it extends it with much more information for analysing comparative advantage.

Hidalgo and Hausmann published a series of papers on the evolution of comparative advantage. These are important literature in the theory of capability-based comparative advantage. In order to measure a country's capability in producing certain products, Hidalgo et al. devised the product space methodology. They measure a country's comparative advantage by product characteristics and the relatedness between products, to uncover the evolution of a country's pathway to latent comparative advantage. In effect it emphasises that a country's industrial upgrading is constrained by its current capabilities. Although factors that affect the industrial division of labour between regions within a country differ from those between countries, the discovery that the factor impacting on the international division of labour is far more complex than factor endowments is an important lesson for research in the industrial division of labour between regions. Thus when we measure the comparative advantage between regions we borrow the product space methodology, a methodology that measures comparative advantage directly at the product level. For the time being, this is the most feasible way to measure a country or a region's capability for industrial upgrade.

2. **Categories of comparative advantage and definition of the flying geese model of industrial upgrade**

When measuring a region's latent comparative advantage from a product's perspective, we should divide products into categories. There are many different methods to do this. For example, by factor contents, products can be divided into labour-intensive, resource-intensive, technology-intensive; or by level of technology, they can be divided into high technology, medium technology or low technology. Here we will use the method by Jesus Felipe et al. This method assumes that the accumulation of capability or knowledge differs from product to product, thus containing different potentials for upgrade. Two indicators are used in measuring the accumulation of a product's capability or knowledge—one for a product's technology content, the other for a product's connectedness. The rationale for such an approach is that it can measure the complexity of an economy: a complexity that is related to the economy's rate of growth or per capita GDP. The reasons why a country gets stuck in middle income trap or why developed economies were confronted with financial crisis in 2008 are all related to the changes in complexity (Felipe et al. 2010; Zhang et al. 2014).

When calculating the technology content of products between regions, we will borrow the PRODY index for measuring export complexity to calculate China's regional product complexity. The formula is:

$$PRODY_i = \sum_c \left[ \frac{xval_{ci} / \sum_i xval_{ci}}{\sum_c \left( xval_{ci} / \sum_i xval_{ci} \right)} \right] \times GDPpc_c$$

$\text{xvalci}_{ci}$ is the production cost for product i in region C, $\text{GDPpc}_c$ is the per capita GDP for region C.

There is a correlation between the product's complexity indicator and that for the product's technology content, but these are not entirely the same. The general approach for measuring a product's technology content is the investment in R&D as a share of sales revenue. For highly complex products, this ratio can be high or it low, and thus the technology content can also be high or low. To a large degree however, a product's complexity reflects its technology content, and we therefore use it to represent a product's technology content.

If the production is determined by a knowledge function, then the technology content of a region's products will reflect the unique nature of the accumulated knowledge for that region. However, when examining the comparative advantage of a region's economy, apart from its unique knowledge, we should also examine its capabilities for diversification. Thus, in addition to categorising products by their levels of technology, we can also categorise them by their capability for diversification. For this kind of capability, we can specifically measure product connectedness. A product's connectedness is the sum of all its proximity. $\varphi_{ij}$ Represents proximity, *path* represents a product's connectedness, then the connectedness of a product can be calculated as:

$$PATH_i = \sum_i \varphi_{ij}$$

A product's proximity measures the likelihood for upgrading the product. The method for calculation is:

$$\varphi_{ij} = \min\{P(RCA_i|RCA_j), P(RCA_j|RCA_i)\}, \quad 0 \le \varphi_{ij} \le 1$$

The concept of proximity was put forward by Hidalgo et al. in 2007. When analysing a product's proximity, because of data constraint, Hidalgo et al. used export data. $\varphi_{ij}$ represents proximity, $P(RCA_i|RCA_j)$ represents the likelihood of product $i$ having revealed comparative advantage when the country's product $j$ has revealed comparative advantage in export. A greater proximity between products indicates that there is a smaller difference in the input mix for producing the two products, with a smaller capability differential. When analysing the product proximity at a regional level, we used regional output data. Therefore, the analysis of *P(RCAi|RCAj)* represents the likelihood of its product i having revealed comparative advantage, when the value added of the region's product j has revealed comparative advantage.

A product's technology content can be divided according to its complexity—high, medium and low, represented by HPR, MPR and LPR respectively; a product's connectedness is divided into three types of high, medium and low, represented by HPA, MPA and LPA respectively. Putting the two together gives nine possible combinations, which we can call Type I, Type II, Type III, Type IV … Type IX. There can be many different types of products produced in a region. According to the products with the most advantage, regions can be classified into different types. A classic flying geese model of upgrade means that economically advanced regions will continuously transfer in sequence from Type IX to Type VIII, VII etc. towards relatively less undeveloped regions.

## 7.2 Has Flying Geese Style Upgrade Already Emerged in China?

1. **Basis of data obtained for measurement**

The methodology put forward by Hidalgo et al. used international trade data. This approach takes full advantage of the superior data contained in international trade data, but its shortcomings is the exclusion of non-tradeable goods. Our method differs from that by Hidalgo et al. who analysed product space at the national level. In categorising regional product types, we used regional production output data, and regional specialisation index was used as a substitute for Hidalgo's revealed comparative advantage index in their calculation of product space proximity.

The analysis of product technology content and the calculation of connectedness are based on data during 2000–2011 from the database of industrial firms. This database contains statistics of firms over the designated size as a whole. The advantage of this database is that it contains detailed data classified by sector. The shortcomings are: what the statistics cover are not uniform for different periods—the statistics during 1998–2006 cover all state-owned enterprises and those non-state owned enterprises with annual revenue of over 5 million yuan; the statistics during 2007–2010 cover industrial firms with annual revenue of over 5 million yuan from their core business; from 2011 onwards the statistics cover industrial firms with annual revenue of over 20 million yuan from their core business. Since there is a big variation in the scope of the statistics in 2011, in the choice of data we selected data prior to 2010 as the basis for analysis.

Although the industrial firm database does not include all the firms in the regions, it includes the important ones. This makes it useful for reflecting on the comparative advantage in the regions, and when using it for analysis there should not be any major bias. We cannot find continuous data on the value added of an industry in this database. Thus, when it comes to calculating correlation, the value added of an industry is substituted by sales volume.

In categorising products by means of connectedness and technology content, we should also consider the stability in product space. For the analysis, it is more appropriate to choose a period in which the product space is relatively stable, that is, a period in which the relationship between the products is relatively stable. The stability in product space can be measured by the standard deviation in the proximity value of the product space. In analysing changes in product space, Hidalgo et al. use 10-year periods for analysis (2007). However, while analysing the product space stability during the 10-year period of 2002–2011, we found a rather high standard deviation in the proximity value. In particular, when examining the standard deviations from the means in the different proximity areas, we found that they are higher than 30%, which shows that the product space during the 10-year period is not stable enough. Thus, we shortened the periods to 6 years, which resulted in much lower standard deviations, with the standard deviation between the different proximity areas reduced to within 0.1. From this, we chose to base the analysis on 6-year periods for classifying products.

Products are classified according to PRODY; the top 1/3 most complex products include specialised and general purpose equipment manufacturing, the chemical industry, instrumentation, cultural and office machinery, communications devices, the manufacture of computing and other electronic devices, cultural and sports equipment manufacturing. Industries at the mid 20 and in a position to steer a course are instrumentation, cultural and office machinery, communications devices, the manufacture of computing and other electronic devices, stationery and sports equipment manufacturing (see Table 7.1). Those industries at the lower 1/3 are mainly resource intensive sectors. The last 20 industries are mainly in the mining industry, ferrous and non-ferrous metals smelting and flat-rolling processing.

When products are classified according to their relatedness, those highly connected are not all high-tech products. Among the last 30 industries, resource intensive industries are in the majority but there are also some high-tech industries. Likewise, highly connected products are not necessarily sophisticated products. Figure 7.1 shows the relationship between the technology content of products and their relatedness. Clearly, there is no linear relationship between the two, i.e. high technology content does not mean that the products are more closely related or otherwise.

**Table 7.1** Types of comparative advantage

| | High relatedness (HPA) | Medium relatedness (MPA) | Low relatedness (LPA) |
|---|---|---|---|
| Technology content (HPR) | High technology-high relatedness (HPR-HPA) | High technology-medium relatedness (HPR–MPA) | High technology-low relatedness (HPR-LPA) |
| Medium technology content (MPR) | Medium technology-medium relatedness (MPR–HPA) | Medium technology-medium relatedness (MPR–MPA) | Medium technology-low relatedness (MPR-LPA) |
| Low technology content (LPR) | Low technology-high relatedness (LPR-HPA) | Low technology-medium relatedness (LPR-MPA) | Low technology-low relatedness (LPR-LPA) |

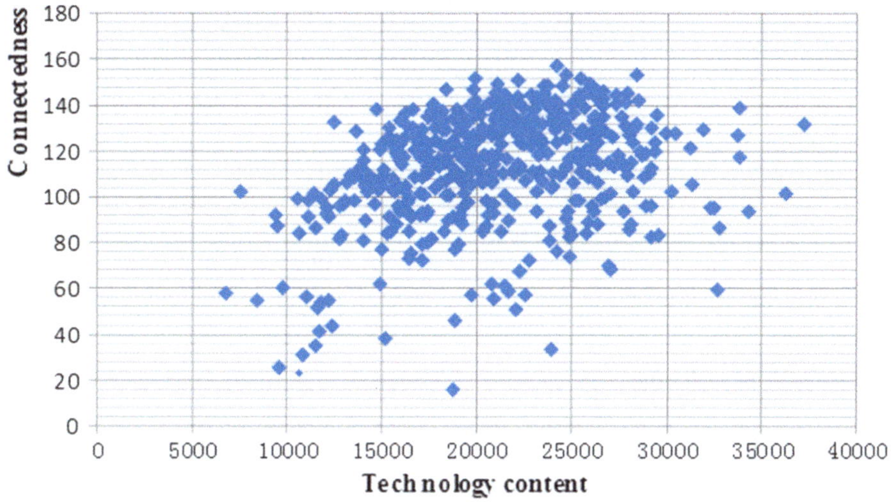


**Fig. 7.1** Relationship between the technology content of products and their connectedness

According to the technology content of products and their connectedness, they are classified into nine types. For the process, we first calculated the average technology content and relatedness of the products during specified periods. According to the technology content, the products are then classified into high, medium and low, each of 1/3. The connectedness of the products is dealt with similarly. From this basis, and the combining technology content and relatedness, products are divided into nine types. There are more types belonging to low connectedness and low technology content, 90 types in total; the next types belong to high connectedness and high technology content—there are 70 types. Approximately, these two account for 16 and 14% respectively of the total product types (Table 7.2).

**Table 7.2** According to a product's technology content and relatedness, products are divided into 9 types (benchmarked against 2005–2010 constant prices)

| | High connectedness | Medium connectedness | Low connectedness |
|---|---|---|---|
| High technology content | Product type: 70<br>Level of technology: 25965<br>Connectedness: 138 | Product type: 56<br>Level of technology: 26573<br>Connectedness: 118 | Product type: 43<br>Level of technology: 27216<br>Connectedness: 89 |
| Medium technology content | Product type: 69<br>Level of technology: 21217<br>Connectedness: 136 | Product type: 54<br>Level of technology: 220672<br>Connectedness: 117 | Product type: 38<br>Level of technology: 20705<br>Connectedness: 83 |
| Low technology content | Product type: 24<br>Level of technology: 17200<br>Connectedness: 134 | Product type: 57<br>Level of technology: 16289<br>Connectedness: 117 | Product type: 90<br>Level of technology: 14446<br>Connectedness: 88 |

The outcome of combining technology content and relatedness of products is different from other ways of classifying products. Table 7.3 reflects the distribution of industries in the different types using the new classification method. It shows the statistical implication for classifying certain industries—they will belong to different categories. According to the traditional classification method, textile and clothing are considered labour-intensive industries, but under new classification criteria, textile and clothing are spread throughout the 9 types. Among the pharmaceutical industry which is traditionally viewed as high technology content, not one product falls within Type I, Type II or Type III.

2. **Evaluation outcome**

Although there are many interpretations of the flying geese model, in terms of evaluating whether the flying geese model of industrial upgrade has emerged among the regions, an often used method is to measure the market share and changes in revealed comparative advantage to find out whether there is transfer of industries from developed regions to relatively less developed regions. Qu Yue and Cai Fang believe that the flying geese model of industrial upgrade has emerged in China since 2004. They have come to this conclusion by analysing changes in the distribution of labour-intensive industries in the regions. Moreover, Cai Fang and others have identified the year 2004 as the Lewis Turning Point (Qu et al. 2013). In Figs. 7.2, 7.3 and 7.4, there is no distinction between industry types, but they show changes to the types of products with revealed comparative advantage in the more developed coastal regions and the central and western regions. The overall trend is a fall in the coastal regions, with a rise in the central and western regions. Therefore, on the basis of a traditional classification of industry types, we can conclude that the flying geese model of industrial upgrade has emerged. However, does this conclusion still stand if we use the new criteria to classify products?

**Table 7.3** Distribution of product types by industry

| | Total types | Type I | Type II | Type III | Type IV | Type V | Type VI | Type VII | Type VIII | Type IX |
|---|---|---|---|---|---|---|---|---|---|---|
| 06 Coal mining and washing | 3 | | | | | | 1 | | | 2 |
| 07 Oil and gas extraction | 2 | | | | | | 1 | | | 1 |
| 08 Ferrous metals mining and ore dressing | 2 | | | | | | | | | 2 |
| 09 Non-ferrous metals mining and ore dressing | 8 | | | | | | 1 | | | 7 |
| 10 Non-metallic mineral mining and dressing | 10 | | | | | | | 3 | 2 | 5 |
| 11 Other types of mining | 1 | | | | | | | | | 1 |
| 13 Agricultural foodstuff processing | 17 | | | | 1 | 2 | | 1 | 8 | 5 |
| 14 Food production | 20 | 1 | 1 | | 2 | 4 | 1 | | 7 | 4 |
| 15 Beverage manufacturing | 13 | | 2 | | 1 | | 1 | 1 | 5 | 3 |
| 16 Tobacco products industry | 3 | | | | | | | | | 3 |
| 17 Textile industry | 21 | 5 | 1 | 3 | 3 | 3 | 3 | | 2 | 1 |
| 18 Textile garments, footwear, hat manufacturing | 3 | 2 | 1 | | | | | | | |
| 19 Leather, fur, down feather and other products | 11 | 1 | 2 | | | 1 | 2 | | 3 | 2 |
| 20 Wood processing, timber, bamboo, palm fibre and straw products | 10 | | | | | 2 | 2 | 1 | 4 | 1 |
| 21 Furniture manufacturing | 5 | 2 | 1 | | 1 | | | 1 | | |
| 22 Paper making and paper products | 6 | | | | 3 | | | 1 | 1 | 1 |
| 23 Printing and reproduction of recorded media | 5 | 1 | 1 | | 1 | | | 1 | 1 | |
| 24 Stationery and sports equipment manufacturing | 17 | 4 | 10 | | 2 | 1 | | | | |
| 25 Petroleum processing, coking and nuclear fuel processing | 2 | | | | | | 2 | | | 1 |
| 26 Chemical raw materials and chemical products manufacturing | 34 | 2 | 3 | | 5 | 2 | 6 | 2 | 6 | 8 |
| 27 Pharmaceutical manufacturing | 7 | | | | 2 | 1 | | | 3 | 1 |
| 28 Chemical fibre manufacturing industry | 7 | | | 3 | 1 | | | 1 | 1 | 1 |

(continued)

**Table 7.3** (continued)

| | Total types | Type I | Type II | Type III | Type IV | Type V | Type VI | Type VII | Type VIII | Type IX |
|---|---|---|---|---|---|---|---|---|---|---|
| 29 Rubber products industry | 9 | 1 | 1 | | 4 | | 1 | | 1 | 1 |
| 30 Plastic products industry | 10 | 2 | 3 | 1 | 1 | 1 | | | 1 | 1 |
| 31 Non-metallic mineral products | 31 | | 1 | | 5 | 5 | 4 | 3 | 5 | 8 |
| 32 Ferrous metals smelting and flat-rolling processing | 4 | | | | 1 | 1 | | | | 2 |
| 33 Non-ferrous metals smelting and flat-rolling processing | 12 | | | | | | 1 | | 1 | 10 |
| 34 Fabricated metal products | 24 | 4 | 5 | 5 | 4 | 5 | | 1 | | |
| 35 General purpose equipment manufacturing | 33 | 9 | 3 | 3 | 8 | 5 | 3 | | 1 | 1 |
| 36 Special equipment manufacturing | 49 | 12 | 5 | 5 | 8 | 6 | 4 | 1 | 3 | 5 |
| 37 Transport equipment manufacturing | 24 | 6 | | 3 | 1 | 1 | 2 | 2 | 5 | 4 |
| 39 Electrical, mechanical and equipment manufacturing | 28 | 5 | 5 | 4 | 10 | 3 | | | | 1 |
| 40 Communications devices, the manufacture of computing and other electronic devices | 20 | 8 | 4 | 5 | 1 | 2 | | | | |
| 41 Instrumentation, cultural and office machinery manufacturing | 23 | 3 | 5 | 7 | 2 | 4 | 1 | | | 1 |
| 42 Crafts and other manufacturing industries | 14 | 2 | 5 | 1 | 2 | 3 | 2 | | 1 | |
| 43 Discarded and waste materials recycling and processing | 2 | | | | 1 | 1 | | | | |
| 44 Production and supply of electricity and heating | 7 | | | 1 | | | 1 | | | 5 |
| 46 Water production and supply | 3 | | | | | 1 | 1 | | | 1 |

*Data source* Author's calculations, the same for other tables below

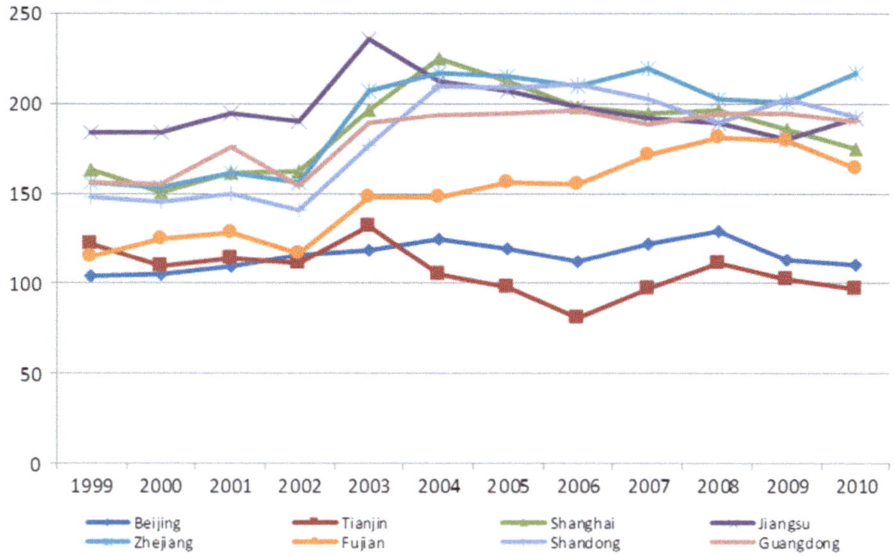


**Fig. 7.2** Changes to the number of industries with revealed comparative advantage in the developed eastern region. *Data source* Author's calculations, the same below

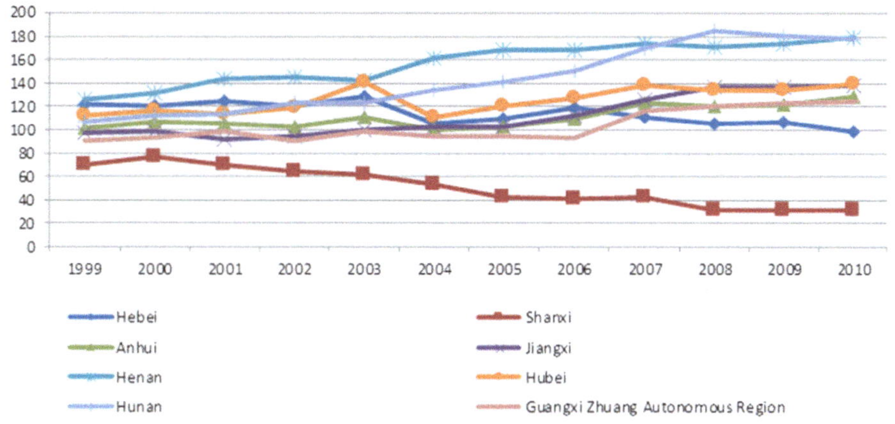


**Fig. 7.3** Changes to the number of industries with revealed comparative advantage in the central region

Table 7.4 lists the number of different industries with declining market share in developed regions, using the new product classification criteria. It clearly shows that in the developed regions the market shares of some industries have declined within their industry. Figures 7.5, 7.6 and 7.7 list the market shares changes of the industries in the developed eastern region for product Types VII, VIII and IX. The examination shows that in the more developed eastern region, the market share of

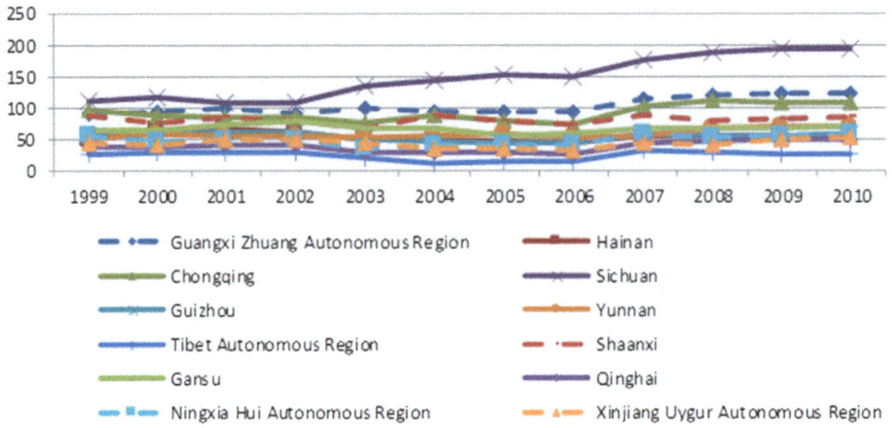


**Fig. 7.4** Changes to the number of industries with revealed comparative advantage in the western region

**Table 7.4** Product types with declining market share in different industries (2008–2010 compared with 2005–2007)

| | I | II | III | VI | V | VI | VII | VIII | IX |
|---|---|---|---|---|---|---|---|---|---|
| Beijing | 49 | 31 | 21 | 47 | 30 | 22 | 15 | 33 | 35 |
| Tianjin | 41 | 23 | 18 | 38 | 27 | 19 | 10 | 32 | 32 |
| Shanghai | 58 | 43 | 31 | 61 | 41 | 24 | 15 | 40 | 33 |
| Jiangsu Province | 24 | 27 | 22 | 35 | 27 | 18 | 17 | 30 | 43 |
| Zhejiang Province | 52 | 34 | 20 | 51 | 35 | 20 | 17 | 43 | 53 |
| Fujian Province | 36 | 29 | 13 | 28 | 15 | 9 | 9 | 25 | 29 |
| Shandong Province | 28 | 24 | 19 | 38 | 24 | 18 | 14 | 42 | 37 |
| Guangdong Province | 43 | 33 | 21 | 45 | 40 | 22 | 17 | 33 | 49 |

*Information source* Author's calculations

industries with lower technology content and connectedness is declining, and the transfer from the east to the west has already been happening. Because the period is quite short, we cannot verify that the inter-region industrial upgrade under the new industry classification method is entirely consistent with the classic pathway of the flying geese model. However, with the industry already transferring from the eastern region to the central and western regions, the implication is that, according to the new industry classification method, we can come to the conclusion that the flying geese model of industrial upgrade is happening in China.

There are two stages in the flying geese model of industrial upgrade. During the first stage more developed regions transfer the industries that have lost advantage to less developed regions while continue to upgrade their own industries. The second stage spells a period of uncertain outlook for the more developed region, while its

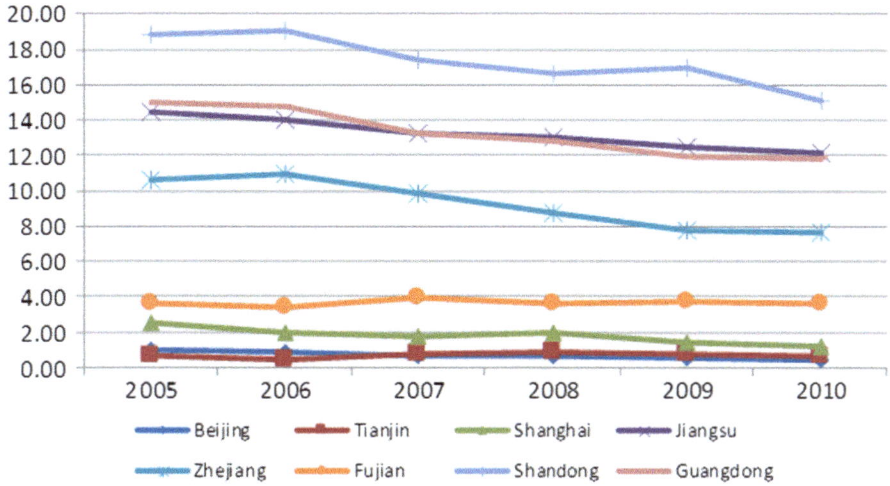


**Fig. 7.5** Changes to the market share of product Type VII in the developed eastern region

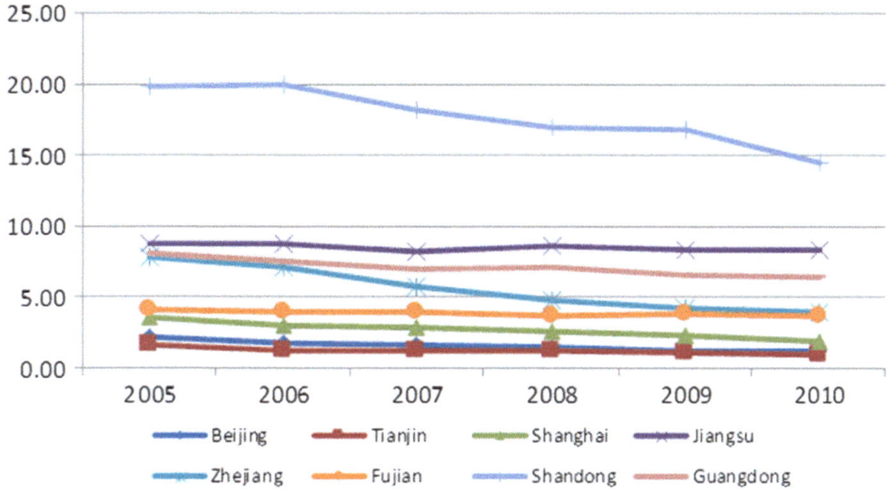


**Fig. 7.6** Changes to the market share of product Type VIII in the developed eastern region

industries are being transferred to less developed regions. To determine at what stage China is in the flying geese model of industrial upgrade, we can assess if the competitiveness of more sophisticated industries is also declining while industries are being transferred from developed regions to less developed regions. If it is declining, this shows that China's flying geese model of industrial upgrade is at the second stage. Figures 7.8, 7.9 and 7.10 list the changes in the market share of three types of more sophisticated industries. Although individual provinces or industries

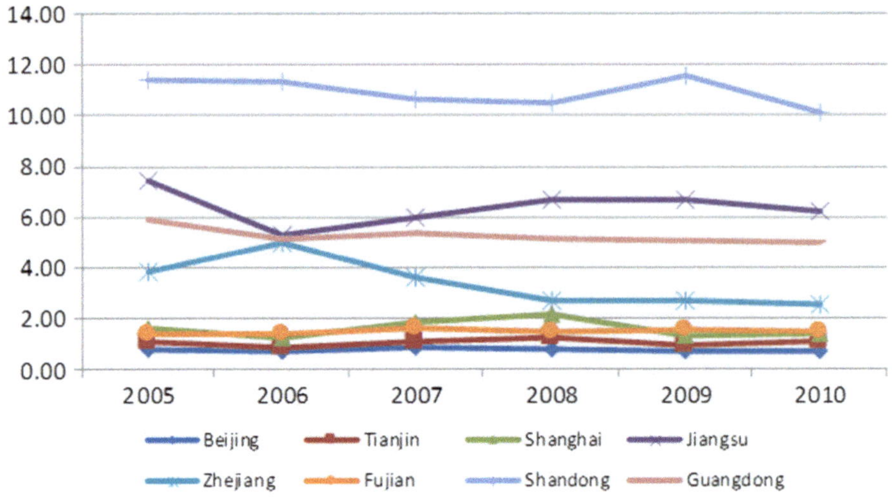


**Fig. 7.7** Changes to the market share of product Type IX in the developed eastern region

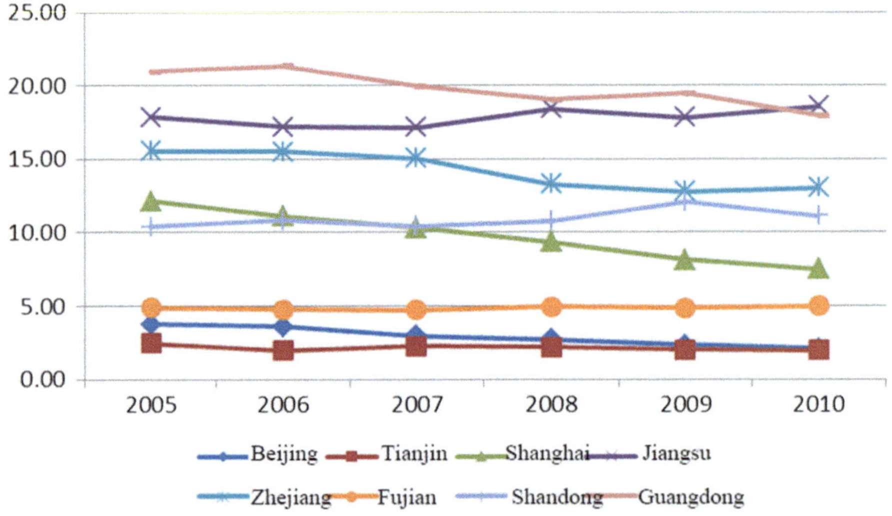


**Fig. 7.8** Changes to the market share of product Type I in the developed eastern region

show upward trends, the overall trend is declining. This downward trend is a signal that China's flying geese model of industrial upgrade is entering the second stage.

Another perspective corroborates this signal that China's flying geese model of industrial upgrade has entered the second stage. In using the flying geese model to analyse the evolution of industrial structure, Ozawa pointed out the changing trend in Japan's industrial structure: from labour-intensive towards economy of scale, from resource-intensive towards undifferentiated industry, then towards a

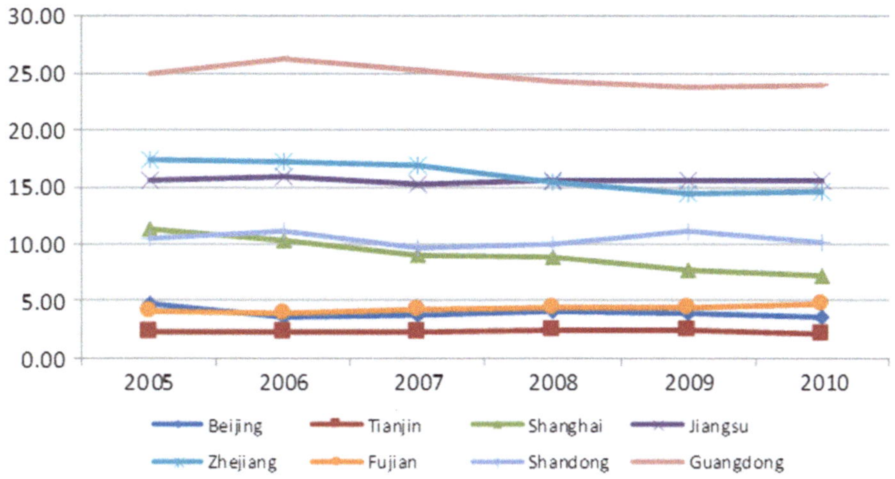


**Fig. 7.9** Changes to the market share of product Type II in the developed eastern region

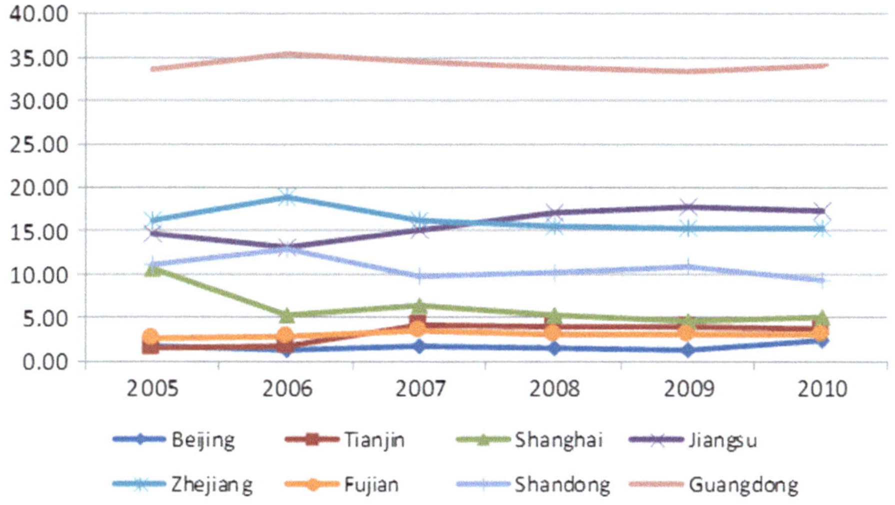


**Fig. 7.10** Changes to the market share of product Type III in the developed eastern region

differentiated Smithian industries such as the automotive industry, further on towards upgrade through Schumpeterian innovation industries, and lastly towards network-oriented industries. The classic industries in the first stage are textile and clothing, steel and the chemical industries in the second stage, the automotive industry in third stage, the electronics industry in the fourth stage, and the information processing and transmission industry in the fifth stage (Ozawa 2005). In terms of industrial development, China has begun the transition from the labour- and resource-intensive stage to a stage driven by innovation, which means going

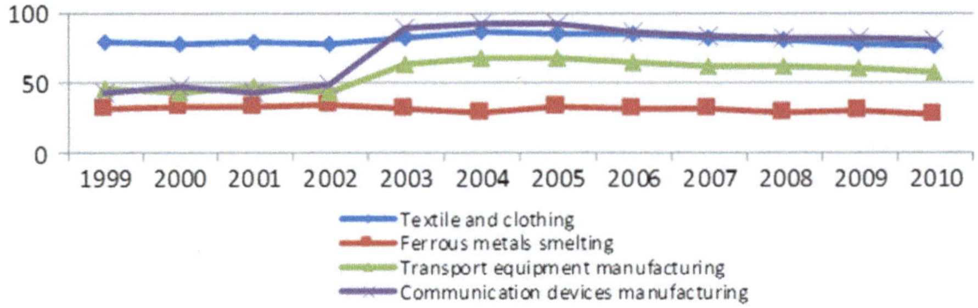


**Fig. 7.11** Changes to the market share of typical industries in the developed eastern region

into the third and fourth stages. Figure 7.11 lists the changing market share of typical industries at these two stages in the eastern region, including Beijing, Shanghai, Tianjin, Jiangsu, Zhejiang, Fujian and Shandong. It shows that in the more developed eastern region, the market share of these industries is declining during these two stages. The signal from this evolving trend is that within China the flying geese model of industrial upgrade is already at the second stage. If this is allowed to go further, then ultimately, a hollowing-out will appear in the developed regions that induce this flying geese model. This in turn will affect the momentum of the geese heading to other regions to transfer the industries, thus hindering the technology transfer from more developed regions to less developed regions and widening the technology gap between the regions.

## 7.3 Risks in the Flying Geese Model of Industrial Upgrade

A country faces different problems at different development stages, maybe falling into the poverty trap or the middle income trap. Economists differ in their opinions as to why these traps appear. According to Lin Yifu, the proponent of new structural economics, these problems can be attributed to how comparative advantage is harnessed. Lin Yifu et al. began in the 1990s to analyse and evaluate the reform in China and its course of development under the theory of comparative advantage. They divided the economic development strategies into two major types: to abide by comparative advantage or to run contrary to comparative advantage. They believe that by following the comparative advantage strategy developing countries can achieve faster economic growth and converge with developed countries sooner (Lin et al. 1994, 1996). Even though many support the idea of following the comparative advantage strategy, there has been no lack of critics either. Professor Gao Hongye argued in 1982 that to undertake production as stipulated by relatively advantageous conditions based on existing ‘naturally endowed’ resources will limit one’s production in the long term to technologically primitive products, and be unable to explore and mobilise one’s own potential, which leaves one always lagging behind (1982). From then on, literature that is critical of the strategy of comparative advantage sums this up as a comparative benefits trap (Hong 1997), or a comparative advantage trap (Xu 2003). Within China, this kind of literature is somewhat lacking in systematic analysis compared with the literature that is supportive of comparative advantage, but the idea proposed has been studied rigorously in Western literature (Matsuyam 1992). Lin Yifu et al. believe that the comparative advantage development strategy is not only compatible at a national level but also at a regional level (Lin and Liu 2003). We can also find critics who question this comparative advantage development strategy at a regional level (Shao and Qi 2008). As a post-development theory, the flying geese model of industrial upgrade has comparative advantage as its basis. Then can a country avoid the comparative advantage trap when the flying geese model occurs within its boundary?

1. **An evolution of a region's comparative advantage**

We can calculate the proportion of product types with comparative advantage in the various regions according to indices for the connectedness and the technology content of the products. Products with the highest ratio in the region will determine under which category the region will fall. A region falling into the comparative advantage trap means that it has comparative advantage in the products with lower technology level and finds it difficult to upgrade to one with comparative advantage for producing high-technology products. It can also mean that as a region having an advantage for producing of low-connectedness products, it finds it difficult to upgrade to one with comparative advantage for producing closely connected products. It can also be both of these. Tables 7.5 and 7.6 list the proportion of product types for different provinces over two periods. During 1999–2004 three provinces (cities) belonged to the high technology-high connectedness category, one belonged to the medium technology-medium connectedness category, 16 belonged to the low technology-low connectedness category, five provinces belonged to the low technology-medium connectedness category, and five provinces belonged to the medium technology-high connectedness category. Jiangxi can be included in the low connectedness category, and also the low technology-low connectedness category (see Table 7.5). During 2005–2010, across the country regions, those belonged to the high technology-high connectedness category include Beijing, Tianjin, Shanghai, Jaingsu, Guangdong and Fujian; 17 provinces (cities) belonged to the low technology-low connectedness category, 17 belonged to the low technology-low connectedness category, five belonged to the low technology-medium connectedness category, and three belonged to the medium technology-high connectedness category (see Table 7.6).

Comparing the regional comparative advantage in 2005–2010 to that in 1999–2004, we find that Beijing moved from the medium technology-medium connectedness category to the high technology-high connectedness category; Tianjin, Jiangsu and Zhejiang moved from the medium technology-high connectedness category to high technology-high connectedness category. Among those regions

**Table 7.5** Categories of regional comparative advantage (1999–2004)

| | High technology high connectedness | Medium technology medium connectedness | Low technology low connectedness | High technology medium connectedness | High technology low connectedness | Medium technology high connectedness | Medium technology low connectedness | Low technology high connectedness | Low technology medium connectedness |
|---|---|---|---|---|---|---|---|---|---|
| Beijing | 15.1 | 18.6 | 9.9 | 13.1 | 6.4 | 15.8 | 8.4 | 3.4 | 9.5 |
| Tianjin | 18.6 | 13.1 | 9.7 | 10.4 | 4.2 | 19.8 | 6.8 | 3.3 | 14.3 |
| Hebei Province | 6.1 | 14.1 | 17.8 | 4.7 | 2.6 | 18.8 | 7.3 | 10.0 | 18.7 |
| Shanxi Province | 5.0 | 10.3 | 35.3 | 6.0 | 3.0 | 8.6 | 6.5 | 7.8 | 17.6 |
| Inner Mongolia Autonomous Region | 3.5 | 10.0 | 46.3 | 0.9 | 3.8 | 4.7 | 4.7 | 5.3 | 21.1 |
| Liaoning Province | 6.5 | 9.0 | 22.9 | 9.2 | 4.1 | 16.4 | 8.7 | 4.1 | 19.3 |
| Jilin Province | 3.9 | 8.2 | 33.9 | 6.1 | 1.8 | 8.5 | 9.4 | 3.9 | 24.5 |
| Heilongjiang Province | 4.4 | 13.9 | 33.1 | 6.3 | 4.4 | 8.8 | 8.5 | 2.8 | 18.0 |
| Shanghai | 23.1 | 12.0 | 4.2 | 15.1 | 7.5 | 22.1 | 4.2 | 3.7 | 8.3 |
| Jiangsu Province | 17.1 | 11.1 | 6.6 | 10.7 | 6.0 | 21.5 | 7.2 | 8.1 | 11.8 |
| Zhejiang Province | 19.0 | 11.7 | 4.7 | 13.0 | 7.0 | 21.0 | 6.1 | 6.7 | 10.9 |
| Anhui Province | 8.4 | 10.7 | 20.2 | 4.8 | 3.5 | 12.4 | 5.1 | 9.4 | 25.6 |
| Fujian Province | 20.4 | 7.4 | 10.9 | 12.2 | 5.2 | 18.2 | 6.7 | 5.4 | 13.8 |
| Jiangxi Province | 3.9 | 8.5 | 25.1 | 7.0 | 3.2 | 14.0 | 4.8 | 8.5 | 25.1 |
| Shandong Province | 10.3 | 12.0 | 14.1 | 6.7 | 3.4 | 20.0 | 8.5 | 8.9 | 16.2 |
| Henan Province | 6.3 | 12.4 | 22.5 | 2.8 | 2.8 | 16.2 | 4.1 | 10.0 | 22.9 |
| Hubei Province | 7.8 | 8.7 | 19.9 | 4.6 | 3.1 | 16.2 | 5.0 | 8.3 | 26.6 |
| Hunan Province | 6.7 | 8.8 | 25.6 | 2.9 | 1.7 | 15.9 | 6.4 | 7.8 | 24.2 |
| Guangdong Province | 22.9 | 13.0 | 5.6 | 14.6 | 6.8 | 16.0 | 6.7 | 5.9 | 8.5 |
| Guangxi Zhuang Autonomous Region | 4.6 | 5.6 | 30.5 | 2.8 | 2.1 | 12.0 | 4.8 | 10.4 | 27.3 |

(continued)

**Table 7.5** (continued)

| | High technology high connectedness | Medium technology medium connectedness | Low technology low connectedness | High technology medium connectedness | High technology low connectedness | Medium technology high connectedness | Medium technology low connectedness | Low technology high connectedness | Low technology medium connectedness |
|---|---|---|---|---|---|---|---|---|---|
| Hainan Province | 9.5 | 12.4 | 24.4 | 2.6 | 2.6 | 15.5 | 7.2 | 4.3 | 21.8 |
| Chongqing | 4.2 | 12.3 | 22.2 | 5.4 | 1.7 | 12.5 | 6.4 | 6.9 | 28.5 |
| Sichuan Province | 6.3 | 13.5 | 28.0 | 2.9 | 1.7 | 11.2 | 7.4 | 7.7 | 21.4 |
| Guizhou Province | 4.1 | 9.7 | 41.2 | 2.4 | 2.4 | 5.6 | 3.5 | 2.9 | 28.5 |
| Yunnan Province | 2.7 | 8.1 | 49.4 | 4.2 | 0.6 | 3.0 | 3.3 | 3.0 | 26.0 |
| Tibet Autonomous Region | 4.8 | 2.7 | 41.5 | 6.8 | 0.0 | 7.5 | 10.9 | 4.1 | 22.4 |
| Shaanxi Province | 5.3 | 11.9 | 24.7 | 4.3 | 6.0 | 10.5 | 7.0 | 7.6 | 22.8 |
| Gansu Province | 2.1 | 15.0 | 33.7 | 7.4 | 2.9 | 10.7 | 3.8 | 5.2 | 19.5 |
| Qinghai Province | 2.8 | 4.6 | 55.8 | 2.8 | 2.3 | 8.3 | 4.6 | 1.4 | 18.0 |
| Ningxia Hui Autonomous Region | 2.9 | 5.0 | 34.8 | 3.9 | 3.2 | 7.2 | 6.8 | 5.4 | 31.2 |
| Xinjiang Uighur Autonomous Region | 3.8 | 12.1 | 40.2 | 1.1 | 3.8 | 5.3 | 10.2 | 3.0 | 20.8 |

**>Table 7.6** Classification by region (2005–2010)

| | High technology high connectedness | Medium technology medium connectedness | Low technology low connectedness | High technology medium connectedness | High technology low connectedness | Medium technology high connectedness | Medium technology low connectedness | Low technology high connectedness | Low technology medium connectedness |
|---|---|---|---|---|---|---|---|---|---|
| Beijing | 19.3 | 15.3 | 10.5 | 18.0 | 3.3 | 15.3 | 6.2 | 1.8 | 10.2 |
| Tianjin | 18.9 | 12.2 | 11.1 | 14.8 | 9.3 | 16.3 | 8.2 | 1.3 | 7.9 |
| Hebei Province | 6.3 | 15.2 | 22.8 | 6.8 | 1.6 | 15.9 | 4.8 | 11.5 | 15.2 |
| Shanxi Province | 5.3 | 7.7 | 53.1 | 2.8 | 0.0 | 3.6 | 5.4 | 3.3 | 18.9 |
| Inner Mongolia Autonomous Region | 1.5 | 9.7 | 43.9 | 1.6 | 0.2 | 5.0 | 8.2 | 5.5 | 24.3 |
| Liaoning Province | 14.9 | 16.3 | 16.8 | 6.3 | 1.4 | 20.0 | 5.3 | 3.5 | 15.5 |
| Jilin Province | 6.2 | 12.6 | 27.4 | 3.2 | 0.5 | 10.3 | 7.5 | 5.8 | 26.6 |
| Heilongjiang Province | 2.7 | 15.5 | 30.8 | 2.9 | 1.1 | 10.8 | 7.6 | 0.9 | 27.7 |
| Shanghai | 28.1 | 11.6 | 2.9 | 18.7 | 8.0 | 20.9 | 3.8 | 1.5 | 4.6 |
| Jiangsu Province | 23.9 | 12.1 | 4.4 | 13.0 | 7.1 | 22.2 | 5.7 | 5.7 | 5.9 |
| Zhejiang Province | 23.5 | 11.3 | 3.2 | 14.2 | 10.6 | 21.4 | 3.6 | 6.3 | 5.8 |
| Anhui Province | 8.5 | 14.0 | 18.6 | 4.2 | 1.9 | 18.3 | 3.0 | 9.6 | 21.9 |
| Fujian Province | 21.9 | 9.3 | 8.2 | 13.8 | 4.3 | 19.3 | 2.2 | 7.2 | 13.9 |
| Jiangxi Province | 8.5 | 12.4 | 18.2 | 3.7 | 1.2 | 15.9 | 4.7 | 12.1 | 23.2 |
| Shandong Province | 11.3 | 11.3 | 14.0 | 6.4 | 3.4 | 21.0 | 7.9 | 7.9 | 16.7 |
| Henan Province | 6.9 | 12.8 | 22.5 | 3.6 | 0.3 | 16.5 | 6.9 | 10.4 | 20.1 |
| Hubei Province | 7.1 | 12.2 | 19.7 | 4.8 | 2.0 | 17.2 | 5.9 | 10.1 | 21.2 |
| Hunan Province | 8.0 | 11.0 | 22.0 | 5.2 | 0.8 | 16.6 | 1.3 | 12.0 | 23.0 |
| Guangdong Province | 24.8 | 7.9 | 4.1 | 18.7 | 14.3 | 18.2 | 3.4 | 4.4 | 4.1 |
| Guangxi Zhuang Autonomous Region | 4.8 | 10.1 | 29.6 | 1.9 | 1.7 | 11.6 | 3.3 | 11.8 | 25.3 |
| Hainan Province | 4.9 | 14.4 | 28.6 | 4.1 | 1.9 | 10.8 | 5.8 | 3.1 | 26.4 |

(continued)

**Table 7.6** (continued)

| | High technology high connectedness | Medium technology medium connectedness | Low technology low connectedness | High technology medium connectedness | High technology low connectedness | Medium technology high connectedness | Medium technology low connectedness | Low technology high connectedness | Low technology medium connectedness |
|---|---|---|---|---|---|---|---|---|---|
| Chongqing | 8.5 | 11.6 | 22.9 | 6.8 | 0.2 | 15.4 | 6.4 | 7.0 | 21.3 |
| Sichuan Province | 9.4 | 10.5 | 20.6 | 2.9 | 1.5 | 17.7 | 6.0 | 8.4 | 22.9 |
| Guizhou Province | 0.6 | 9.0 | 60.9 | 0.9 | 3.1 | 4.0 | 1.6 | 0.6 | 19.2 |
| Yunnan Province | 0.0 | 5.1 | 56.4 | 1.8 | 0.0 | 3.4 | 5.8 | 4.8 | 22.6 |
| Tibet Autonomous Region | 0.0 | 0.8 | 48.4 | 1.8 | 0.0 | 6.1 | 6.9 | 6.1 | 29.8 |
| Shaanxi Province | 4.8 | 13.2 | 32.0 | 6.4 | 2.5 | 13.9 | 7.0 | 2.7 | 17.5 |
| Gansu Province | 2.4 | 7.0 | 51.8 | 1.0 | 0.0 | 8.5 | 3.7 | 6.1 | 19.5 |
| Qinghai Province | 0.9 | 11.8 | 58.5 | 0.9 | 0.0 | 4.4 | 4.6 | 1.5 | 17.4 |
| Ningxia Hui Autonomous Region | 1.2 | 7.7 | 52.7 | 3.4 | 0.0 | 10.0 | 5.8 | 5.2 | 14.0 |
| Xinjiang Uighur Autonomous Region | 0.0 | 9.7 | 44.8 | 0.8 | 0.4 | 8.6 | 4.8 | 3.0 | 27.9 |

that in the previous period belonged to the low technology-low connectedness category, Liaoning upgraded to the medium technology-high connectedness category, Jiangxi and Hunan upgraded to the low technology-medium connectedness category, Sichuan upgraded to the low technology-medium connectedness category. There has been no material change to other regions. What's more, regions that were predominantly of low technology-low connectedness have seen this becoming more acute, which means the emergence of a 'comparative advantage trap'.

2. **How are comparative advantage traps formed**

As there are different explanations for the emergence of comparative advantage traps, attributing it to international trade as not entirely competitive (Gao 1982; Wang 2002), the attempt by developed countries to hamper sustainable development in developing countries through technology barriers and international order, creating a comparative advantage trap with their dominance in international trade and discourse (Shao and Liu 2013). But it is difficult for a region within a country to maintain its comparative advantage through such measures. Matsuyama (1992) points out that precisely because of a comparative advantage in the agricultural sector that a greater proportion that country's labour is concentrated in the agricultural sector, and when the increasing returns to scale of 'learn while you work' mentality exists in the industrial sector, that country's relative weakness in the industrial sector will become more acute as time goes on. This explanation is based on assumptions in two sectors and cannot explain the reasons for the emergence of a comparative advantage trap where there are many sectors and many regions. Another explanation put forward in recent years is the theory of product space by Hausmann and R. Jesus Felipe. This theory attributes the comparative advantage trap to the position occupied by the product space in the economy (Hausmann et al. 2007; Felipe et al. 2010). According to this theory, whether a country or a region can successfully transform from the existing comparative advantage to a new one is determined by the capability differential between the two, and if there is a big differential the probability for success will be very low.

According to the theory of product space, in which direction will a region upgrade its industry, or whether it can do so, is dependent to a large degree on whether its existing capability can support industrial upgrade. Figure 7.6 shows capability differentials and the probability for achieving industrial upgrade. The horizontal axis represents 'capability differential'—the smaller the number, the greater the differential. It shows that as the differential increases, the ratio for industrial upgrade will reduce, which means that in upgrading their industries, the regions basically go by their comparative advantage. Table 7.7 lists how capability differentials limit the probability for industrial upgrade, and the proportion of industrial upgrade under different product space conditions. We can easily see that with existing capacity constraint, a region's probability for success is higher if it adopts a strategy to upgrade nearby. From this we can infer that a region gets stuck in a comparative advantage trap because to transform from the existing comparative

**Table 7.7** Capability distance between various products

| | HPR-HPA | HPR-MPA | HPR-LPA | MPR-HPA | MPR-MPA | MPR-LPA | LPR-HPA | LPR-MPA | LPR-LPA |
|---|---|---|---|---|---|---|---|---|---|
| HPR-HPA | 0.42 | | | | | | | | |
| HPR-MPA | 0.37 | 0.33 | | | | | | | |
| HPR-LPA | 0.27 | 0.28 | 0.28 | | | | | | |
| MPR-HPA | 0.35 | 0.17 | 0.19 | 0.28 | | | | | |
| MPR-MPA | 0.27 | 0.23 | 0.15 | 0.28 | 0.24 | | | | |
| MPR-LPA | 0.18 | 0.16 | 0.13 | 0.19 | 0.17 | 0.15 | | | |
| LPR-HPA | 0.27 | 0.19 | 0.13 | 0.33 | 0.26 | 0.18 | 0.44 | | |
| LPR-MPA | 0.20 | 0.15 | 0.08 | 0.28 | 0.25 | 0.17 | 0.36 | 0.34 | |
| LPR-LPA | 0.14 | 0.12 | 0.08 | 0.197 | 0.18 | 0.15 | 0.26 | 0.273 | 0.276 |

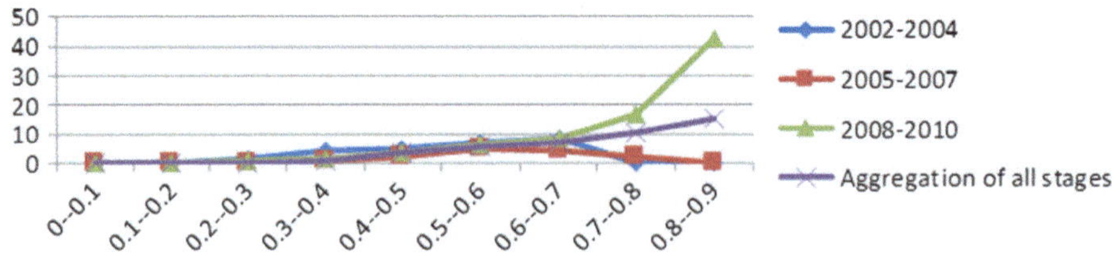


**Fig. 7.12** Probability for industrial upgrade under different capability distances

advantage to another new comparative advantage, it needs to jump over a greater capability distance. Table 7.7 lists the different capability distances between different product types. It shows that two categories of regions will encounter difficulties in transforming comparative advantage. One is those with products in the low technology-low connectedness category because these products are at a great capability distance from others, apart from products within its own sector and of low technology-low connectedness or low technology-high connectedness. The other type, products of medium technology-low connectedness, is also at a great capability distance from other product types, so that it is more difficult for a region to transform its comparative advantage if it is dominated by this type of products (Fig. 7.12).

## 7.4 Conclusion and Policy Recommendation

A country's economic development can be regarded as continuously making full use of its comparative advantage and a continuous process of transformation. A country at a high level of economic development, due to its being at the forefront of science and technology, possesses comparative advantage in its capital- and technology-intensive industries. Countries at a lower level of economic development have abundant low cost labour and so they possess comparative advantage in labour-intensive industries. For countries at a middle income level, as they are not comparatively advantaged in either of the above; they encounter a vacuum in comparative advantage and so easily fall into the 'middle income trap' (Cai 2011). Can a large country with uneven development avoid a 'comparative advantage vacuum' by a reconfiguration of space in its industries? Prior to the international financial crisis, China's economic growth is characterised by its being driven by the high speed economic growth in the coastal region. Following the international financial crisis, the economic growth in China's central and western regions picked up speed. At the moment developed regions are transferring their uncompetitive industries to the central and western regions. With the emergence of this kind of flying geese model (Cai et al. 2009), China effectively avoided the impact from the international financial crisis. But can this effect be sustained and thus resolve the 'middle income trap' problem for China?

Postulated by Japanese scholars, the flying geese model is a well-known catch-up strategy adopted by countries in post-development. The early model has three stages that industries in an open economy in post-development will experience: import—import substitution—export. However, Kaname Akamatsu did not explain adequately how countries in post-development successfully implement import substitution. His analysis shows that countries in post-development are driven by the next wave of countries in post-development to transfer their industries, but he did not explain why there is such an impetus. The modern version of the flying geese model puts emphasis on multi-national corporations and outward investment. In transferring industries that have lost comparative advantage, the direction of the flying geese heads towards economies at the next lower level that are relatively less developed. Having been provided with capital goods and technology, these economies gain competitive advantage in these industries. At the same time, the leading geese gain by increased output in capital goods and exports, as well as increased competitive advantage by reassigning resources in industries that have lost competitive advantage. Therefore, we have a challenge to overcome in the formation of a flying geese model for industrial development in regional economies and in its success: the head of the flying geese must possess sustained creativity in order that it can drive forward the flock of geese.

For industrial transfers between countries the emphasis is on the capability distance between the recipient country and the transferor country, and this factor should not be overlooked either for transfer of industries within the boundaries of a country. However, what is more important is whether the transferor can continue to transform and upgrade its industries, making room and providing impetus for the transition. From a long term perspective, if the advanced eastern region lacks sustained creativity to create new advantages and renewed impetus for transferring industries, then the flying geese model of industrial upgrade cannot be sustained, which also leaves the problem of a 'comparative advantage vacuum' unresolved for countries in middle income. In recent years, the advanced coastal region in east China has given impetus to the economic development of the central and western regions through industrial transfers. However, if the capability and impetus for industrial transfers, and the opportunities provided from these regions continue with the downward trend, then there are major risks involved in adopting the strategy of the flying geese model for industrial upgrade, for harmonising regional development to help China successfully cross over the middle income trap. This issue has yet to attract attention from the Chinese government. In the process of implementing harmonised regional development, the emphasis in China is how to transfer industries from advanced regions to economically less developed regions, but there has been insufficient attention to advanced regions for industrial upgrade and making more room for industries. For example, in the Twelfth Five-Year Plan, the strategy to integrate Beijing, Tianjin and Hebei has been largely interpreted as the transfer of industries out of Beijing to be taken on by Tianjin and in the Hebei region. However, the reality is that a large number of industries have already been transferred from Beijing, with very limited industries remaining that can be transferred. In pushing for further transfers, if no industry with advantage comes forward, the social and economic development of Beijing will be greatly affected.

What is the new direction in industrial upgrade for economically advanced regions? The way to explore this is by selecting industries based on the strategy for import substitution. There is another method, which is to investigate development in the new high-tech industry put forward by many countries after the international financial crisis. Following the international financial crisis, the question of re-industrialisation was frequently raised in the USA and Europe—how to achieve re-industrialisation? Since 2010, re-industrialisation in developed countries has been generally called a new industrial revolution, and while some call it the third industrial revolution, others call it the fourth industrial revolution. The articles on the third industrial revolution British magazine *the Economist* in 2010 attracted much attention in China. In 2012 Germany's Industry 4.0 Working Group released a special report on Industry 4.0. The report calls Industry 4.0 the fourth industrial revolution. The first industrial revolution began with the invention and application of hydro- and steam-powered engines. The second industrial revolution began with the invention and application of electricity in driving standardised production from the early 20th century. The third industrial revolution is the invention of information technology which gave impetus to industrial automation beginning in the 1970s. From now on the fourth industrial revolution is upon us. In June 2013 the theme at an international trade fair, the Hanover Fair in Germany, was on integrated industry, with a presentation of the template for Industry 4.0. The trade fair in 2014 was simply on Industry 4.0. Following Industry 4.0, the research in China on the key direction for revolutionising future industries was being obscured, with the tendency to use concepts such as new industrial revolution and new industry revolution in place of the third revolution or the fourth revolution. Although this tendency prevents new concepts continually appearing and getting confused with old concepts, China may have lost the focus for resolving key problems which may possibly emerge from this new industrial revolution.

Germany's industry is very advanced in manufacturing, and German Industry 4.0 is based on 'Germany's High-tech Strategy' and 'Germany's High-tech Strategy 2020'. Germany is a key exporter of machinery. The country's enterprises, including small and medium enterprises, are very competitive. However, with deepening globalisation, they face ever greater challenges. These come not only from Asia, but also from the USA. The ultimate goal of Germany's Industry 4.0 is to raise industrial competitiveness. In order to advance the fourth industrial revolution, Germany has put forward a series of policy measures, with other nations also taking actions and initiating all kinds of scientific programmes. Economically advanced regions in China are closer to the international forefront in technology. They should seize the opportunities from the fourth industrial revolution, making full use of existing strengths to make room for the development of new industries.

1. Place emphasis on existing strengths. After the international financial crisis, some developed countries attempt to carry out planning and assessment on the future of science and technology and industrial development.

This kind of planning and assessment will of course explore patterns of science and technology and industrial development. However, one of the purposes for their timing is also to attempt to influence the process for development in technology and industry, coordinating and consolidating various resources into processes more conducive for national development. The concerns of this new round of industrial revolution are far and wide, and for countries to become dominant in new industries they have to make the most of their own strengths. As the new industrial revolution was taking off, instead of endorsing plans by other countries, Germany put forward Industry 4.0, with the aim to make the most of their traditional strengths. These are: as leader in the mechanical installations market; as key supplier of capabilities in global information technology; as global leader for embedded systems and innovation in automation engineering; having a highly skilled and proactive labour force; close cooperation between supplier and user; having excellent research and training institutions. China's position in this new round of industrial revolution is also to make the best of her existing strengths. Following a thorough analysis and with a firm grasp on the pattern and characteristics of the new industrial revolution, China should formulate a strategic plan, setting out her role for the fourth industrial revolution, and make a strong presence for a place in the dominant discourse concerning the development of new technology and the industrial revolution.

2. Inter-disciplinary working group or platform to implement 'Industry 4.0' Germany's three major trade associations

The Federal Association for Information Technology, Telecommunications and New Media (BITKOM), the German Engineering Federation (VDMA), and the German Electrical and Electronic Manufacturers' Association (ZVEI)—cooperated and established the 'Industry Platform 4.0' which was launched in April 2013, with the aim to attract and coordinate all the resources associated with this revolution. Given that the concerns of the fourth industrial revolution are far and wide, with the requirement for, and the consolidation of many resources and technologies, China should also set up a similar organisation or platform, encompassing scientists and experts in natural sciences, engineering technology, social sciences, businesses, etc., for in-depth research concerning scientific patterns, special technology, and the socio-economic impact, as well as to follow closely on its progress globally for timely strategic response by China. There is a need to strengthen the manufacturing capability for mechanical equipment, and close cooperation between the ICT and equipment manufacturing sectors and factories are needed in order to work towards the fourth industrial revolution.

3. Changes and the notion of cooperation between the central and western regions In regional cooperation, the central and western regions should not be treated solely as recipients but to become partners in regional cooperation for creating new strengths. The flying geese formation is a model not only for transferring

industries from advanced regions to relatively less developed regions, but, with these regions cooperating together, it is also a model for enhancing the capability of advanced regions to stride ahead towards the forefront of industries.

## Bibliography

Akamatsu, K. 1962. A historical pattern of economic growth in developing countries. *Journal of Developing Economies* 1 (1): 3.

Cai, Fang. 2011. Middle income trap—Theory, experience and relevance. *Economic Perspectives* (12).

Cai, Fang. 2013. Is the flying geese model of economy possible in China? *People's Tribune* (10) (Part 1).

Cai, Fang, Dewen Wang, and Yue Qu. 2009. Analysing the flying geese model in China's industrial upgrading. *Economic Research Journal* 44 (9): 1.

Felipe, Terutomo, Utsav Kumar, and Arnelyn Abdon. 2010. How rich countries became rich and why poor countries remain poor: It's the economic structure. Duh! Working Paper No. 644.

Gao, Hongye. 1982. The comparative cost theory should not constitute the basis of China's strategy in developing foreign trade. *Inquiry into Economic Issues* (4).

Hausmann, R., J. Huwang, and D. Rodrik. 2007. What your export matters. *Journal of Economic Growth* 12 (1): 25.

Hidalgo, C., B. Klinger, A.L. Barabasi, and R. Hausmann. 2007. The product space conditions the development of nations. *Science* 317 (7): 482.

Hong, Yinxing. 1997. From comparative advantage to competitive advantage—Discussing the weakness of the comparative benefits theory in international trade. *Economic Research Journal* (6).

Kasahara, S. 2004a. The flying geese paradigm: A critical study of its application to East Asian regional development. In *United Nations conference on trade and development*. Discussion Paper.

Kasahara, Shigehisa. 2004b. The flying geese paradigm: A critical study of its application to East Asian regional development. http://mpra.ub.uni-muenchen.de/21881/,2004.

Kojima, Kiyoshi. 1960. Capital accumulation and the course of industrialisation, with special reference to Japan. *The Economic Journal* 70 (280): 757.

Lin, Yifu, and Peilin Liu. 2003. China's economic development strategy and regional differences in pay. *Economic Research Journal* (3).

Lin, Yifu, Fang Cai and Zhou Li. 1994. Reflecting on the catch-up strategy. *Strategy and Management* (6).

Lin, Yifu, Fang Cai and Zhou Li. 1996. Resources upgrade, misunderstanding the catch-up strategy. *Strategy and Management* (1).

Matsuyam, K. 1992. Agricultural productivity, comparative advantage and economic growth. *Journal of Economic Theory* 58: 317–3341.

Ono, Susumu. 2008. Japan's multifaceted model of economic development (MMED): The East Asian development model (part 2). *Japan Research* 18 (1): 213.

Ozawa, Terutomo. 2005. Asia's L = labour-driven economic development, flying-geese style: An unprecedented opportunity for the poor to rise. APEC Study Centre, Colorado state University, Discussion paper, No. 40.

Qu, Yue, Fang Cai, and Xiaobo Zhang. 2013. Has the 'flying geese model' arrived?—An analysis of Chinese manufacturing 1998–2008. *Economics Quarterly* (4).

Ruan, Jianqing, and Xiaobo Zhang. 2010. Do geese migrate domestically? Evidence from the Chinese textile and apparel industry. IFPRI Discussion Paper 01040 (10).

Shao, Shuai, and Zhongying Qi. 2008. Energy development and economic growth in the western region: An empirical analysis on the resource curse hypothesis. *Economic Research Journal* (4).
Shao, Bang, and Xiaoyang Liu. 2013. The comparative advantage trap: its nature, causes, and how to overcome. *Contemporary Economy and Management* (12).
Wang, Diankai. 2002. The comparative advantage trap and choosing China's trade strategy. *Economic Review* (2).
Xu, Yuankang. 2003. A study in comparative advantage as an appropriate strategy for China's economic development. (5).
Zhang, Qizi, et al. 2014. *Transforming Industrial Competitiveness*. Beijing: Social Sciences Academic Press.

# Chapter 8
# Implications of Increased Regional Economic Complexity

**Qizi Zhang, Yejun Wu and Lei Wang**

Within the Solow-Swan neo-classical framework for growth, economic growth is driven by physical capital, raw materials, labour and technology. It disregards the role of knowledge in the product itself. In recent years, inspired by Kaldor (1967)'s theory of structural transformation and Romer (1986)'s new growth theory with endogenous knowledge, scholars studying international trade and economic growth began to pay attention to how knowledge and capability impact on the economic growth of a nation or region. Theories on product space and the evolution of comparative advantage put forward by Hausmann and Rodrik (2003) emphasise that products are output by individuals and groups using productive knowledge. The product itself reflects that the economic agent possesses this kind of production capacity. For a country or a region, economic development and structural transformation means that firms are discovering the products they are good at producing, and the process in learning and accumulating the capability for producing those products.

Hidalgo et al. (2007, 2009) then took this to the national level, and emphasised for the first time the significance of economic complexity. They believe that economic complexity comes from the combined efforts by countries and regions through production. It reflects the knowledge belonging to and consolidated by the country or region. Economic complexity is closely related to the many and varied kinds of production knowledge embedded in the products that are produced. Countries cannot just produce what they need in terms of products and services, but what they are capable of producing. Therefore, the level of complexity in an economy is determined by the knowledge mix they possess and their ability to consolidate the knowledge. In highly complex economies, they integrate the people and organisations that are needed in the production of complex products—design, R&D, marketing, finance, technology, human resources management, capital and

Q. Zhang (✉) · Y. Wu · L. Wang
Chinese Academy of Social Sciences, Beijing, China
e-mail: zhangqizi65@126.com



Q. Zhang (ed.), *Transforming Economic Growth and China's Industrial Upgrading*,
Research Series on the Chinese Dream and China's Development Path,
https://doi.org/10.1007/978-981-13-0962-5_8

trading regulations etc.—into interactive networks. The large volumes of knowledge possessed by these people and groups are consolidated, for use in producing many diverse and complex knowledge-intensive products. Economies at a low level of complexity lack the capability to gather or consolidate this kind of knowledge, and therefore can only produce very few and simple products, which are not of the same level of complexity.

Based on the network theory of knowledge and capabilities, Hidalgo et al. (2007, 2009) believe that economic development is essentially a process of self-discovery in learning how to produce and export more complex products. Economic complexity reflects a country's capability of diverse production, and in particular its capability to produce more complex products. An economy's performance is closely related to the complexity in its overall structure in manufacturing. As a trial, they first used multi-national cross-sectional data and carried out an empirical analysis of the relationship between a country's economic complexity and performance, and pointed out that the difference in economic complexity between countries is the main reason for the difference in economic performance. However, there is currently no academic research on the relationship between regional economic complexity and economic growth and the mechanisms that influence these within the boundaries of a nation.

In particular for a geographically extensive country like China undergoing change, economic development is very uneven, and regional differences are widening all the time. How to narrow regional differences is a major challenge for China in maintaining sound, sustainable growth. To narrow the widening regional differences, it is necessary to find the causes. The majority of scholars studying regional economic growth believe that the root causes are differences in resource endowments, the geographical location of the economy, foreign direct investment, infrastructure, industry clusters, policy bias, and trade openness. Most of these studies start from a neo-classical position in explaining external influences on regional economic growth. However, they cannot explain the internal mechanisms for improving technology and knowledge in the production function. Neither can they explain the role that a local agent has in regional economic development. They cannot find the mechanism that can enhance regional economic sophistication and regional economic growth.

Clearly, according to the theory on the evolution of knowledge- and capability-based comparative advantage, local capacity and its capability to consolidate knowledge are particularly important for regional economic development. Thus, the purpose of this chapter is to validate how the theory on the evolution of comparative advantage can explain the difference in regional economic performance in China. Working within the framework of this theory that emphasises capability and knowledge, we will analyse the relationship between economic complexity and economic growth in China. On this basis, we will analyse the mechanism that economic complexity drives economic growth, as well as factors that influence regional economic complexity.

## 8.1 Theoretical Analysis and Hypothesis

How can we expound on the internal mechanism between regional economic complexity and economic growth in China? This chapter will attempt to elaborate on this within the growth paradigm. According to the convergence hypothesis in the neo-classical school on growth, economies with similar technology and preferences will tend towards the same stable equilibrium point. The root cause for the differences in economic growth between nations and regions is that they have different capital-labour ratio. But based on diminishing marginal returns, which is the core of neo-classical production function, underdeveloped countries and regions may quicken their growth in order to catch up, so that ultimately economic growth in both developed and underdeveloped regions will converge. This implies that there will be no difference in their economic performance or in their positions, and that ultimately these different economies will converge at the same steady state, in other words, achieving absolute convergence. However, whether looking at it worldwide or within China, the gap is widening between developed and underdeveloped countries and regions. For example, at constant 2000 prices in US dollars and adjusted purchasing power parity, we can see in the worldwide income distribution that the per capita income in the top developed countries is actually more than 30 times that in the least developed countries. In China, since the reform and opening up, the gap in economic development between regions is also widening; the convergence predicted by the neo-classical growth model has not materialised.

So exactly what has caused the difference in economic performance between the regions in China? According to the conditional convergence hypothesis espoused by Barro et al. (2004), the differences are due to regional heterogeneity or some unique characteristics closely related to the process of growth. It means that with these unique regional characteristics, divergence and differentiation occur during economic growth, and where convergence occurs, it is conditional. Going forth from this assumption of conditional convergence, economists began to investigate the reasons for the different economic performance and regional differences in China. Within the framework of growth accounting, factors that have attracted the attention of scholars on the progress of Chinese regional markets include: human capital, policies, protectionism at a local level, economic structure, foreign direct investment, geographical location, trade openness, institutional structure, technology spillover, and history. For example, Fan et al. (2010) devised an index on market-oriented development to measure 31 Chinese provinces, municipalities and autonomous regions, and carried out an analysis on market-oriented development and its impact on China's regional economic growth. The study by Fleisher et al. (2010) found that the effect of human capital spillover was very acute prior to 1994, so more regional investment in human resources can narrow the gap between the regions, and can be effective for promoting regional economic growth. Prior to

1994, foreign direct investment had an even greater impact on regional economic growth but has since diminished or is statistically insignificant. Chen and Wu (2005) also found that foreign direct investment has contributed significantly to China's regional economic growth. Peng (2005) pointed out that regional differences in China are mainly due to their different economic structures. The level of contribution to regional economic growth can vary greatly with the economic structure, which in turn causes regional differences. Based on the theoretical analyses carried out in 1994 and 1999 (Lin et al. 1994, 1999, 2003) point out further that development strategy is a key factor in explaining China's regional economic growth and income distribution.

Without doubt, research carried by economists has been thorough on factors that determine regional economic growth in China. However, there has not been one unified theoretical framework and logic that can analyse causes that influence Chinese regional growth, explain the different characteristics emerging thereof, and the impact of heterogeneity on regional economic growth. On the basis of the work by Hausmann et al. (2003), Hidalgo et al. (2007), Hausmann and Klinger (2007), as well as Hidalgo et al. (2009) constructed a unified theoretical framework for explaining factors that motivate economic development, i.e. product space structure and the theory on the evolution of comparative advantage. Their theory is based on knowledge and capability, integrating methodologies from the modern comparative advantage theory, new theory of economic growth, evolutionary economics, and the social network theory. The fundamental view of this theory is that a product is a knowledge medium embodying the capability of an economy to consolidate input factors and to integrate production knowledge in human capital, marketing management, natural resources, raw materials, process flow, R&D, etc. They use product sophistication and economic complexity to measure the technology content contained within a product and the various production capabilities in an economy. The more capabilities there are in an economy, the better able it is to consolidate production knowledge. The higher the technology content of its product also means a higher degree of economic complexity. The degree of economic complexity varies with different economies, and it indicates the difference in economic performance. Economies with a high degree of complexity develop soundly, whereas economies with a low degree of complexity perform poorly. Economic complexity is a comprehensive index constructed from product or output mix; it measures factors that influence economic growth. It comprehensively reflects a series of tangible and intangible factors including investment in human capital, foreign direct investment, policy and institutional differences, economic structure, marketing management, natural resources, factor endowments, technology spillovers, value chains etc., as well as the mechanisms for applying such knowledge in production.

Hence, based on the theories of product space and the evolution of comparative advantage and our initial analysis above, we can infer that economic complexity makes a positive contribution to economic growth. However, since the reform and opening up, there are vast differences in Chinese regional economic structures, policy and institutions, geographical location of economies, climatic conditions, the adoption of market principles, progress in urbanisation, historical starting point for economic development, etc. The degree of openness as well as the adoption of market principles vary from region to region. Compared with the western region, the economy is more developed in the central and eastern regions. We can infer that the economic complexity in the eastern and central regions contributes more to economic growth than that in the western region.

**The basic hypothesis**: Increasing economic complexity is conducive to China's economic growth, but this positive impact varies by region.

## 8.2 The Empirical Model and Approach

1. **The empirical model**

All of existing empirical studies conduct econometric analyses on the relationship between economic complexity and growth in an economy with multinational cross sectional data. However, for the purpose of this study and in terms of data sample, cross sectional data sample at provincial level will not yield meaningful calculations and empirical findings. In order to increase the data sample, this study has constructed a balanced panel dataset that covers 31 provinces (municipalities, autonomous regions) during 2002–2007, which can adequately depict the dynamic influence of regional economic complexity on economic growth at different times. In order to test this influence, we need to establish a function for economic growth factors. Wei (2002) has found that in the eastern region foreign direct investment had a significant influence on economic growth, but the influence in the undeveloped western region is not obvious. Ninety percent of the difference in economic performance between the eastern and western regions can be attributed to foreign direct investment. Cai et al. (2002) have found that distortion in the labour market widened the regional difference, as barriers to the movement of labour between regions greatly impeded economic growth in China. Lu et al. (2009) have found that regional market integration and its progress had a significant influence on the difference in regional economic performance, but protectionism at a local level and market segmentation are conducive to growth in the local economy. Zhang et al. (2011) used provincial level panel data from China during 1994–2007 to analyse the relationship among local government investment behaviour, monopoly by local administration and economic growth, and found that at the time monopoly by local administration had an inverted U effect, and in most cases monopoly by the provincial administration promoted economic growth. Wang (2002) points out that the extent and progress in urbanisation at the local level also serves as a positive momentum for regional economic growth. Bao (2008) points out that trade openness plays strong role in regional economic growth in China, whereas human capital makes a negative contribution. Huang et al. (2010) have come to a similar conclusion. Using sample data from 222 prefecture-level cities in China during

2001–2008, Shao et al. (2011) carried out an empirical examination of the relationship between export specialisation and regional economic growth, and found that concentration in exports clearly had a positive correlation with economic growth locally. Emurger (2001) used panel data from 24 provincial cities in China during 1985–1998 to examine the effect of transport infrastructure on China's economic growth and found transport infrastructure promotes economic growth in China, with different geographical locations and the conditions for transport infrastructure playing an important role in the process. Chen Liang et al. used panel data from 31 Chinese provinces, municipalities and autonomous regions during 2001–2008 to examine the effect of information infrastructure on China's economic growth and found that information infrastructure promoted economic growth in China, but its contribution varies by region and was at odds with the economic growth. Xu (2010) also carried out an empirical study on how progress in information infrastructure contributes to local economic growth, and found that it had a positive impact, and that uneven development in information infrastructure directly affects socio-economic development and was an important reason for regional differences. Shao et al. (2010) found that although having an abundance of natural resources in itself was conducive to economic growth, the reliance on the resource industry can clearly constrain regional economic growth. This is a clear reminder of the resource curse.

Here, we use the definition of economic complexity as defined by Hidalgo et al. (2007, 2009); we have taken account of research literature on economic growth, and have fully considered the possible omitted variables, multicollinearity and endogenous variables. On this basis, we brought together the structure and characteristics of the sample data, and designed the econometric model for this study as follows:

$$\ln rpgdp_{it} = \alpha + \beta eci_{it} + \partial X_{it} + \varsigma_i + \varsigma_t + \varepsilon_{it} \tag{8.1}$$

In the calculations in model (8.1), i and t represent province (municipality, autonomous region) and year respectively. ln $rpgdp_{it}$ represents the logarithm for the actual GDP per capita in *t* year *i* region. $eci_{it}$ represents the regional economic complexity index. $X_{it}$ represents a series of other vector variables and controlled variables that explain economic growth. we also use $\varsigma$ to control the heterogeneity unobserved by businesses in year and provincial (municipality, autonomous region) characteristics. $\varepsilon_{it}$ represents random errors. In order to accurately reflect the relationship between economic complexity and economic growth and to avoid endogenous problems caused by omitted variables, we made controlled variables $X_{it}$ include foreign direct investment, institutions, trade openness, degree of export specialisation, the state of infrastructures, endowed natural resources, human capital, urbanisation, and the geographical location of the economy, according to results from existing studies.

2. **Calculating key indicators, data and descriptive statistics**

(1) Key economic indicators—measuring regional economic complexity

In view of the many shortcomings of using export data and income information to calculating product sophistication and economic complexity, such as the methodology adopted by Hidalgo et al. (2009), this study for the first time measured product sophistication in China's regional production mix and economic complexity from an output perspective based on data of 827 four-digit code industries from the 'China Industrial Enterprise Database' and through aggregating data at the enterprise and sector levels. With the controlled size of the regional economy and product market, the location quotient (LQ) is the statistical indicator reflecting whether a certain product produced in a certain region in China has comparative advantage. Essentially it is the indicator for revealed comparative advantage in manufacturing, with its definition and formula also similar to that of the revealed comparative advantage index. Let us first define the LQ for producing a certain product in a region: the value added of this product in a region as a proportion of regional GDP is compared to the value added of this product in the whole country as a share in the country's GDP. The specific formula is as follows:

$$LQ_{c,p,t} = \frac{VAD_{c,p,t} / \sum_p VAD_{c,p,t}}{\sum_c VAD_{c,p,t} / \sum_{c,p} VAD_{c,p,t}}$$

Here, $LQ_{c,p,t}$ represents the LQ in year t and region c for product p. $VAD_{c,p,t}$ represents the value added in year t and region c for product p. The location quotient $\left(LQ_{c,p,t}\right)$ is treated as a network linking a region and the products it produces. On this basis, we calculate the product sophistication and economic complexity in two steps.

Firstly, if $LQ_{c,p,t}$ is greater than or equal to a specified critical value $LQ^*$, then let us set $LQ_{c,p,t} = 1$, if it is smaller than the critical value, then $LQ_{c,p,t} = 0$. According to the theory of knowledge- and capability-based product space by Hidalgo et al. (2009), the assumption made in the comparative advantage theory and the characteristics of LQ, let us have $LQ^* = 1$, then when $LQ_{c,p,t} \geq 1$, it means that relative to other regions in the country, the product produced in year t and region c has revealed comparative advantage. Then that region has the capability needed for producing that product. In order to avoid confusion, it is calculated as $M_{c,p,t} = 1$, otherwise $M_{c,p,t} = 0$. Then, we aggregate the data of products in this region with LQ greater than or equal to 1, and treat the result as the connectedness or degree of the LQ network, represented by $k_{c,t} = \sum_p M_{c,p,t}$. Apart from region c's degree, $k_{c,t}$ also represents this region's production mix diversification level, measured by the number of products with advantage in the region. Similarly, the number of regions in the LQ network that produce certain products with advantage is defined as that product's ubiquity, represented as $k_{p,t} = \sum_c M_{c,p,t}$.

Next, with the reflection method, iterative correction is made to the regional diversity in the network structure and information on product ubiquity. Within the constraints of the country's initial diversification and product ubiquity, and subject to conditional convergence, we have the following two vectors $\vec{k}_{c,t,n}$ and $\vec{k}_{p,t,n}$, with n as the number of iterations. The real reason for using the reflection method is to take full advantage of the information in the network structure to correct each other so as to obtain more accurate indicators that measure regional economic complexity and product complexity.

According to the definition by Hidalgo et al. (2009) on elements in vectors after iteration, $k_{c,t,1}$, after corrected by the product complexity index, represents the average product complexity for that region. The higher this value is, the higher the special capability in that region's productive structure is. And a high value indicates a high degree of regional economic complexity, and vice versa. This means that the average product complexity $k_{c,t,1}$ is a measurement of the overall complexity of that region's productive structure. Take $eci_{it} = k_{c,t,1}$, here i and c are equivalent, representing the same region, t represents time, 1 is the number of iteration.

(2) On data, defining variables and descriptive statistics

The data sources used in this section for econometric analysis mainly come from the 'China Statistical Yearbook', 'China Industrial Enterprise Statistical Database', 'Index of market adoption in China: a report on the relative progress of market adoption by regions in 2009', and from annual special surveys in the national statistical databases which analysed 31 provinces, municipalities and autonomous regions in China. The sample period is 2002–2007[1] i.e. the period since China's accession to the WTO and before the financial crisis, when the Chinese economy was experiencing rapid growth.

The indices frequently used for measuring the variables explained in this section —regional economic growth are mainly GDP, per capita GDP and their growth rates. In this study, we have chosen the actual GDP per capita logarithm (1nrpgdp) as the indicator for economic growth. The regional GDP per capita data is taken from the 'China Statistical Yearbook' for the years 2002–2008, and the actual value is converted from the regional GDP deflator using 2002 as the base period.

Data for calculating the regional economic complexity index (ECI) is taken from the 'China Industrial Enterprise Statistical Database' which includes data during 2002–2007 for all state-owned enterprises and non-state-owned enterprises of designated size (revenue from core business is over 5 million *yuan*). The statistical sample encompasses over 400,000 industrial enterprises in 827 four-digit code industries of 39 key categories by standard industrial classification: categories 06–11 in mining (type B), categories 13–43 in manufacturing (type C), and categories 44–46 in the production and supply of electricity, fuel and water (type D). The

[1]Moreover, after 2002, GB/T4754-2002 became the new standard industrial classification in China. In selecting 2002–2007 as the sample period, we have ensured consistency between the industry classification used and statistical indicators.

database contains the most detailed sample on enterprises, the most finely categorised industries, and the most complete statistical information. Specifically, the database contains indices such as total output, value added, export shipment, total workforce, as well as information at a micro, enterprise level such as financial statistics on enterprise assets and liabilities. Generally speaking, the finer the categorisation of industries, the more similarities there are in the enterprises in the sector. In order to calculate regional economic complexity from an output perspective, it is necessary to employ information on industries at a local level and even at a product level, and this is the reason for our original intention in choosing this database for the calculation. Even though this database does not include the service industries or the agricultural industry, this database is an appropriate choice for measuring regional economic complexity, because 80% of the regional differences in China can be attributed to the industrial sector (Peng 2005), hence from the perspective of selecting sample.

Since the sample is very large, there are abnormal values and erroneous records in the 'China Industrial Enterprise Statistical Database'. In calculating regional economic complexity, we have deleted those erroneous records or obvious abnormal observed values, such as where the age of enterprises that is smaller than 0, where total values on output; value added, new product output and export shipment are negative; where total inputs (intermediate inputs, net fixed assets, total workforce, original value of fixed assets) are smaller than 0; where the value added or intermediate inputs are greater than the total output; and abnormal regional code, etc. Deletions are also made where records are duplicated, where the observed value of the industry workforce is smaller than 10, the receivables are smaller than 0; where the observed value of core business revenue is smaller than 5 million *yuan* this is eliminated from the sample. This study differs from past studies that used export data in calculating economic complexity. In this study, we select an enterprise's value added as the essential data for calculating regional economic complexity. During calculation, this study first deflated the value added in the regional GDP deflator for the 2002 base period.

The institutional variable, as indicated by $market_{it}$, represents the institutional environment in the various regions. It is measured by using the 2002–2007 regional market adoption index published by Fan et al. (2010). A characteristic of this index is that it is based on large volumes of statistical and field survey data from five areas, including the level of government intervention in 31 Chinese provinces (municipalities, autonomous regions), the development of non-state-owned enterprises, product and factor markets, market intermediaries, and the legal environment, and the index is calculated from the weighted aggregation of the market-oriented development index in these five areas.

Trade openness ($open_{it}$) represents the economic connection of the various regions with foreign markets. It is measured by the total amount of regional export as a proportion of the GDP. Foreign direct investment ($FDI_{it}$) represents the actual total amount of foreign investment into the various regions. The data source for measuring trade openness and foreign direct investment comes from the annual 'China Statistical Yearbook'.

Transport infrastructure is measured by the railway route mileage (in ten thousand kilometres) and road length (in ten thousand kilometres), indicated by $railway_{it}$ and $road_{it}$ respectively. Information infrastructure is measured by fibre optic cables installed for users over long distances (in ten thousand kilometres) and broadband internet access (in ten million units), represented by $cable_{it}$ and $access_{it}$. The data is taken from the 'China Statistical Yearbook'. When carrying out the empirical analysis, we began with road length and fibre optic cable length as reference variables, with railway route mileage and internet broadband access as proxy variables to check for robustness.

Since there are numerous kinds of mineral resources, in working out the regression, this study used coal reserve as an indicator of natural resources endowment, indicated by $coal_{it}$. The reason for choosing this indicator is that coal accounts for 60% as a share of China's energy consumption structure—it is the main energy used in industrial production. Also, coal is fairly widely distributed in China, an important mineral resource in various regions. The data on coal reserve comes from the annual special surveys in the national statistical database.

According to Lucas' model (2001) of endogenous economic growth, such growth in technology is manifested chiefly in human capital, which is also an important medium for technological progress. Frequently used measurements include indices for public spending in education, number of years in education, number of students in all the different stages in education, illiteracy rate, etc. This study uses local government spending in education (a hundred million *yuan*) as a share of GDP as the indicator that measures human capital, represented by $Edu_{it}$, and the data comes from the annual special survey in the national statistical database.

Urbanisation is measured by the population in towns and cities of the region as a proportion of the overall population, indicated by $city_{it}$. The geographical location of an economy has influences on the performance in regional economic growth. In order to reflect on such influences, this study selects the climate in provincial capitals as controlled variables, which are mainly annual averages in daylight hours, rainfall, relative humidity, and temperature. These are indicated by $sun_{it}$, $rain_{it}$, $wet_{it}$ and $tem_{it}$. Measurements for urbanisation and climate conditions are taken from data in the annual 'China Statistical Yearbook'.

This study has constructed the balanced panel data in the 31 provinces (municipalities, autonomous regions) in China during 2002–2007. The results of the descriptive statistics on the variables are listed in Table 8.1.

## 3. Empirical approach and estimation

This study focuses on the impact of economic complexity on economic growth. Our approach in the empirical analysis is to first control other factors that can influence regional economic growth, and to examine the effects of regional economic complexity. Next, we test the robustness of the correlation identified in the

**Table 8.1** Variables and descriptive statistics

| | Name of variable | Symbol of variable/ variable operator | Obs | Mean | Standard deviation | Smallest value | Largest value |
|---|---|---|---|---|---|---|---|
| Variable explained | Logarithm for actual per capita GDP | lnrpgdp | 186 | 9.18 | 0.53 | 8.09 | 10.64 |
| Complexity variable | Regional economic complexity | **ECI** | **186** | **23.32** | **1.70** | **20.04** | **27.22** |
| Institutional variable | Adoption of market principles index | Market | 186 | 6.32 | 2.10 | 0.63 | 11.71 |
| Urbanisation variable | Percentage of urbanisation (%) | City | 186 | 41.48 | 15.56 | 0.00 | 84.50 |
| Trade openness variable | Total trade in import and export as a share of GDP | topen | 186 | 0.04 | 0.05 | 0.00 | 0.23 |
| | Export as a share of GDP | Open | 186 | 0.02 | 0.02 | 0.00 | 0.12 |
| Foreign direct investment variable | Total FDI used (100 million US dollars) | FDI | 186 | 25.87 | 37.53 | 0.03 | 218.92 |
| Transport infrastructure variable | Railway route mileage (ten thousand kilometres) | Railway | 182 | 0.25 | 0.15 | 0.02 | 0.67 |
| | Road length (ten thousand kilometres) | Road | 186 | 7.75 | 5.12 | 0.63 | 23.87 |
| Information infrastructure variable | Broadband internet access (100 million units) | Access | 149 | 0.25 | 0.35 | 0.00 | 2.56 |
| | Length of fibre optic cables (ten thousand kilometres) | Cable | 186 | 2.02 | 1.09 | 0.06 | 5.59 |
| Natural resource endowments | Coal reserve for mining (10 million tons) | Coal | 150 | 110.92 | 225.94 | 0.12 | 1056.13 |
| Human capital variable | Spending in education (10 million yuan)/ GDP (%) | Edu | 186 | 0.06 | 0.51 | 0.01 | 6.94 |

(continued)

**Table 8.1** (continued)

| | Name of variable | Symbol of variable/ variable operator | Obs | Mean | Standard deviation | Smallest value | Largest value |
|---|---|---|---|---|---|---|---|
| Geographical location of economy variable | Number of annual daylight hours (hours) | Sun | 186 | 1980.58 | 516.40 | 777.00 | 3181.00 |
| | Annual average relative humidity (%) | Wet | 186 | 64.07 | 10.72 | 33.83 | 83.00 |
| | Annual rainfall (mm) | Rain | 186 | 840.49 | 447.39 | 74.90 | 2175.70 |
| | Annual average temperature (°C) | Tem | 186 | 14.51 | 5.06 | 4.70 | 25.40 |
| | Economic belt | Region | 186 | 2.03 | 0.86 | 1 | 3 |

quantitative analysis. In order to arrive at a reliable and consistent outcome, there is a need to deal with the following problems:

(1) The multicollinearity between variables
The empirical model used in this study contains many variables, and during analysis we often encounter problems of collinearity where there are too many explanations for variables, i.e. a problem of badly controlled variables. To solve estimation biases caused by this serious problem during quantitative analysis, we first select more targeted and important explanatory variables, and calculate their variance inflation factor (VIF) by an auxiliary regression, in order to identify and eliminate the controlled variables with serious collinearity in variable $X_{it}$ in empirical model (1). According to Hidalgo et al. (2009) our findings in the examination of multicollinear variables, we find that natural resource endowments, export specialisation, investment in human capital and foreign direct investment all correlate strongly with regional economic complexity. Hence, the regression process later on in this study will reject these variables.
(2) Selecting an appropriate prediction methodology
For an accurate measurement of the relationship between economic complexity and economic growth, the choice of a model is critical in the empirical analysis. As a benchmark model, this study first carried out a mixed least squares regression. With this method, we know that in econometrics the best linear unbiased estimator can only be arrived at when the conditions for a classic Gauss-Markov assumption have been established. By examining heteroscedasticity and multicollinearity of the mixed least squares method, and comparing the estimate with the fixed effects model, the outcome of test F rejects the null hypothesis. Hence, between the mixed least squares and the fixed effects models, the latter is chosen. This study then compared the fixed

effects and random effects models, and the outcome of the Hausmann test rejects the null hypothesis. Therefore, the final choice of an empirical model for this study is the fixed effects model. In fact, unobserved heterogeneity by region and period will clearly impact on regional economic growth because they correlate with random perturbations. Our choice is therefore appropriate for this study from an economics point of view.

(3) Problems of an endogenous nature

Political and economic variables can be both cause and effect with regards economic growth. It is also possible that important variables are included in the empirical model, resulting in a problem with omitted variables and endogenous problems in simultaneous equations. To correct endogenous problems, this study adopts the generalised method of moments (GMM) put forward by Arellano and Bover (1995) and Blundell and Bond (1998). System GMM corrects the problem of a weak instrumental variable in the differenced GMM model due to lagged and subsequent first differences. It has been widely used for solving endogenous problems with variables in narrow panel models (N-sectional width, short time period T). This method makes full use of standard and differenced information from short time period large cross sectional dynamic panel data, and so is more effective than difference GMM. In taking full account of orthogonality conditions for lagged explained variables and random perturbation, GMM can acquire more instrumental variables to overcome endogenous problems caused by biased simultaneous equations and omitted variables and reach more accurate, effective and consistent estimation. Blundell et al. (1998) point out that given limited samples, bias from the system GMM estimator is smaller than that from the difference GMM estimator, and as an improved estimator it can reduce bias in limited samples. Moreover, system GMM in itself can be a way of checking the robustness of the regression outcome.

## 8.3 Analysing the Outcome of the Empirical Study

1. **Analysing the regression outcome for all regions**

Table 8.2 shows the calculation outcome on the relationship between regional economic complexity and economic growth for the data sample with controlled heterogeneity in location and time period. Considering the growing differences in regional and industrial development in China since the reform and opening up, especially in the 21st century, in order to overcome possible yet unidentified heteroscedasticity or autocorrelation, the Generalised Least Squares approach is normally used for corrections. However, this approach is more appropriate for wide panel data models (i.e. big time series T, small cross sectional N). For the narrow panel data model with large N and small T used in our study, normally the mixed

**Table 8.2** How regional economic complexity affects growth

| | (1) | (2) | (3) | (4) | (5) | (6) | (7) |
|---|---|---|---|---|---|---|---|
| Variable Explained | lnrpgdp | lnrpgdp | lnrpgdp | lnrpgdp | lnrpgdp | lnrpgdp | lnrpgdp |
| ECI | 0.102*** | 0.021*** | 0.021*** | 0.022*** | 0.020*** | 0.019*** | 0.019*** |
| | (0.006) | (0.009) | (0.009) | (0.009) | (0.007) | (0.007) | (0.008) |
| Market | | 0.070*** | 0.070*** | 0.074*** | 0.066*** | 0.063*** | 0.062*** |
| | | (0.007) | (0.008) | (0.009) | (0.009) | (0.010) | (0.010) |
| City | | | 0.000 | 0.000 | −0.000 | −0.000 | −0.000 |
| | | | (0.001) | (0.000) | (0.000) | (0.000) | (0.000) |
| Open | | | | −1.284* | −0.995 | −0.902 | −1.017 |
| | | | | (0.602) | (0.586) | (0.603) | (0.663) |
| Road | | | | | 0.004* | 0.004* | 0.003 |
| | | | | | (0.001) | (0.001) | (0.002) |
| Cable | | | | | | 0.011 | 0.010 |
| | | | | | | (0.010) | (0.010) |
| Sun | | | | | | | −0.000 |
| | | | | | | | (0.000) |
| Wet | | | | | | | −0.001 |
| | | | | | | | (0.001) |
| Rain | | | | | | | −0.000 |
| | | | | | | | (0.000) |
| Tem | | | | | | | 0.002 |
| | | | | | | | (0.007) |
| _cons | 6.793*** | 8.258*** | 8.256*** | 8.223*** | 8.300*** | 8.316*** | 8.365*** |
| | (0.147) | (0.171) | (0.173) | (0.169) | (0.139) | (0.144) | (0.190) |
| Time-fixed effects | YES | YES | YES | YES | YES | YES | YES |
| Province-fixed effects | YES | YES | YES | YES | YES | YES | YES |
| N | 186 | 186 | 186 | 186 | 186 | 186 | 186 |
| Adj. R-sq. | 0.541 | 0.849 | 0.848 | 0.853 | 0.865 | 0.866 | 0.865 |

Standard errors in parentheses: $^{*}p < 0.05$, $^{**}p < 0.01$, $^{***}p < 0.001$

*Note* Driscoll-Kraay standard errors in parentheses. *, **, *** indicate significance levels at 5, 1 and 0.1% respectively in statistical tests

least squares method or the fixed effects Driscoll-Kraay standard errors method is used to obtain a robust estimation, and Table 8.2 shows the coefficients obtained via the latter.

The regression outcome in Table 8.2 shows that the adoption of market-oriented index is a significant positive in the different provinces. This means that where this index is high in the regions, economic development is also rapid. This is consistent with the conclusion in the research by Fan et al. (2010). However, it is different from the research outcome by Wang (2002) who found that the urbanisation coefficient hovers around 0. The level of regional urbanisation in China and the GDP per capita does not display a stable, positive relationship; in other words, regional urbanisation has not brought significant increase in GDP per capita to the region. Past research shows that the relationship between urbanisation and economic growth is not conclusive. According to Shen et al. (2007), urbanisation can drive economic growth through two mechanisms: on the one hand urbanisation brings agglomeration economy, which accelerates the accumulation of physical, human and knowledge capital, and thus promotes economic growth; on the other hand, urbanisation helps to move excess labour from the rural areas to the cities, optimising the primary sector and promoting the development of non-agricultural industries, while at the same time development in the secondary and tertiary sectors further accelerate upgrade of the industrial structure, and thereby promoting economic growth. In other words, urbanisation first acts on factor accumulation and structural change, and then indirectly promotes economic growth. Through their empirical study in economic growth and urbanisation in China, they found that physical, human and knowledge capital as well as industrial structure are ways through which urbanisation can impact on economic growth. In addition, currently for China, human capital and structural change can have significant effects on urbanisation and per capita output. Shen (2004) studied the experience of Japanese urbanisation and economic growth and found that there may be an inverse relationship between the level of urbanisation and economic growth. The empirical study carried out by Zhan et al. (2006) on the relationship between Chinese urbanisation and economic growth found that although urbanisation has a positive role in economic growth, it was very minimal. However, the empirical outcome is not statistically significant and is unstable, which is basically similar to the conclusion reached in this study.

The regional trade openness coefficient is negative but is statistically insignificant according to the standard errors. A possible reason for this outcome is the correlation between regional openness and the adoption of market principles, resulting in problems for the regression. Moreover, according to Lu et al. (2009), increased trade openness exacerbates local governments' protectionism, which implement policies that divide up the market obstruct regional economic growth. To consider the effect of transport infrastructure on regional economic growth, this research has examined the effect of regional road length as seen in Table 8.2 columns (5)–(7). The result from the regression shows that regional transport infrastructure has a significant role in the actual GDP per capita. This result validates some of the findings in the empirical study by Emurger (2001), that is, there is a stable and significant positive relationship between transport infrastructure in Chinese provinces and economic growth. Specifically, he believes that transport infrastructure is one of the most important factors for uneven regional economic development. This conclusion is different from those by Chen et al. (2011) and Xu (2010), who concluded that information infrastructure is weakly positive in promoting regional economic development. A possible reason for the different conclusions is that in this study the data we use is absolute numbers for the length of fibre optic cables, whereas in the above literature they use metrics corrected by population size. Regarding other geographical variables such as climate, the results from regressions are not significant in this study. This shows that the climate factor has no significant effect on regional economic performance in China. This differs from the findings by Bao et al. (2002). The reason we have come to different conclusions is that in this study we used a sample period different from that used by Bao et al. (2002), which means for the data chosen in the two studies, the Chinese regions are at two different stages. The sample used by Bao et al. (2002) is for the period 1978–1998. At this stage agriculture still accounted for a large proportion in many areas in China. As agriculture is susceptible to climate conditions, the climate condition can significantly affect regional economic growth. During 2002–2007 China entered a period of industrialisation in heavy industries. In this period, markedly improved conditions in agricultural production and a further decline of agriculture as a share of the regional economy. For example, in 2007, at regional level, the value added of agriculture as a proportion of the economy only averaged 12.27%, the lowest being 0.82%. Also, the manufacturing and service industries are less susceptible to climatic conditions, therefore regional climate has no significant impact on regional economic growth.

We are most concerned with the effect of economic complexity on economic growth. The regression outcome in Table 8.2 shows that there is a stable and positive relationship between them. This means that a region with a high degree of economic complexity is also more developed. For every one percentage point increase in regional economic complexity, there is an actual GDP per capita increase of around 2%. This demonstrates that enhancing economic complexity is important for regional economic growth. From the perspective of export commodity mix, Jarreau and Poncet (2012) discussed the effect of increased complexity in China's regional exports on regional economic performance. They found that the complexity of a region's export commodity mix is highly positively correlated to economic growth, but the export commodity mix is highly correlated to the production mix. This implies that external factors such as exports may indirectly influence regional economic growth through acting on the complexity in production mix. The relationship between regional economic complexity and growth may be one of self-perpetuation: economically developed regions can more easily attract factors of production, resources and knowledge, resulting in spillovers which enable micro actors to produce more and more complex goods; this in turn increases the overall complexity of the production mix for the region. In regions which has high economic complexity, producers have access to more technology and knowledge which they can consolidate in manufacturing for greater productivity, and thus promoting sustainable growth for the region.

The adoption of market principles index is also positive in the different provinces, which means that where this index is high in the regions, economic development is also rapid. This is consistent with the conclusion in the research by Fan et al. (2010). The urbanisation coefficient hovers around 0. The level of urbanisation in Chinese regions and their GDP per capita do not display a stable, positive relationship. A higher degree of urbanisation has not brought increased GDP per capita to the region. The trade openness coefficient for the region is negative but is statistically insignificant, which means that regional trade openness does not play an important role in economic growth. The regression outcome also shows that developing regional transport infrastructure is very important for growth, whereas information infrastructure is weakly positive in promoting regional development. This result confirms the conclusion in Emurger's (2001) empirical study.

2. **Analysis of the regression outcome by region**

Next, we separate out the provinces into eastern, central and western regions to further examine the effect of regional economic complexity on growth. In this part, we are mainly concerned with the influence of regional economic complexity on economic growth, because we have established that the coefficient of other variables is basically similar to the regression results for the overall region. When all controlled variables are taken into account, the economic complexity index (eci) coefficient for the eastern region is 0.017, indicating a positive effect on economic growth for the eastern region but is not very statistically significant. For the central region there is a stable, positive correlation between economic complexity and growth, and the coefficient is 0.040. This indicates that for one unit of increase in the economic complexity index, the economy grows by 4%. Next we take a look at the western region. The ECI coefficient is 0.024, indicating that there is a positive correlation between the region's economic complexity and growth. However, it is not statistically significant (Table 8.3).

The impact of economic complexity on growth is not significant in the eastern and western regions. The possible reasons are: (1) The data sample for the eastern and western regions is bigger, but is relatively small for the central region; (2) Testing errors—the central region is home to traditional heavy industries with a good manufacturing base; while in the eastern region, which is more open to the outside world and has adopted market principles, its service industry as a share of the regional production mix has been growing while that of the secondary sector is falling; the western region is less developed, and, its secondary sector as a share of the national economy is smaller than that of the central region. However, in calculating the regional economic complexity, this study used data mainly from the secondary sector, which might have undervalued the ECI for the eastern and western regions, and overvalued that for the central region. Therefore, we carry out regressions on a combined eastern and central region, and a combined central and western region, then re-examine the impact of economic complexity on growth. Table 8.4 columns (1)–(3) show the regression outcome for the combined eastern and central region, columns (4)–(6) for the combined central and western region. As we can see there is no fundamental change to the signs of the controlled variables or the significance level. The result is basically the same as the regression outcome in Table 8.2. Taking all the controlled variables into account, in column (3) the ECI

**Table 8.3** Effect of economic complexity on growth by region

| | (1) East | (2) East | (3) Central | (4) Central | (5) West | (6) West |
|---|---|---|---|---|---|---|
| Variable explained | lnrpgdp | lnrpgdp | lnrpgdp | lnrpgdp | lnrpgdp | lnrpgdp |
| ECI | 0.024 | 0.017 | 0.039 | 0.040 | 0.017 | 0.024 |
| | (0.011) | (0.010) | (0.017) | (0.018) | (0.015) | (0.017) |
| Market | 0.048*** | 0.049*** | 0.078*** | 0.068* | 0.080* | 0.082* |
| | (0.009) | (0.008) | (0.012) | (0.015) | (0.020) | (0.019) |
| City | 0.001 | 0.001 | 0.004 | 0.003 | 0.001 | 0.001 |
| | (0.001) | (0.001) | (0.004) | (0.004) | (0.002) | (0.002) |
| Open | −0.120 | −0.474 | −4.458 | −6.604 | 3.628* | 3.039 |
| | (0.671) | (0.687) | (2.353) | (3.688) | (0.825) | (1.429) |
| Railway | 0.341 | 0.932 | −0.533 | −0.126 | 1.146 | 0.954 |
| | (0.793) | (0.846) | (0.655) | (0.786) | (0.748) | (0.686) |
| Access | 0.005 | 0.011 | 0.071 | 0.041 | 0.013 | 0.032 |
| | (0.012) | (0.010) | (0.041) | (0.039) | (0.030) | (0.028) |
| Sun | | 0.000 | | −0.000* | | 0.000 |
| | | (0.000) | | (0.000) | | (0.000) |
| Wet | | −0.002 | | −0.004* | | −0.001 |
| | | (0.002) | | (0.002) | | (0.002) |
| Rain | | −0.000 | | 0.000 | | −0.000 |
| | | (0.000) | | (0.000) | | (0.000) |
| Tem | | 0.020 | | 0.021 | | 0.013 |
| | | (0.010) | | (0.011) | | (0.012) |
| _cons | 8.706*** | 8.523*** | 7.626*** | 7.761*** | 7.637*** | 7.367*** |
| | (0.183) | (0.400) | (0.258) | (0.362) | (0.409) | (0.543) |
| Time-fixed effects | YES | YES | YES | YES | YES | YES |
| Province-fixed effects | YES | YES | YES | YES | YES | YES |
| N | 53 | 53 | 38 | 38 | 56 | 56 |
| Adj. R-sq. | 0.909 | 0.922 | 0.944 | 0.959 | 0.901 | 0.904 |

*Note* Driscoll-Kraay standard errors in parentheses. *, **, *** indicate significance levels at 5, 1 and 0.1% respectively in statistical tests

coefficient is statistically significant at 0.024, which shows that economic complexity has a positive effect on growth for the eastern and central regions; in column (6) the ECI coefficient is 0.026, which means that economic complexity also plays a positive role in growth for the central and western regions. Through the above quantitative analysis, we have found that economic complexity has an important role for growth in the different regions in China, and although the impact varies by region, the fundamental assumption stands.

**Table 8.4** The impact of economic complexity on growth in the eastern and central region, and the central and western region

| | (1) East-Cen | (2) East-Cen | (3) East-Cen | (4) Cen-West | (5) Cen-West | (6) Cen-West |
|---|---|---|---|---|---|---|
| Variable explained | lnrpgdp | lnrpgdp | lnrpgdp | lnrpgdp | lnrpgdp | lnrpgdp |
| ECI | 0.016 | 0.024* | 0.024 | 0.024 | 0.024 | 0.026* |
| | (0.008) | (0.011) | (0.012) | (0.012) | (0.012) | (0.012) |
| Market | 0.069*** | 0.069*** | 0.065*** | 0.066*** | 0.065*** | 0.065*** |
| | (0.007) | (0.007) | (0.008) | (0.011) | (0.012) | (0.012) |
| City | 0.000 | 0.000 | 0.000 | 0.003* | 0.003 | 0.003 |
| | (0.000) | (0.000) | (0.001) | (0.001) | (0.002) | (0.002) |
| Open | −1.028* | −1.391* | −1.490* | 1.292 | 1.204 | 0.621 |
| | (0.444) | (0.660) | (0.636) | (2.538) | (2.834) | (2.881) |
| Railway | | 0.078 | 0.310 | | 0.707 | 0.610 |
| | | (0.574) | (0.544) | | (0.632) | (0.603) |
| Access | | 0.018 | 0.014 | | 0.009 | 0.010 |
| | | (0.014) | (0.011) | | (0.027) | (0.026) |
| Sun | | | −0.000 | | | −0.000 |
| | | | (0.000) | | | (0.000) |
| Wet | | | −0.002 | | | 0.000 |
| | | | (0.001) | | | (0.001) |
| Rain | | | −0.000 | | | 0.000 |
| | | | (0.000) | | | (0.000) |
| Tem | | | 0.019* | | | 0.017* |
| | | | (0.005) | | | (0.008) |
| _cons | 8.580*** | 8.355*** | 8.417*** | 7.852*** | 7.621*** | 7.382*** |
| | (0.153) | (0.203) | (0.315) | (0.246) | (0.308) | (0.349) |
| Time-fixed effects | YES | YES | YES | YES | YES | YES |
| Province-fixed effects | YES | YES | YES | YES | YES | YES |
| N | 114 | 91 | 91 | 120 | 94 | 94 |
| Adj. R-sq. | 0.900 | 0.918 | 0.932 | 0.860 | 0.900 | 0.905 |

*Note* Driscoll-Kraay standard errors in parentheses. *, **, *** indicate significance levels at 5, 1 and 0.1% respectively in statistical tests

3. **Robustness testing**

The relationship between economic complexity and growth identified in the above fixed effects regression model is an initial step, because in measuring regional economic growth, this study used the logarithm of the actual GDP per capita for the region. As such, the correlation identified earlier may be peculiar to the index used by this study for measuring regional economic growth. For this

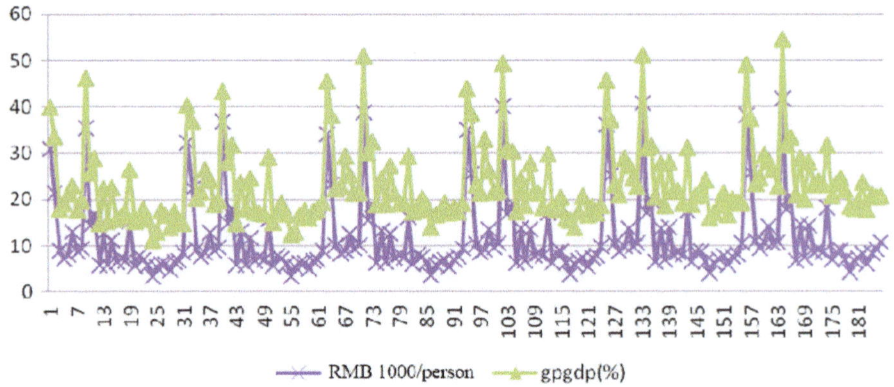


**Fig. 8.1** Regional GDP per capita growth and actual GDP per capita for the region

reason, this study will re-examine the effect of regional economic complexity on growth with the GDP per capita for the region. From Fig. 8.1 which shows the correlation between regional real GDP per capita and its growth rate, we can see that the two are highly correlated. This means that using the regional GDP per capita growth to measure economic growth is appropriate and feasible.

In order to test the robustness of the relationship between regional economic complexity and growth, we carried out another regression analysis on the empirical model using regional economic complexity and GDP per capita growth rate. The regression outcome is shown in Table 8.5. After measuring regional economic growth using the regional GDP per capita growth rate, the ECI coefficient is still positive and has become more significant than that in Table 8.2, making it statistically more significant. Moreover, when other controlled variables are taken into account, the correlation between economic complexity and growth is still robust, with hardly any changes to the signs and no significant change to the relationship between other variables and economic growth.

For example, the regression coefficient in Table 8.5 column (7) has increased from 0.019 to 0.869, the value of t has increased from 2.37 to 3.38. This clearly demonstrates that there is a stable, positive correlation between regional economic complexity and growth. Enhancing regional economic complexity is conducive to regional economic development. The economic relationships identified in Table 8.2 are reliable, robust and conclusive.

To further verify the robustness of the regression outcome in Table 8.2, this study has adopted the following methods: (1) Substituting railway route mileage (railway) and broadband internet access (access) for road length (road) and fibre optic cables (cable) respectively, as measurements for transport and information infrastructure. (2) Considering that exports as a share of GDP can only partially reflect regional openness, here the total amount of regional import and export as a share of GDP is used to measure the overall regional openness. Table 8.6 shows the

**Table 8.5** Robustness testing

| | (1) | (2) | (3) | (4) | (5) | (6) | (7) |
|---|---|---|---|---|---|---|---|
| | gpgdp | gpgdp | gpgdp | gpgdp | gpgdp | gpgdp | gpgdp |
| ECI | 1.747*** | 0.874*** | 0.854*** | 0.915*** | 0.898*** | 0.844* | 0.869* |
| | (0.249) | (0.206) | (0.209) | (0.231) | (0.244) | (0.240) | (0.257) |
| Market | | 0.746*** | 0.900*** | 1.097*** | 1.040*** | 0.841* | 0.824* |
| | | (0.202) | (0.218) | (0.224) | (0.264) | (0.315) | (0.316) |
| City | | | −0.028 | −0.026 | −0.027 | −0.027 | −0.029 |
| | | | (0.024) | (0.022) | (0.022) | (0.023) | (0.023) |
| Open | | | | −62.228* | −60.128* | −54.021 | −51.456 |
| | | | | (24.994) | (25.704) | (27.760) | (25.558) |
| Road | | | | | 0.027 | 0.016 | 0.065 |
| | | | | | (0.057) | (0.054) | (0.058) |
| Cable | | | | | | 0.717 | 0.598 |
| | | | | | | (0.372) | (0.392) |
| Sun | | | | | | | 0.001 |
| | | | | | | | (0.001) |
| Wet | | | | | | | −0.055 |
| | | | | | | | (0.044) |
| Rain | | | | | | | 0.001 |
| | | | | | | | (0.001) |
| Tem | | | | | | | −0.373 |
| | | | | | | | (0.339) |
| _cons | −28.823*** | −13.184* | −12.524* | −14.124* | −13.566* | −12.514* | −6.892 |
| | (5.812) | (4.379) | (4.471) | (5.021) | (5.478) | (5.449) | (8.792) |
| Time-fixed effects | YES | YES | YES | YES | YES | YES | YES |
| Province-fixed effects | YES | YES | YES | YES | YES | YES | YES |
| N | 186 | 186 | 186 | 186 | 186 | 186 | 186 |
| Adj. R-sq. | 0.355 | 0.432 | 0.437 | 0.467 | 0.465 | 0.478 | 0.488 |

Standard errors in parentheses: $*p < 0.05$, $**p < 0.01$, $***p < 0.001$

*Note* Driscoll-Kraay standard errors in parentheses. *, **, *** indicate significance levels at 5, 1 and 0.1% respectively in statistical tests

outcome following the re-examination for robustness. We find that there is no fundamental change to the signs of the variable or statistical significance, which demonstrates again that the regression outcome in this study is robust and reliable.

4. **(3) Dealing with endogeneity**

This part focuses on endogeneity of variables as a result of reverse causality caused by omitted variables and biased simultaneous equations. For example, even though the above fixed effects model predicts a stable and significantly positive

**Table 8.6** Robustness re-examination

| | (1) | (2) | (3) | (4) | (5) | (6) | (7) |
|---|---|---|---|---|---|---|---|
| | lnrpgdp | lnrpgdp | lnrpgdp | lnrpgdp | lnrpgdp | lnrpgdp | lnrpgdp |
| ECI | 0.102*** | 0.021* | 0.021* | 0.021* | 0.022* | 0.025* | 0.026* |
| | (0.006) | (0.009) | (0.009) | (0.009) | (0.009) | (0.009) | (0.010) |
| Market | | 0.070*** | 0.070*** | 0.070*** | 0.074*** | 0.071*** | 0.069*** |
| | | (0.007) | (0.008) | (0.008) | (0.009) | (0.010) | (0.011) |
| City | | | 0.000 | 0.000 | 0.000 | −0.000 | 0.000 |
| | | | (0.001) | (0.001) | (0.000) | (0.001) | (0.001) |
| topen | | | | | −0.791** | −0.827* | −0.886* |
| | | | | | (0.278) | (0.354) | (0.393) |
| Railway | | | | | | 0.859 | 0.857 |
| | | | | | | (0.493) | (0.485) |
| Access | | | | | | 0.004 | 0.007 |
| | | | | | | (0.020) | (0.019) |
| Sun | | | | | | | −0.000 |
| | | | | | | | (0.000) |
| Wet | | | | | | | −0.001 |
| | | | | | | | (0.002) |
| Rain | | | | | | | −0.000 |
| | | | | | | | (0.000) |
| Tem | | | | | | | 0.012 |
| | | | | | | | (0.007) |
| _cons | 6.793*** | 8.258*** | 8.256*** | 8.256*** | 8.222*** | 7.966*** | 7.839*** |
| | (0.147) | (0.171) | (0.173) | (0.173) | (0.170) | (0.224) | (0.307) |
| Time-fixed effects | YES | YES | YES | YES | YES | YES | YES |
| Province-fixed effects | YES | YES | YES | YES | YES | YES | YES |
| N | 186 | 186 | 186 | 186 | 186 | 186 | 186 |
| Adj. R-sq. | 0.541 | 0.849 | 0.848 | 0.848 | 0.854 | 0.888 | 0.893 |

Standard errors in parentheses: $^{*}p < 0.05$, $^{**}p < 0.01$, $^{***}p < 0.001$

*Note* Driscoll-Kraay standard errors in parentheses. *, **, *** indicate significance levels at 5, 1 and 0.1% respectively in statistical tests

correlation between regional economic complexity, adoption of market principles and growth, according to our theoretical analysis and the existence of bias in the simultaneous equation, economic complexity is endogenous given certain conditions. Our study has found that increased economic complexity can promote regional growth. However, economically well-developed regions have access to productive knowledge as well as the capability for knowledge intensive production, and therefore their economy is also relatively complex. In addition, where the index is high in the adoption of market principles, with increased competition and a greater degree of openness, the need for adopting market principles for regional development will also change in the process. For example, Lu et al. (2009) found that a higher degree of regional openness exacerbates protectionism in order to promote local economic development. In other words, there may be a reverse causal relationship between the adoption of market principles and regional economic growth, which means that the relationship is endogenous. Clearly this kind of endogenous variables has been overlooked in the regression outcome shown in Table 8.2. Serious endogeneity in the regression model leads to inconsistent and biased outcome.

To counter possible endogeneity in regional economic complexity and the adoption of market principles, methods that are commonly used include instrumental variables and System GMM. According to the characteristics of the panel data in our study, we have selected System GMM to deal with this potential problem of endogeneity. Table 8.7 shows the regression model using GMM to deal with endogeneity. In all the equation estimation results, concomitant probability $p$ values tested by Arellano-Bond AR (2) and Sargan are all greater than 0.05. Such a result cannot reject the null hypothesis, confirming the rationale and effectiveness of the instrumental variables. The Arellano-Bond AR (1) test rejects the null hypothesis that the residuals do not possess first step serial correlation. Therefore, it is appropriate to use System GMM to deal with endogeneity in the empirical equations in this study.

Because System GMM can make use of information from both the level and differenced models, it can produce good estimations for narrow panel data with 'few time periods but big sample'. In Table 8.7 columns (1)–(3), the outcome shows that the key variables—the sign of the ECI and the statistical significance—have intrinsically changed, meaning that the regression is robust. Compared with the result in Table 8.2, the coefficient estimates in the equations for regional economic complexity have all increased at different levels. This demonstrates that endogeneity in economic complexity causes a downward bias in the fixed effects estimation, underestimating the effect of economic complexity on growth. Moreover, after taking into account other controlled variables, the economic complexity coefficient has fallen somewhat, but is still statistically significant despite the slight drop, and will not fundamentally weaken the conclusion in this paper.

Compared with the previous one, this regression and its controlled variables sees intrinsic changes in the sign for other variables and the statistical significance, apart from the reversal of the signs for institutional (market) and transport (road) infrastructures. This demonstrates that the regression outcome is still quite robust. The information infrastructure coefficient has a positive sign and its significance is much increased, which means that the endogenous variables led to a downward bias of the effect of information infrastructure on regional economic growth in Table 8.2. After overcoming endogeneity, the conclusion reached is consistent with that by Chen et al. (2011) and Xu (2010).

The positive sign of the adoption of market principles has changed to negative but is statistically insignificant, which means that adopting market principles probably does not impact on regional economic growth, or that it does not have an active role. It is possible that the policy of dividing the market by the local government is more beneficial for that region's economic growth, which means that

**Table 8.7** Regression outcome having dealt with endogenous variables

| | (1) | (2) | (3) |
|---|---|---|---|
| | lnrpgdp | lnrpgdp | lnrpgdp |
| L.lnrpgdp | 1.070*** | 1.125*** | 1.113*** |
| | (0.035) | (0.043) | (0.046) |
| ECI | 0.031*** | 0.026*** | 0.023*** |
| | (0.004) | (0.004) | (0.004) |
| Market | 0.007 | −0.003 | −0.002 |
| | (0.004) | (0.005) | (0.005) |
| City | −0.000 | −0.000 | −0.000 |
| | (0.000) | (0.000) | (0.000) |
| Open | −1.579** | −1.449** | −1.423*** |
| | (0.501) | (0.456) | (0.408) |
| Road | −0.004*** | −0.005*** | −0.004*** |
| | (0.001) | (0.001) | (0.001) |
| Cable | | 0.029*** | 0.021*** |
| | | (0.004) | (0.005) |
| Sun | | | 0.000 |
| | | | (0.000) |
| Wet | | | −0.002* |
| | | | (0.001) |
| Rain | | | −0.000 |
| | | | (0.000) |
| Tem | | | 0.001 |
| | | | (0.003) |
| _cons | −1.294*** | −1.683*** | −1.417** |
| | (0.355) | (0.423) | (0.437) |
| Time-fixed effects | YES | YES | YES |
| Province-fixed effects | YES | YES | YES |
| Sargan | 0.0761 | 0.1381 | 0.2186 |
| AR (1) | 0.0043 | 0.0028 | 0.0083 |
| AR (2) | 0.0811 | 0.4341 | 0.2236 |
| N | 155 | 155 | 155 |

*Note* Driscoll-Kraay standard errors in parentheses. *, **, *** indicate significance levels at 5, 1 and 0.1% respectively in statistical tests. Sargan and AR values are Arellano-Bond tests for statistical $p$ values, to test whether an instrumental variable is over-identified, and whether differenced one-step and two-step autocorrelations exist in random perturbation

promoting markets is not necessarily beneficial for a region's economic development. According to Lu et al. (2009), segmenting the market has an inverted U-shape effect on local economic growth. When the market is not highly segmented, dividing it further can be conducive to economic growth. However, when the market is segmented beyond a critical point, it can negatively impact on economic growth. They find that given the current stage of regional development in China, segmentation is conducive to economic growth; moreover, for provinces that are economically more open, dividing up the market can promote growth locally. To an extent this confirms that increasing the adoption of market principles does not necessarily promote regional economic growth.

The sign of the transport infrastructure has changed completely, which means that the effect of regional transport infrastructure on economic growth identified in Table 8.2 may have errors—Table 8.2 identifies a negative correlation. A possible reason is that the accumulating effect from transport infrastructure makes it more convenient to transfer production factors to more developed regions, reinforcing the negative spillover effect for undeveloped regions. This means that more investment in transport infrastructure will not necessarily bring higher output per capita. In fact, how investment in transport infrastructure contributes to economic development is not a simple linear relationship. A linear model may lead to wrong estimations, and even selecting different variables can produce different results. Infrastructure services function like networks. They can only play a role when ancillary facilities are able to keep up. However, given limited public resources, building the transport infrastructure may divert investment from social infrastructures, and can instead inhibit economic growth. When social infrastructure is inadequate compared with transport, reducing investment proportionally in the economic infrastructure can in fact improve growth, and is better for economic development. At such times, there a is greater need to build the social infrastructure for science, education, health, governance and the environment, etc., and to completely overhaul the investment portfolio for infrastructure. Since 2002, there has been a 'great leap forward' in the transport infrastructure in different parts of China, but the ancillary facilities have not kept up, so that the transport infrastructure has not played an active role in regional economic growth.

## 5. **Conclusion and policy implication**

In recent years, there has been a large number of literature on the complexity of Chinese exports measured using PRODY and EXPY indices put forward by Hausmann et al. (2007). However, the significance of economic complexity as put forward by Hidalgo et al. (2007, 2009) has been neglected. Economic complexity definitely has a significant impact on growth, but so far there has not been any empirical study on this subject, and this paper attempts to fill this void. In view of the shortcomings of the PRODY and EXPY indices, this paper uses enterprise level data from the 'China Industrial Enterprise Database', and for the first time Chinese regional economic complexity has been measured from a manufacturing perspective. A balanced panel dataset has been constructed for 2002–2007 on 31 Chinese provinces (municipalities and autonomous regions) in an attempt to confirm the effect of regional economic complexity on growth. This is the first time such an examination has been carried out within the boundaries of a nation. In addition, it reveals the source for Chinese regional economic growth, and helps us learn more about the reasons for the differences in regional economic growth.

Findings from the empirical analysis show that there is a stable, positive relationship between Chinese regional economic complexity and growth, and that increasing the complexity is important for growth. This conclusion is robust and reliable because it is immune to controlled variables and endogeneity. For the first time the theories of product space and evolutionary comparative advantage put forward by Hidalgo et al. (2007, 2009) have been tested within the boundaries of a nation, and these are shown to be applicable for explaining the differences in the regional economic performance in China. From the study described earlier, we reach the following conclusions and their implication for policy: (1) In terms of theory, this study accurately measures regional economic complexity and carries an empirical analysis on the relationship between regional economic complexity and growth. In furthering the empirical work on the theories of product space and evolutionary comparative advantage and strengthening their explanatory power, we have demonstrated their theoretical and application values through our research. (2) In terms of policy, in order to promote sustainable and healthy regional growth, local governments have a role in allowing and encouraging the movement of production factors and knowledge, increasing the capability for knowledge consolidation, to fully harness a region's comparative advantage, optimise its production portfolio, and continuously increase its economic complexity. As the Chinese economy develops, and the transfer of industries is beginning to take place locally and globally. Local governments should take this opportunity to take a lead in policies, do the groundwork to attract investments, transfer out old industries to make room for new ones (Zhang 2008) and reconfigure regional industries to increase the overall complexity of the production mix.

# Chapter 9
# Industrial Policy Design

**Qizi Zhang and Hao Li**

## 9.1 Debating the Role of Industrial Policy

Prior to 1970 many developing countries were influenced by old structuralist economics. They adopted strategies for import substitution, protecting or subsidising nascent industries. With the emergence of the debt crisis in Latin America, however, the role of industrial policy was called into question. In the 1980s, Latin American countries began to undergo changes, guided by the so-called Washington Consensus for their reforms. These reforms made contribution to the Latin American economy, but such policy results paled in comparison with the rapid growth in East Asian countries, and industrial policy was still much debated in the world of economics.

By the 21st century, with the miracle growth of the Chinese economy and the international financial crisis in 2008, the role of industrial policy again came up for debate. However, this time there was a strong voice for industrial policy. Dani Rodrik pointed out explicitly that the talk of the demise of industrial policy was an exaggeration. Industrial policy has always been there in real life and is necessary for the 21st century, having still a big role within the constraints of international guidelines (2004, 2008). After the international financial crisis, industrial policy was renewed in various countries. In the heartlands of free trade such as the USA, policies were adopted to develop emerging industries. Even international organisations, such as the World Bank for whom the market is a venerated yardstick, have begun to reconsider the role of industrial policy. When Professor Lin Yifu started working for the World Bank, he also pushed for it to provide advice to developing countries on how to formulate industrial policy. Ha-Joon Chang, the renowned

Q. Zhang (✉) · H. Li
Chinese Academy of Social Sciences, Beijing, China
e-mail: zhangqizi65@126.com



Q. Zhang (ed.), *Transforming Economic Growth and China's Industrial Upgrading*,
Research Series on the Chinese Dream and China's Development Path,
https://doi.org/10.1007/978-981-13-0962-5_9

development economist, said that developed countries got rich by protecting their nascent industries. The secret of getting rich for Britain, the birth place of free competition, is an entirely free market economy. What is claimed as free trade by developed nations is in fact the exclusion of developing countries from the ladder to prosperity (2009).

Although there is growing consensus on the need for industrial policy, the debate continues on how it can play a part. The most fundamental argument is whether industrial policy works with or against comparative advantage. Two renowned economists, Lin Yifu from China and Ha-Joon Chang from Korea, engaged in an earnest debate over this matter. The *2009 World Bank Development Policy Review* published the debate between these two eminent scholars entitled "Should industrial policy in developing countries conform to comparative advantage or contravene it?"

This debate on industrial policy is not about the relationship between government and market or whether government should intervene. Both sides in this debate believe that governments should intervene. The crux of the disagreement is the direction of government intervention. For Lin Yifu, the emphasis should be on industrial upgrade and restructuring when promoting economic growth, as well as the government's role within it. However, on how the government should intervene, he believes that a government's role is one of facilitation in helping the private sector to exploit comparative advantage. This is along the same line of thinking in his research on the origin of the Chinese economic miracle. He believes that the optimal industrial structure is inherent in the composition of a country's factor endowments, which manifest as labour, skills, capital and natural resources. Industrial structure upgrade has to start with enhancing the endowed factors, otherwise we are left with an industrial structure that will hamper development. For him the reason that industrial policies fail in some countries is because 'they fix their sight and policy on an ideal industrial structure linked to modernisation, but this kind of structure is usually capital—and technology-intensive, a characteristic in countries where income is higher than in their own'. "This kind of thinking is contrary to comparative advantage and the cost is high for quality governance in finance and government" (Lin and Chang 2009). Ha-Joon Chang holds the same view as Lin Yifu on the role of government intervention for economic growth, but at the beginning of the debate he stressed that the main difference between his and Lin's view is that, 'Yifu believes that the important role of government intervention is mainly in exploiting a country's comparative advantage. But for me, this is important but is only the baseline; if a country wants to upgrade its industries, it needs to defy its comparative advantage" (Lin and Chang 2009).

During their discussion, Lin Yifu and Ha-Joon Chang used case studies to illustrate their points of view. However, neither provided systematic evidence to show whether countries are generally working with or against comparative advantage in implementing industrial policy. The aim of this study is to use relatively systematic data to test which is more factually faithful.

Whether industrial policy should conform or defy comparative advantage is not entirely a matter of different schools of thought, but a fundamental problem that needs to be resolved in the process of implementing the policy. It impacts on the outcome as well as whether the industrial policy should be implemented at all. As an advocate of industrial policy, Rodrik believes that finding out the actions required and the policies that can bring optimal outcome are key to what the government should intervene (Rodrik 2009, 141). However, if we cannot identify the scope of intervention, then the industrial policy cannot be implemented. This can be sufficient argument against adopting industrial policy. An important reason against government intervention in economics is a question of its feasibility.

## 9.2 Measuring Comparative Advantage

Examining whether a country's industrial policy works with or against comparative advantage is to make a comparison between revealed and latent comparative advantage. A small difference indicates conformity with comparative advantage, whereas a very big difference indicates defiance. Thus the key question for methodology is how to measure latent comparative advantage.

Comparative advantage is one of the most mature concepts in economics, but when used to analyse a country's competitiveness, it is not as simple as implied in theory. In the debate between Lin Yifu and Ha-Joon Chang, they used the same case studies but came to different conclusions. One of the reasons is that they have different interpretations for comparative advantage. So, unless we solve the problem of how to measure comparative advantage, we cannot reach a consensus as to whether a country develops by conforming with or defying its comparative advantage.

Adam Smith put forward a theory of absolute advantage in *The Wealth of Nations*, in which he pointed out that countries that produce the same products have different productive advantage, caused by an absolute difference in labour productivity. Ricardo put forward the comparative advantage theory in his representative work *On the Principles of Political Economy and Taxation*, in which he said that the basis of international trade was the relative difference in technology (rather than absolute difference). Although Ricardo's theory explains how a country can position itself in the international division of labour given its disadvantage in production, the measurement of a country's comparative advantage is still labour productivity.

Ricardo's comparative advantage theory assumes that only one factor of production was put in, but in reality in economics inputs are not limited to one factor. Heckscher-Ohlin put forward the resource endowments theory which states that if the level of technology in producing a product by different countries is the same, the price difference between two countries would be due to a difference in cost, which is a result of a difference in the price of the factors of production. The latter is determined by its relative abundance in the country, i.e. the relative difference in endowments. Hence, Heckscher-Ohlin's model can measure a country's comparative advantage using their factor endowments. If a country has higher capital stock per capita than another, then it is relatively capital abundant. In a general sense this theory also measures a country's comparative advantage by the relative abundance of its input factors. Measuring comparative advantage from an input perspective makes it difficult to really resolve some issues in practice: what type of input factors are to be included, and when there are many factors it is difficult to carry out international comparisons on a large scale. If only several simple factors are considered, it is easier to measure a country's comparative advantage but the implication for practical application will be greatly weakened, and will be of limited guidance in implementing industrial policy. Take for example the two factors of capital and labour, different countries can be classified as relatively abundant in capital and relatively abundant in labour. Capital-abundant countries have advantage in producing capital-intensive goods, labour-abundant countries have advantage in producing labour-intensive goods. However, there is a huge number of products that can be included within these two types. How should decision-makers choose? Moreover, the capability needed for the products are not entirely interchangeable. Steel and automotive are both capital intensive productions. Workers and capital used in steel production cannot be used for producing cars without outlay costs.

Adam Smith's theory on absolute comparative advantage, Ricardo's theory on comparative advantage, and Heckscher-Ohlin's theory on resource endowments are all static theories, which are in contrast with a dynamic model of comparative advantage. One of the most important ideas in a dynamic model is that of learning-by-doing, which stresses experience and practice. According to this theory, a country's comparative advantage in aircraft manufacturing depends on whether it has already done so. Hence, a country's comparative advantage can be measured from the output end.

A long-standing indicator for measuring this is the revealed comparative advantage index. However, the problem with this method is how to judge that the output measured is real comparative advantage. Unless we can come to an assessment benchmark for comparative advantage from measuring output, we would have to stick to using factor endowments to assess the appropriateness of revealed comparative advantage. To solve this problem in measuring output, we introduced the product space method to measure a country's comparative advantage.

The theory of product space treats proximity between two products as the difference in production capability or technology. In moving from one product to another, a high degree of proximity means less initial investment, lower cost, and a smaller difference in technology. For example, in proximity comparisons, product A is closer to B than it is to C, and product B is closer to C than product A is. This means that for countries that already make product A, they have greater comparative advantage when making product B; countries that already make product B will have greater comparative advantage when making product C. The specific method for calculating product proximity is:

$$\phi_{i,j} = \min\{P(RCA_{\chi_i}/RCA_{\chi_j}, P(RCA_{\chi_j}/RCA_{\chi_i}\}$$

i and j represent two products, $\phi_{I,\ j}$ represents the proximity between two products, and RCA represents the revealed comparative advantage index (Hidalgo et al. 2007).

The simplest model for explaining a country's comparative advantage from an input perspective, is to assume that for two countries, this country and a foreign country, to produce two products such as cheese and wine, there is only one factor, such as labour. If the labour input ratio for this country to produce one pound of cheese is smaller than that for the foreign country to produce one gallon of wine, then this country has comparative advantage in cheese production (Paul and Obstfeld 1998, p. 17). After simple modification, this model can explain a country's comparative advantage from the perspective of its product space. There are two countries, this country and a foreign country, if this country turns to produce cheese and the difference in technology it has to overcome is smaller than that for the foreign country to turn to produce wine, when compared with the foreign country, this country has comparative advantage in changing to cheese production. This can be explained in two steps. Step one, let us assume that this country turns to produce one pound of cheese and requires a new input of $a_c$, and for one gallon of wine it is $a_l$; the foreign country turns to produce one pound of butter and one gallon of wine and requires new input of $a^*_c$ and $a^*_l$ respectively. Step two, the increase in new input is directly proportional to the technology distance between the products. If $a_c/a_l < a^*_c/a^*_l$, it means that for this country to turn to produce cheese, the technology distance to be overcome is a smaller ratio than that for the foreign country to produce wine.

Using the product space method to discover a country's comparative advantage, we get results not for the current stage but for the next. Thus this measurement for comparative advantage can also be called latent comparative advantage. If the distance is small between the products to be produced and the current products with comparative advantage, then those new products is considered as in line with comparative advantage. To find out whether industrial upgrade conforms with or defies comparative advantage, we can examine the success rate in upgrading for current products with high proximity, and compare it to those with low proximity.

Figures 9.1, 9.2, and 9.3 represent the levels of conformity or defiance in comparative advantage for industrial upgrades. The horizontal axis represents the distance in technology between products, the vertical axis represents the success rate in product upgrade, i.e. the number of products changing from not revealed to revealed comparative advantage as a proportion of products with latent comparative advantage. This is called the industrial upgrade success ratio. Figure 9.1 shows countries conforming with comparative advantage. It shows that when the technology distance exceeds a certain critical value, businesses do not have the momentum for transformation and upgrade, but latent advantage is fully exploited up. Figure 9.2 shows the situation that contravenes comparative advantage. In this situation, the possibility for a successful industrial upgrade is inversely proportional

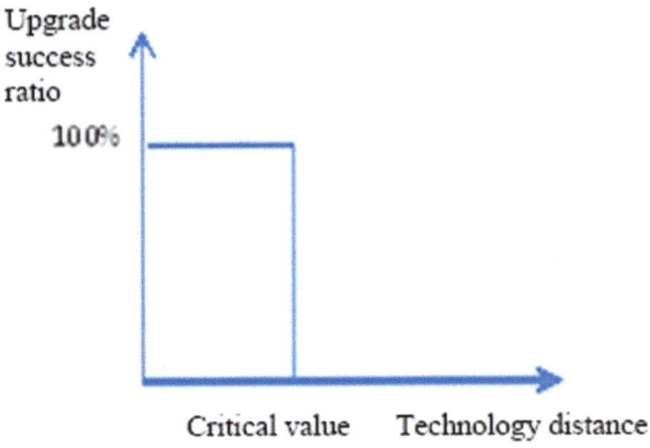


**Fig. 9.1** Conforming with comparative advantage

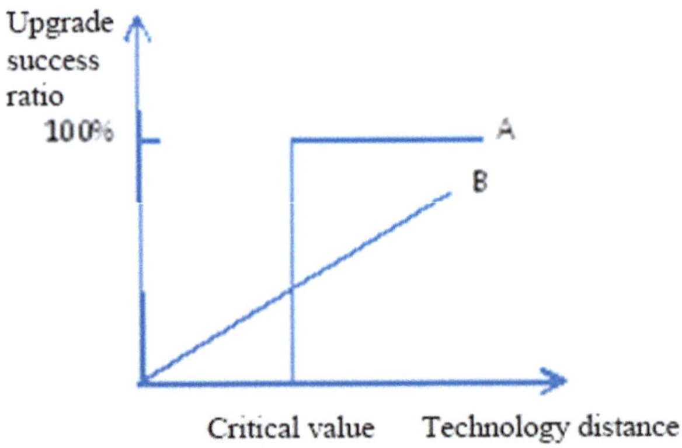


**Fig. 9.2** Contravening comparative advantage

to the distance in technology; this extreme scenario is the complete opposite to that in Fig. 9.1. Figure 9.3 shows an in-between scenario. In this situation products that are in closer proximity have a higher success rate than those of lower proximity. This means that industrial policy should not completely contravene comparative advantage; neither should it conform completely. It should seek a balance between the two extremes.

## 9.3 Data Source, Methodology and Empirical Outcome

1. **Constructing the global product space**

To measure comparative advantage in the countries using the product space method, we first need to construct a global product space. The global product space is made up of products with revealed comparative advantage from around the world and their relationship. Relationship refers to the spatial proximity between products.

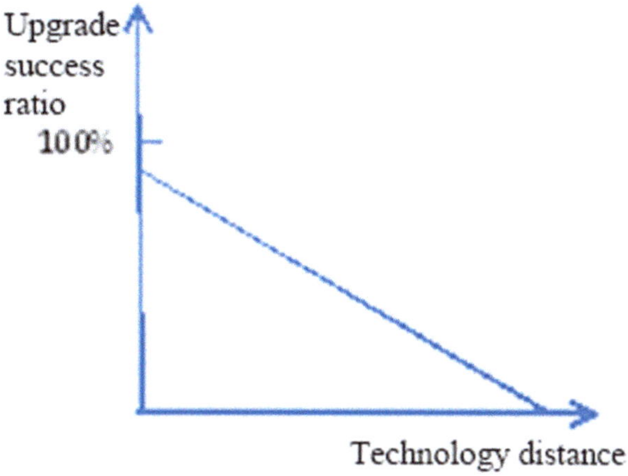


**Fig. 9.3** In-between scenario

The structure of the global product space is based on export data. Currently an authoritative record of country—specific trade data is the UN Comtrade database. We will use this as the basis for measuring the countries' comparative advantage. The UN Comtrade database includes data from different classification standards, such as SITC rev1, SITC rev2, SITC rev3. They start in different years and include different number of products. SITC rev1 includes a total of 1374 products of five-digit codes and uncategorised four-digit codes. SITC rev2 includes 1836, and SITC rev3 includes 3118.

A possible criticism for using the product space structure to measure comparative advantage is that current products may not reflect a country's comparative advantage. In a given year certain exports in a country may indeed be affected by casual factors. A method that can overcome this problem is the use of an average value from data over a longer time period to measure changes in a country's comparative advantage. Here we have chosen a five-year period for calculating a country's revealed comparative advantage. For some products, if their revealed comparative advantage index is greater than one during three out of five years, then they will be defined as having comparative advantage.

2. **Measuring the comparative advantage of the various countries and the ratio of industrial upgrade given the difference in technology**

In analysing the stability and volatility of product space, we have chosen a 10-year time span for investigating industrial upgrade; a country's comparative advantage during the last five years is analysed based on its first five years. The criteria used in selecting products with comparative advantage are: in the first five years, products whose comparative advantage is greater than or equal to one for three out of the five years; and, in the second five years, products whose highest proximity is greater than the critical value of proximity.

In calculating the proportion of products with latent advantage that can be realised under different distances, we constructed the product space structure with the average proximity value between products during the 10 benchmark years and used the proximity between potential products and products with revealed comparative advantage as the distance for upgrade between products or the distance in technology. Based on this principle, calculations were carried out using SITC rev1, rev2 and rev3 data, and the results are shown in Table 9.1. Table 9.1 shows that where potential and established products (products with comparative advantage in the previous stage) are in close proximity and with a small difference in technology, the probability for upgrade is high. The overall picture is that there is a greater chance for attaining industrial upgrade where a smaller distance is to be overcome. Therefore, with reference to a country's comparative advantage, on the whole its industrial upgrade is in line with this. However sometimes the upgrade is achieved on a bigger distance, so industrial policy is not entirely in line with comparative advantage (see Table 9.1 for details), but being more like the in-between scenario shown in Fig. 9.3.

Table 9.1 shows the global picture. Table 9.2 shows the success rate for different countries in industrial transformation and upgrade in different periods. For most countries, the industrial transformation and upgrade does not run entirely in line or counter to comparative advantage. The data demonstrates that more countries succeed in upgrading their industries where the difference in technology is small. This is the trend within the distance range of 0.3–0.9. Outside of this range there are some exceptions in individual periods, where there is a relatively high number of countries succeed in upgrading (where the technology distance is >0.9) or a smaller number (where the technology distance is smaller than 0.3). The reason why such anomalies appear is that out of this distance range most of the countries do not have products with latent advantage, and hence if a few countries are within this range, their rate of success in upgrading will show a percentage that is either relatively high or relatively low.

3. **Product space stability**

When we examine a country's revealed comparative advantage over a long period, we may encounter issues of stability in the structure of product space. In using the product space structure to measure a country's comparative advantage, we need to calculate the proximity of various products. With progress in technology and industrial restructuring, there may be changes to the relationship between products. Unstable product space structure will affect the resulting comparative advantage for the next period. Therefore, in using the 10-year average value to calculate proximity and making it the basis for working out latent industries, we need to analyse whether there have been major changes to product relationship during this period. In other words, we need to study the stability of the product space.

**Table 9.1** Percentage of industrial transformation and upgrade for different technology distances under rigorous standards (unit: %)

| SITI rev1 Percentage of industrial upgrade for different distances | | | | | | | | |
|---|---|---|---|---|---|---|---|---|
| Year | 1–0.9 | 0.9–0.8 | 0.8–0.7 | 0.7–0.6 | 0.6–0.5 | 0.5–0.4 | 0.4–0.3 | 0.3–0.2 |
| 1968–1972 | 0.00 | 0.04 | 0.37 | 0.98 | 2.24 | 4.09 | 6.17 | 14.37 |
| 1973–1977 | 0.00 | 0.14 | 0.46 | 1.29 | 2.94 | 4.76 | 9.07 | 7.14 |
| 1978–1982 | 0.06 | 0.22 | 0.57 | 1.43 | 2.86 | 4.66 | 8.83 | 9.38 |
| 1983–1987 | 0.00 | 0.07 | 0.49 | 1.15 | 2.31 | 3.51 | 6.53 | 13.21 |
| 1988–1992 | 0.00 | 0.12 | 0.66 | 2.08 | 4.34 | 7.00 | 9.06 | 10.00 |
| 1993–1997 | 0.00 | 0.17 | 0.46 | 1.58 | 3.37 | 5.24 | 8.27 | 6.10 |
| 1998–2002 | 0.00 | 0.11 | 0.28 | 1.09 | 2.31 | 4.10 | 7.26 | 10.61 |
| 2003–2007 | 0.00 | 0.10 | 0.53 | 1.45 | 2.86 | 4.84 | 8.60 | 10.20 |
| 2008–2011 | 0.28 | 0.16 | 0.33 | 0.94 | 1.87 | 3.17 | 5.88 | 4.12 |
| Totals in different periods | 0.03 | 0.12 | 0.47 | 1.32 | 2.76 | 4.50 | 7.59 | 9.60 |
| SITI rev2 Percentage of industrial upgrade for different distances | | | | | | | | |
| Year | 1–0.9 | 0.9–0.8 | 0.8–0.7 | 0.7–0.6 | 0.6–0.5 | 0.5–0.4 | 0.4–0.3 | 0.3–0.2 |
| 1987–1991 | 0.00 | 0.09 | 0.52 | 1.62 | 3.35 | 6.72 | 10.97 | 15.76 |
| 1992–1996 | 0.00 | 0.20 | 0.60 | 1.86 | 3.79 | 6.09 | 8.13 | 6.79 |
| 1997–2001 | 0.00 | 0.11 | 0.37 | 0.94 | 2.33 | 3.92 | 5.32 | 6.94 |
| 2002–2006 | 0.13 | 0.42 | 0.46 | 1.26 | 2.55 | 4.31 | 6.53 | 8.94 |
| 2007–2011 | 0.00 | 0.25 | 0.57 | 1.36 | 2.70 | 4.46 | 6.04 | 8.29 |
| Aggregation | 0.07 | 0.29 | 0.51 | 1.38 | 2.89 | 5.02 | 7.28 | 9.10 |
| SITI rev3 Percentage of industrial upgrade for different distances | | | | | | | | |
| Year | 1–0.9 | 0.9–0.8 | 0.8–0.7 | 0.7–0.6 | 0.6–0.5 | 0.5–0.4 | 0.4–0.3 | 0.3–0.2 |
| 1997–2001 | 0.00 | 0.07 | 0.29 | 0.75 | 1.94 | 3.73 | 5.58 | 7.09 |
| 2002–2006 | 0.08 | 0.08 | 0.37 | 1.14 | 2.40 | 4.26 | 6.05 | 7.73 |
| 2007–2011 | 0.00 | 0.15 | 0.57 | 1.18 | 2.43 | 4.24 | 5.89 | 7.46 |
| Aggregation | 0.05 | 0.11 | 0.44 | 1.09 | 2.28 | 4.04 | 5.78 | 7.37 |

The stability and volatility of product space can be measured by the 'standard deviation in proximity'. Using data from SITC rev1 for 1963–2011, SITC rev2 for 1982–2011, and SITC rev3 for 1992–2011 to calculate the standard deviation in proximity, we have the following: the mean of the standard deviations for all connecting proximities during 1963–2011 for SITC rev1 products is 0.1122; during 1982–2011 for SITC rev 2 it is 0.0956; during 1992–2011 for SITC rev 3 products it is 0.0791. Shortening the period of investigation to 10-year time spans the results are: during each 10-year period the mean of the standard deviation for all product proximities in the product space are 0.0467–0.0756 for SITC rev1 during 1963–2011; 0.0494–0.0747 for SITC rev2 during 1982–2011; 0.0646–0.0656 for SITC rev3 during 1992–2011. As we can see, as the time spans are shortened, there is less proximity volatility in the product space.

**Table 9.2** Distribution of countries that have succeeded in industrial upgrade under different technology distances (unit: %)

| SITI rev1 Country distribution in terms of industrial upgrade success ratio | | | | | | | | |
|---|---|---|---|---|---|---|---|---|
| 1968–1972 | 1–0.9 | 0.9–0.8 | 0.8–0.7 | 0.7–0.6 | 0.6–0.5 | 0.5–0.4 | 0.4–0.3 | 0.3–0.2 |
| <10% | 98.15 | 95.52 | 94.03 | 94.03 | 83.58 | 60.61 | 55.56 | 32.26 |
| >20% | 0.00 | 0.00 | 0.00 | 0.00 | 1.49 | 7.58 | 9.26 | 48.39 |
| 100% | 0 | 0 | 0 | 0 | 0 | 0 | 0 | 3.2 |
| 1973–1977 | 1–0.9 | 0.9–0.8 | 0.8–0.7 | 0.7–0.6 | 0.6–0.5 | 0.5–0.4 | 0.4–0.3 | 0.3–0.2 |
| <10% | 100 | 95.95% | 91.89% | 79.73% | 62.16% | 54.17 | 36.67 | 65.70% |
| >20% | 0 | 0.00 | 0.00 | 0.00 | 4.054 | 13.69 | 31.42 | 22.85 |
| 100% | 0 | 0 | 0 | 0 | 0 | 0 | 1.67% | 2.90% |
| 1978–1982 | 1–0.9 | 0.9–0.8 | 0.8–0.7 | 0.7–0.6 | 0.6–0.5 | 0.5–0.4 | 0.4–0.3 | 0.3–0.2 |
| <10% | 97.83 | 90.91 | 84.42 | 75.32 | 66.23 | 44.59 | 41.94 | 45.45 |
| >20% | 0 | 5.19 | 0.00 | 1.30 | 3.9 | 18.18 | 37.93 | 78.57 |
| 100 | 0 | 0 | 0.00% | 0.00 | 0 | 0 | 0 | 14.30 |
| 1983–1987 | 1–0.9 | 0.9–0.8 | 0.8–0.7 | 0.7–0.6 | 0.6–0.5 | 0.5–0.4 | 0.4–0.3 | 0.3–0.2 |
| <10% | 100 | 98.7 | 91.89 | 82.43 | 60.81 | 50.00 | 38.24 | 50.00 |
| >20% | 0 | 0.00 | 0.00 | 1.35 | 8.11 | 20.27 | 45.59 | 31.25 |
| 100% | 0 | 0.00% | 0.00% | 0 | 0 | 0 | 7.35% | 15.63 |
| 1988–1992 | 1–0.9 | 0.9–0.8 | 0.8–0.7 | 0.7–0.6 | 0.6–0.5 | 0.5–0.4 | 0.4–0.3 | 0.3–0.2 |
| <10% | 100.00 | 87.84 | 86.49 | 70.27 | 50.00 | 27.03 | 40.63 | 70.59 |
| >20% | 0 | 0.00 | 0.00 | 1.33 | 10.67 | 26.67 | 43.75 | 28.60 |
| 100% | 0.00 | 0.00 | 0.00 | 0 | 0.00 | 0.00 | 1.56 | 11.43 |
| 1993–1997 | 1–0.9 | 0.9–0.8 | 0.8–0.7 | 0.7–0.6 | 0.6–0.5 | 0.5–0.4 | 0.4–0.3 | 0.3–0.2 |
| <10% | 100 | 89.23 | 84.06 | 72.46 | 53.03 | 30.77 | 42.86 | 75.76 |
| >20 | 0 | 1.61 | 0.00 | 4.55 | 7.58 | 18.18 | 33.33 | 32.40 |
| 100% | 0 | 0 | 0.00% | 0 | 0 | 0% | 0 | 16.22 |
| 1998–2002 | 1–0.9 | 0.9–0.8 | 0.8–0.7 | 0.7–0.6 | 0.6–0.5 | 0.5–0.4 | 0.4–0.3 | 0.3–0.2 |
| <10% | 98.15 | 98.68 | 92.21 | 88.31 | 71.43 | 46.75 | 41 | 62.86 |
| >20% | 0 | 1.32 | 0.00 | 0.00 | 0.00 | 1.30 | 40.54 | 34.29 |
| 100% | 0 | 0 | 0.00 | 0.00 | 0.00 | 0.00 | 0.00 | 8.57 |
| 2003–2007 | 1–0.9 | 0.9–0.8 | 0.8–0.7 | 0.7–0.6 | 0.6–0.5 | 0.5–0.4 | 0.4–0.3 | 0.3–0.2 |
| <10% | 98.31 | 94.07 | 91.53 | 78.81 | 58.47 | 46.55 | 46.67 | 73.33 |
| >20% | 1.69 | 1.69 | 0 | 0.0 | 3.39 | 46.55 | 40.00 | 26.67 |
| 100% | 0 | 0 | 0 | 0.00 | 0 | 1.69 | 3.81 | 10.00 |
| 2008–2011 | 1–0.9 | 0.9–0.8 | 0.8–0.7 | 0.7–0.6 | 0.6–0.5 | 0.5–0.4 | 0.4–0.3 | 0.3–0.2 |
| <10% | 97.73 | 97.44 | 98.31 | 89.83 | 78.81 | 89.83 | 58.72 | 78.72 |
| >20% | 2.27 | 1.69 | 1.69 | 0.00 | 0.85 | 7.63 | 19.27 | 18.75 |
| 100% | 0 | 0 | 0 | 0.00% | 0 | 0 | 0 | 8.33% |
| SITI rev2 Country distribution in terms of industrial upgrade success ratio | | | | | | | | |
| 1987–1991 | 1–0.9 | 0.9–0.8 | 0.8–0.7 | 0.7–0.6 | 0.6–0.5 | 0.5–0.4 | 0.4–0.3 | 0.3–0.2 |
| <10% | 100.00 | 87.10 | 87.10 | 75.81 | 53.23 | 30.65 | 27.42 | 32.26 |

(continued)

**Table 9.2** (continued)

| SITI rev2 Country distribution in terms of industrial upgrade success ratio | | | | | | | | |
|---|---|---|---|---|---|---|---|---|
| 1987–1991 | 1–0.9 | 0.9–0.8 | 0.8–0.7 | 0.7–0.6 | 0.6–0.5 | 0.5–0.4 | 0.4–0.3 | 0.3–0.2 |
| >20% | 0.00 | 1.61 | 1.61 | 1.61 | 1.61 | 16.13 | 40.32 | 35.48 |
| 100% | 0.00 | 0.00 | 0.00 | 0.00 | 0.00 | 0.00 | 0.00% | 4.44 |
| 1992–1996 | 1–0.9 | 0.9–0.8 | 0.8–0.7 | 0.7–0.6 | 0.6–0.5 | 0.5–0.4 | 0.4–0.3 | 0.3–0.2 |
| <10% | 1 | 90.91 | 87.88 | 76.81 | .57.57 | 30.76 | 32.30 | 43.07 |
| >20% | 0 | 3.22 | 1.51 | 15.15 | 3.03 | 16.921 | 36.92 | 40.00 |
| 100% | 0 | 0 | 0 | 0 | 0 | 0 | 0 | 8.89 |
| 1997–2001 | 1–0.9 | 0.9–0.8 | 0.8–0.7 | 0.7–0.6 | 0.6–0.5 | 0.5–0.4 | 0.4–0.3 | 0.3–0.2 |
| <10% | 0 | 97.33 | 93.33 | 88 | 74.66 | 44 | 35.13 | 49.23 |
| >20% | 0 | 2.66 | 0 | 0 | 1.33 | 4.00 | .24.32 | 43.93 |
| 100% | 0 | 0 | 0 | 0 | 0 | 0 | 0.13 | 0.15 |
| 2002–2006 | 1–0.9 | 0.9–0.8 | 0.8–0.7 | 0.7–0.6 | 0.6–0.5 | 0.5–0.4 | 0.4–0.3 | 0.3–0.2 |
| <10% | 97.97 | 97.97 | 93.27 | 93.57 | 63.30 | 47.22 | 43.13 | 48.71 |
| >20% | 10.10 | 0 | 0.91 | 1.83 | 0 | 13.88 | 42.15 | 39.74 |
| 100% | 0 | 0 | 0 | 0 | 0 | 0 | 0.98 | 6.41 |
| 2007–2011 | 1–0.9 | 0.9–0.8 | 0.8–0.7 | 0.7–0.6 | 0.6–0.5 | 0.5–0.4 | 0.4–0.3 | 0.3–0.2 |
| <10% | 85.48 | 94.16 | 93.33 | 83.33 | 67.50 | 0.45 | 39.83 | 55.12 |
| >20% | 3.22 | 2.5 | 0 | 0 | 0.83 | 12.5 | 31.35 | 34.61 |
| 100% | 0 | 0 | 0 | 0 | 0 | 0 | 0 | 7.69 |
| SITI rev3 Country distribution in terms of industrial upgrade success ratio | | | | | | | | |
| 1997–2001 | 1–0.9 | 0.9–0.8 | 0.8–0.7 | 0.7–0.6 | 0.6–0.5 | 0.5–0.4 | 0.4–0.3 | 0.3–0.2 |
| <10% | 100 | 87.30 | 96.82 | 87.30 | 76.19 | 47.61 | 38.09 | 40.67 |
| >20% | 0 | 3.17 | 1.58 | 0 | 0 | 1.58 | 20.63 | 37.28 |
| =100% | 0 | 0 | 0 | 0 | 0 | 0 | 0 | 3.38 |
| 2002–2006 | 1–0.9 | 0.9–0.8 | 0.8–0.7 | 0.7–0.6 | 0.6–0.5 | 0.5–0.4 | 0.4–0.3 | 0.3–0.2 |
| <10% | 100 | 100 | 93.85 | 87.72 | 60.52 | 35.08 | 25.22 | 48.10 |
| >20% | 0 | 0 | 0.87 | 0 | 0 | 10.52 | 42.34 | 36.70 |
| 100 | 0 | 0 | 0 | 0 | 0 | 0 | 3.60 | 6.32 |
| 2007–2011 | 1–0.9 | 0.9–0.8 | 0.8–0.7 | 0.7–0.6 | 0.6–0.5 | 0.5–0.4 | 0.4–0.3 | 0.3–0.2 |
| <10% | 100 | 96.22 | 85.32 | 79.81 | 65.13 | 42.20 | 33.66 | 55.12 |
| >20% | 0 | 1.83 | 0 | 0 | 0 | 9.17 | 25.74 | 32.05 |
| 100 | 0 | 0 | 0 | 0 | 0 | 0 | 0 | 7.69 |

Each year different countries and products are included in the UN Comtrade database, and therefore the number of countries varies in the calculations for the different time periods. In SITC rev1 there are 36 countries for 1963–2011, 67 countries for 1963–1972, 77 countries for 1973–1982, 74 countries for 1983–1992, 77 countries for 1993–2002, and 117 countries for 2003–2011. In SITC rev2 there are 42 countries for 1982–2011, 63 countries for 1982–1991, 75 countries for 1992–2001, and 120 countries for 2002–2011. In SITC rev3 there are 53 countries for 1992–2011, 63 countries for 1992–2001, and 106 countries for 2002–2011. The problem is that changes to the number of country samples affect the standard deviation, and the more countries there are in the sample, the smaller the standard deviation. Judging from the calculation results, there is a small number of country samples that exceed 10-year periods, whereas in the 10-year period data, there are more country samples the nearer we get to the present. The effect of this on the calculations of the 10-year period data is to make the standard deviation smaller than that for longer periods, and even smaller for the periods that are nearer to the present. The results from the standard deviation also reflect this trend: if the country samples for the other periods can be extended, the actual proximity deviations can also be further reduced, which confirms that the product space structure is actually quite stable in the 10-year periods.

## 9.4 In-Between Industrial Policy

During the process of upgrading industries, countries do not always follow their comparative advantage, and deviating from it is quite normal. This fact provides insight for the role that industrial policy will play, and also confirms the need for industrial policy. The meaning of industrial policy not only lies in overcoming barriers to comparative advantage, but can in acting against comparative advantage to a degree.

Will a certain degree of defiance of comparative advantage in industrial policy cause economic failure? In theory, when a country works counter to its comparative advantage, its resources are not optimally allocated, and some industries that are uncompetitive have to survive by government support. Hence when a country's industrial upgrade runs counter to its comparative advantage, its economy may not produce the best performance. However, the reality is not like this. The textile industry was a new high-tech industry in 15th century Europe. Initially Britain lagged behind, with its comparative advantage in producing and exporting cotton. Britain's income from wool export was quite impressive, but from Henry VII's point of view those abroad who could turn wool into garments were making more profits. To help develop the textile industry, Britain adopted a range of measures, such as a ban on the export of raw materials and semi-finished garments, and taxes on manufactured goods from other countries. The result was that Britain became the most important exporter of textile goods in the world (Chang 2009, pp. 28–29). After the Second World War, the economy was growing rapidly in Japan and Korea, and it is recognised that industrial policy was widely adopted in these countries. The way that their industrial structure changed was not entirely in line with their comparative advantage but followed an in-between path (see Figs. 9.4, 9.5, 9.7, 9.8, 9.10 and 9.11 for details). The achievement of China's economy since the reform and opening up caught the world by surprise. The Chinese economy was

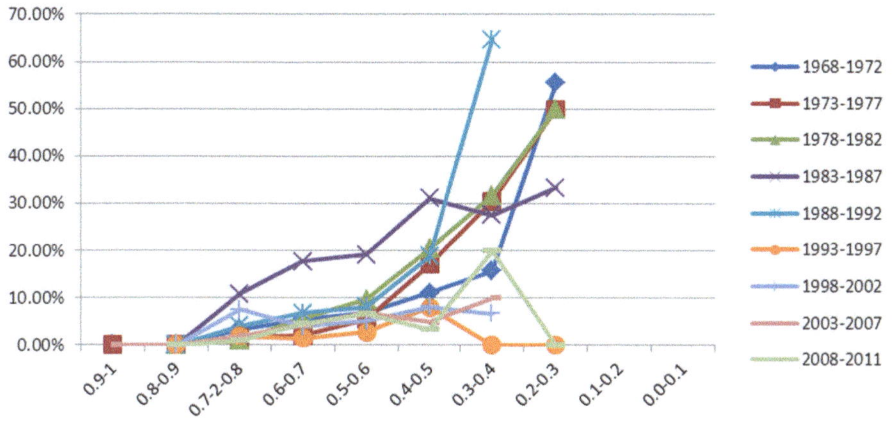


**Fig. 9.4** Japanese industrial upgrade (SITI rev1)

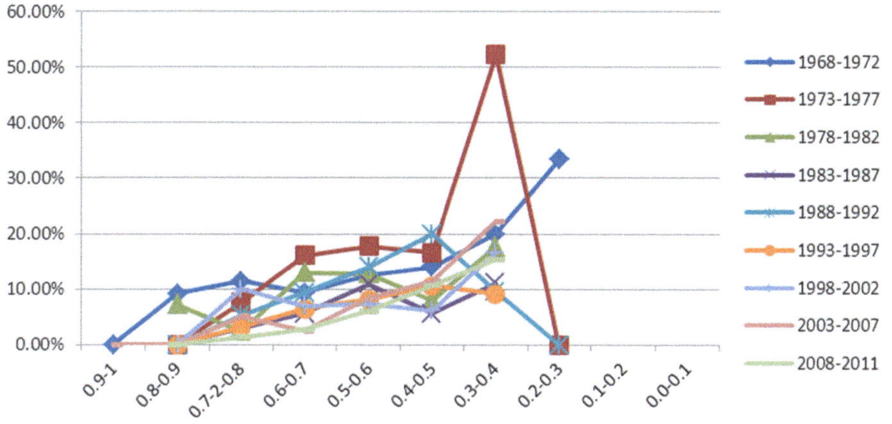


**Fig. 9.5** Korean industrial upgrade (SITI rev1)

transforming from an entirely planned one to a market economy. Resource allocation was reconfigured where previously there was a large degree of deviation from comparative advantage. However, its success again was not entirely built on conforming with its comparative advantage (see Figs. 9.6, 9.9 and 9.12 for details). These examples show that in not complying with its comparative advantage, a country can still achieve good results. However, it is noteworthy that although industrial upgrades in Japan, Korea and China did not entirely follow their comparative advantage, neither did they work against it. The graph shows that as the distance in technology shrinks, the success rate for upgrade rises. Hence the success in these countries is also determined by not having deviated too far from their comparative advantage.

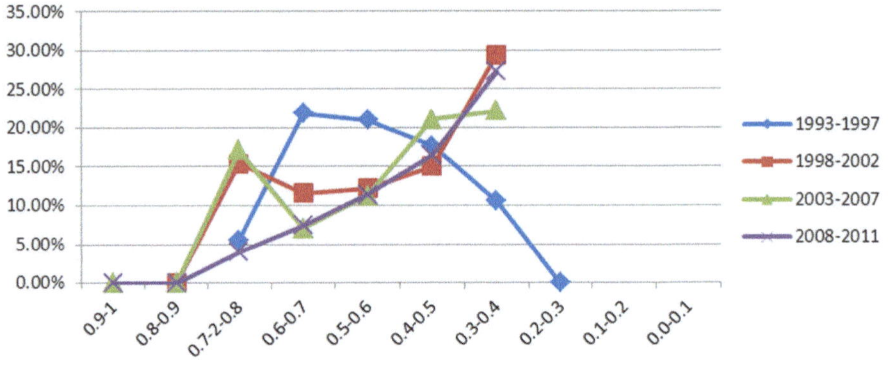


**Fig. 9.6** Chinese industrial upgrade (SITI rev1)

**Fig. 9.7** Japanese industrial upgrade (SITC rev2)

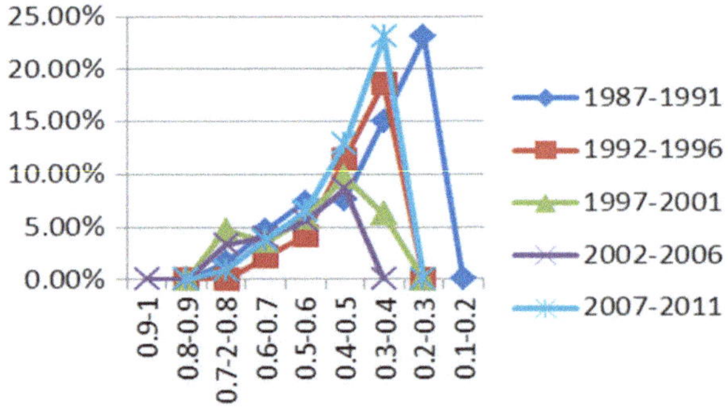


**Fig. 9.8** Korean industrial upgrade (SITC rev2)

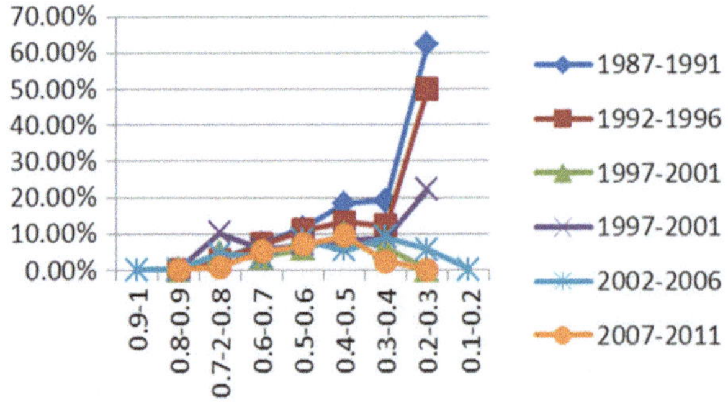


When industrial policy runs counter to comparative advantage, or put another way, why is a country still internationally competitive when it does not conform to its comparative advantage? A dynamic model of the comparative advantage theory may provide an answer. The explanation from this is similar to that provided by Ha-Joon Chang to explain the deviation of industrial policy from comparative advantage. Although the theory addresses this issue of deviation, it is not

**Fig. 9.9** Chinese industrial upgrade (SITC rev2)

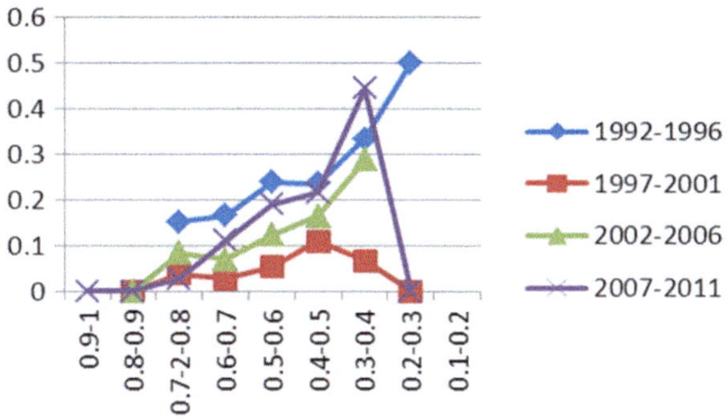


**Fig. 9.10** Japanese industrial upgrade (SITI rev3)

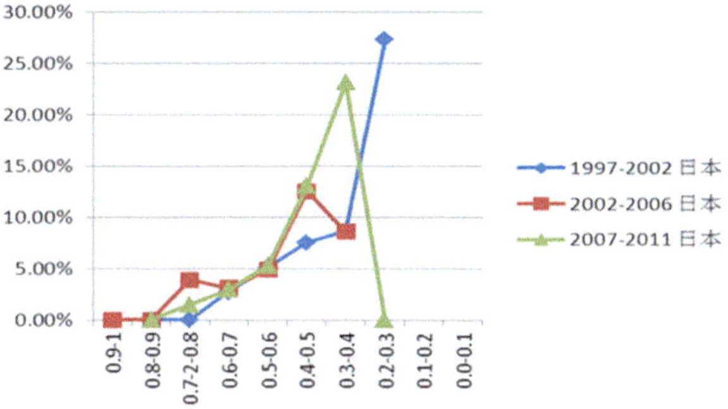


**Fig. 9.11** Korean industrial upgrade (SITI rev3)

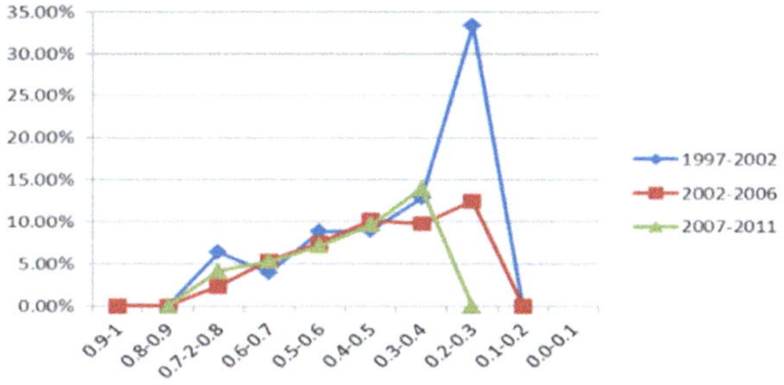


**Fig. 9.12** Chinese industrial upgrade (SITI rev3)

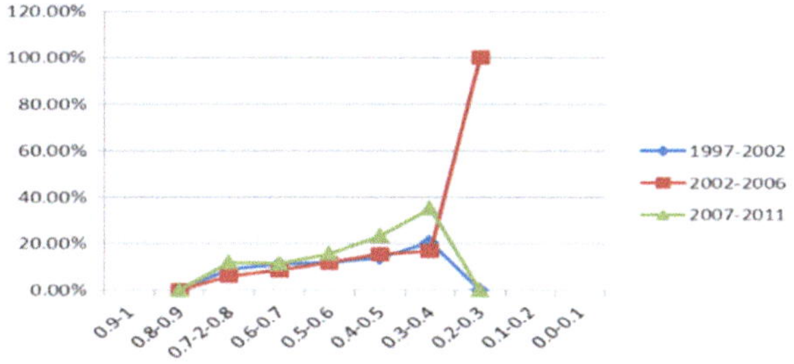

convincing in explaining whether industrial policy should be in line with comparative advantage in the long run. Similarly, this theory cannot foresee that a country's economic development and product diversity display an inverted U shape (Imbs 2003).

Here we provide another explanation, inspired by the real options theory, on industrial policy to defy comparative advantage. For a long time, enterprises have used the standard net present value in resource allocation. The focus of this method is on measurable cash flow rather than on strategic returns generated by competitive advantage and having development implications but are difficult to grasp strategically (Lenos 2007, p. 5). However, from a real options perspective, some investments become negative in standard cash value terms, but many strategic investments produce a series of opportunities which can be treated as a series of cash flows plus options combined (Amram and Kulatilaka 2001, p. 6). Although this theory is specifically aimed at businesses, its logic is equally applicable for formulating strategies at a national level. In defying comparative advantage industrial policy has future rights which are options. When uncertainties exist options are valuable.

This theory appears similar to the dynamic model of comparative advantage because they both emphasise the importance of the future. However, there are significant differences between the two. The dynamic model of comparative advantage puts the emphasis on the accumulation of capability, technology and knowledge, whereas for the real options theory, the emphasis is on managing and planning strategic investment and on dealing with uncertainties. Of course the two are not in conflict but are complementary.

From a real options perspective, it is easy to understand why industrial upgrade in all the countries does not concentrate on the areas of highest proximity. Our past research found that when the proximity threshold exceeds 0.5 in the various countries, the number of products with latent advantage drop sharply (Zhang and Li 2013). This implies that within this area, a country's options drop sharply. To prevent this, it is necessary to extend product lines.

From the real options perspective, we can also understand why economic development and product diversification appear as an inverted U. In order to explain this, it is necessary to introduce the concept of product degree. The concept relates to a product's upgrade opportunities (Zhang 2008). A country's opportunity for industrial upgrade is product line multiplied by the product's industry degree. After comparing the product space structure of developing and developed countries, we found that competitive products of developed countries are located within the core of the global product space, whereas those of developing countries are located in the periphery (Zhang and Li 2013). In other words, in developed countries, industry degree is high, and the overall product space is denser; while in developing countries, the industry degree for individual products is lower, and the product space is less dense. This means that if developing countries are to have more upgrade opportunities, they need to extend product lines. As there are more products with a higher industry degree, there will be less need to rely on extending product lines for industrial upgrade opportunities.

From cross border evidence, this study has found that industrial policy does not need to completely comply with comparative advantage and can have a role while it runs counter to it. However, in implementing industrial policy with a certain degree of deviation from comparative advantage does not necessarily bring success. Cross border experience shows that to achieve remarkable economic development, a country cannot do without industrial policy, but its implementation is no guarantee for economic success. Whether industrial policy succeeds or fails is not only a matter of the direction of intervention, but also depend on whether policymakers have a correct understanding of industrial policy and appropriate institutional design. This does not need to mean that an omniscient planner can implement the best Pigouvian tax to internalise all externalities, what it does is that this is a strategic interaction between the private and public sectors (Rodrik 2009, p. 141).

Our findings can be insightful for understanding the relationship between current economic growth and restructuring in China. There are two different views on this issue. One argues that there is no conflict between restructuring and economic growth, whereas the other argues for the opposite. Our research findings support the latter view. Restructuring actually means fostering new comparative advantage. This cannot be done by complying with existing conditions for comparative advantage. If comparative advantage is not given full play, then the potential for economic growth cannot be fully harnessed and growth will be slowed down. A necessary condition for achieving restructuring is to lower the growth target for the short term, which is conducive to the economy's long term, stable growth.

## References

Chang, Ha-Joon. 2002. *Kick away the ladder*. Anthem Press.

Chang, Ha-Joon. 2009. *The hypocrisy of rich countries*, trans. Yan, Rong. Social Sciences Academic Press.

Hidalgo, C. A., B. Klinger, A. L. Barabasi, and R. Hausman. 2007. The product space conditions the development of nations. *Sciences* 317.

Imbs, Jean, and Roman, Wacziarg. 2003. Stage of diversification. *American Economic Review* 93 (1).

Lenos, Trigeorgis. 2007. *Real options*, trans. Qian, Lin. Tsinghua University Press.

Li, Hao, and Qizi, Zhang. 2013. An evolution of the global product space structure. In *The blue book: A report on Chinese industrial competitiveness*, No. 3, ed. Zhang, Qizi. Social Sciences Academic Press.

Lin, Yifu, and Ha-Joon, Chang. 2009. Should industrial policy in developing countries conform to comparative advantage or defy it? A debate between Justin Lin and Ha-Joon Chang Justin Lin. *Development Policy Review* 27 (5).

Martha, Amram, and Nalin, Kulatilaka. 2001. *Real options*, trans. Wei Zhang et al. Machinery Industry Press.

Paul, Krugman, and Maurice, Obstfeld. 1998. *International economics*, trans. Wen, Hai, Wei, Liu, Qi, Qin, and Meiqun, Xiao. China Renmin University Press.

Rodrik, D. 2004. Industrial policy for the twenty first century. *CEPR Discussion Papers*, 4767.

Rodrik, Dani. 2008. Normalizing industrial policy. Working Paper No. 3, Commission on Growth and Development, World Bank, Washington, DC.

Rodrik, Dani. 2009. One economics, many recipes, trans. Junkuo, Zhang, and Yongzhi, Hou. Beijing: CITIC Press.

Zhang, Qizi. 2008. An evolution of comparative advantage and China's choice for a route to industrial upgrade. *Industrial Economy of China* (9).

Zhang, Qizi, and Li, Hao. 2013. Identifying opportunities for Chinese industrial upgrade. *China Industrial Economics* (5).